Love & the American Delinquent

Steven L. Schlossman

Love & the American Delinquent

The Theory and Practice of
"Progressive" Juvenile Justice, 1825-1920

The University of Chicago Press
Chicago and London

The University of Chicago Press, Chicago 60637
The University of Chicago Press, Ltd., London
© 1977 by The University of Chicago
All rights reserved. Published 1977
Printed in the United States of America
82 81 80 79 78 77   9 8 7 6 5 4 3 2 1

Steven L. Schlossman received his Ph.D. in history from Columbia University and is assistant professor of education at the University of Chicago.

Library of Congress Cataloging in Publication Data

Schlossman, Steven L
  Love and the American Delinquent.

  Bibliography: p.
  Includes index.
  1. Juvenile courts—United States—History.
2. Juvenile justice, Administration of—United States—
History.   3. Juvenile courts—Milwaukee—History.
4. Juvenile justice, Administration of—Milwaukee—
History.   I. Title.
KF9709.S3   345'73'08   76-17699
ISBN 0-226-73857-4

To my devoted and loving parents

Contents

Preface

No, this book is not about the sexual practices of juvenile delinquents. Rather, it is a selective historical inquiry into the theory and practice of American juvenile justice. Almost inevitably, the questions I ask are pertinent to today's controversies on the treatment of delinquents, especially the virtues of "deinstitutionalization" and "diversion." That is well, for I believe that historians can do much to enlighten ongoing policy debates and, moreover, that lack of historical research serves to buttress the status quo. Still, my primary goal is not reformist but historical, to shed new light on juvenile justice in its formative period.

In an era of widespread disenchantment with correctional and other educational facilities, there is a temptation to foreshorten history, to search for and locate the sources of a rotten present in the rotten past. I have endeavored not to do this, but neither have I sacrificed a naturally critical bent. I make no pretense at objectivity, yet at the same time I have attempted not to evaluate the past mainly in light of present-day policy perspectives and sensibilities. In other words, within the limitations of my own source materials, conceptual abilities, and interests, I have tried not to oversimplify or caricature. That my effort remains imperfect I know only too well.

Acknowledgments Many friends, teachers, and colleagues have lent guidance and encouragement for this work during the several years of its preparation. It began as an essay—a rather simple inquiry into the constitutional origins of the juvenile court in Stanley Kutler's free-wheeling and challenging seminar in legal history at the University of Wisconsin. The book began to assume its present form after I became a student of American educational history at Columbia University, and especially after a brilliant colloquium on the history of the family taught by David Rothman. Whatever merit there is in the final product derives from my fortunate association with Lawrence Cremin, now president of Teachers College, under whose tutelage I grew along with my work, and who provided an example of generosity and excellence which was, unequivocally, inspirational.

The scholarly influence of Stanley Schultz and Carl Kaestle on my work is obvious, but I want to thank them more for the enthusiasm that they conveyed from the beginning. I also want to thank Douglas Sloan, Alfred Kahn, and Gerald Grob for their comments on an earlier draft; Arthur Mann for combining encouragement and skepticism in just the right doses; and Sheldon Messinger for helping me figure out what the numbers were all about.

The sections on Milwaukee juvenile justice could not have been completed without the gracious assistance of Robert Stolhand, chief probation officer of the Milwaukee Children's Court, whose informative and lively conversation made my weeks in the basement thoroughly educational as well as bearable.

I received financial assistance from the Center for Studies in Criminal Justice, Law School, the University of Chicago; my sincere thanks to Norval Morris, Franklin Zimring, and Ben Meeker. The Center for the Study of Law and Society, University of California, Berkeley, provided a stimulating and congenial setting in which to bring this work to conclusion; I am grateful to Jerome Skolnick for inviting me.

A final note for Steffi: thanks for all the sunshine.

The Theory of "Progressive" Juvenile Justice

Introduction to Part 1

Our modern system of juvenile justice came into existence in the nineteenth and early twentieth centuries. The two main types of reformatories still in use—congregate and cottage (also called the family system)—were designed and put into operation before the Civil War. Although a variety of private ventures developed over the next century, often under religious auspices, these represented only slight variations on the congregate and cottage themes (save perhaps for the George Junior Republics). Around 1900 the second principal component of our modern system, the juvenile court, emerged and quickly swept the country. Within little more than a decade nearly every state, with those in the South lagging behind, had adopted this dual institutional framework (although significant differences remained in law, design, personnel, and financing). Since that period no state has abandoned the juvenile court, despite much spirited argument pro and con, and only one, Massachusetts, has eliminated reformatories (at least as traditionally conceived).

In part one these institutional developments are placed in the context of American legal, social, and intellectual history.

My emphases are highly selective; this is far from being a comprehensive examination of juvenile corrections. My primary intent is to trace the origins and nature of publicly sponsored, "progressive" correctional programs: that is, ideas and institutional designs self-consciously advanced and adopted in the post-Jacksonian period as alternatives to the correctional status quo. My focus will be on the cottage reform school and the juvenile court: especially on when they first began to interest lay and governmental sponsors, where they differed from previous correctional strategies and from each other, and how they intersected with related developments in social thought and social policy.

Chapter one briefly sketches the legal framework of American juvenile justice, paying special attention to the policy implications of the *parens patriae* doctrine. Chapter two examines the nation's first juvenile reformatory in Jacksonian New York City, less to probe its social and intellectual roots than to analyze its rehabilitative goals. Chapter three concentrates on the cottage reform school as a neglected correctional innovation of the mid-nineteenth century which sheds light on, and is in turn illuminated by, more traditional themes in Victorian social thought and policy. Chapter four attempts to reinterpret the rise of the juvenile court against the backdrop of earlier "progressive" rehabilitative ideas, and to ascertain precisely what was and was not new about it.

To be sure, it would be desirable to spend much more time on the political, economic, social, and intellectual milieu in which "progressive" ideas first became popular. One can imagine an almost endless research agenda, given the paucity of research on the history of American criminal law and corrections. Such subjects as the personal beliefs and activities of diverse spokespersons and groups for correctional change; the institutional networks impinging on corrections, notably schools, jails, charitable agencies, and police; the evolution of family structures, community cohesiveness, work and recreational opportunities, and so forth, among the urban poor; and the fluctuating roles of public and private agencies, to name only a few, require sustained attention. Only then will a truly convincing explanation be possible of why institutional innovations appeared when they did, and how they were integrated into particular communities and the nation as a whole.[1] What follows should be regarded as an overview of the correctional scene in the nineteenth and early twentieth centuries, not a definitive account of the changes that came about, the reasons for their appeal, or their impact on the treatment of juvenile delinquents throughout the nation.

‖

Precedent and Policy: The Law of American Juvenile Justice

Before examining the institutional phases of correctional change in the nineteenth and early twentieth centuries, it will be useful to outline the legal rationale of the juvenile justice system as a whole.[1] Unfortunately, the legal foundations of juvenile justice have given rise to much confusion, most of it traceable to the attempts of Progressive era reformers to analogize between juvenile courts and medieval equity courts.[2] Whether this elaborate theorizing was legally or intellectually necessary remains moot; there is reason to think sufficient judicial and policy precedents already existed to justify the comprehensive powers of intervention sought.[3] Nonetheless, the debates on juvenile law in the early twentieth century were significant in that they pointed up long-standing ambiguities in our penal codes—ambiguities which remain troublesome to this day, leaving room for abuse of governmental power and sanctioning a system of justice that intentionally discriminates according to age and social status.[4]

These ambiguities were nowhere better revealed than in the numerous appellate court decisions upholding the constitutionality of reformatories and juvenile courts.

Parens Patriae and the Juvenile Reformatory

The law of juvenile justice stands as something of an anomaly in the history of American social reform. On the one hand, ameliorative legislation for such measures as restriction of child labor or minimum wage regulations faced stiff constitutional tests because they proposed relatively new areas for governmental intervention. Proponents of these laws argued that bold judicial as well as legislative assaults on anachronistic legal traditions were essential for social progress.[5] On the other hand, new legislation on juvenile justice in the early nineteenth century emerged without serious constitutional challenge. From the creation of reformatories in the 1820s to the establishment of juvenile courts three-quarters of a century later, the principal legal justification was the doctrine of *parens patriae*.[6]

A medieval English doctrine of nebulous origin and meaning, *parens patriae* sanctioned the right of the Crown to intervene into natural family relations whenever a child's welfare was threatened. True, the doctrine appears to have applied at first only where the property of well-to-do minors was at issue. But a broader construction gradually became popular, and was legitimated by the famous *Wellesley* decision rendered by Lord Eldon in 1827.[7] During the course of the nineteenth century, as part of its legal inheritance from Britain, every American state affirmed its right to stand as guardian or superparent of all minors.[8]

The seminal decision incorporating *parens patriae* into American juvenile law was *Ex parte* Crouse, delivered in 1838, a dozen years after the opening of the state's first reformatory (thus attesting the primacy of legislative initiatives in generating juvenile law).[9] Upon her mother's complaint, Mary Ann Crouse was committed to the Philadelphia House of Refuge by an alderman who also (as was common) served as justice of the peace. Mr. Crouse (for reasons that are not clear in the official opinion) remained unaware of his wife's intention until it was too late; Mary Ann was already behind bars. As quickly as possible, he filed a habeas corpus petition, which was denied, and then hired a lawyer to press suit on Sixth Amendment grounds, charging that his daughter's incarceration without a jury trial was unconstitutional. In rebuttal the managers of the House of Refuge denied the Bill of Rights applied to children, and employed a series of arguments which the court incorporated into its unanimous decision to approve Mary Ann's imprisonment until the age of twenty-one.[10]

The opinion revealed at least two important themes in Jacksonian social thought which remained central, if largely implicit, in the correctional literature of the next three-quarters of a century. First, the doctrine of *parens patriae* served as the basis for a concept of community which hearkened back to the early colonial period. An anachronistic vision of proper social organization underlay the judges' legal reasoning: the judges were tied to a concept of community which time, demographic shifts, commercial developments, and secularization had long since eroded. Their reasoning was not very different from what one might have expected in the rulings of Puritan magistrates.[11] Asserting the government's power to remove children from family situations which *might* lead to criminality, the court asked:

> May not the natural parents, when unequal to the task of education, or unworthy of it, be superseded by the *parens patriae*, or common guardian of the community? It is to be remembered that the public has a paramount interest in the virtue and knowledge of its members, and that, of strict right, the business of education belongs to it. That parents are ordinarily entrusted with it, is because it can seldom be put into better hands; but where they are incompetent and corrupt, what is there to prevent the public from withdrawing their faculties, held as they obviously are, at its sufferance?[12]

As moral guardians of the community, the judges were loath to countenance challenge. Notwithstanding the fact that Mary Ann was not a convicted criminal, that her father was able to care for her, and that her mother had acted without first consulting the father, the judges claimed a special prescience to predict a dire future for her. Mary Ann, they asserted, "had been snatched from a course which must have ended in confirmed depravity: and not only is the restraint of her person lawful, but it would have been an act of extreme cruelty to release her from it." Thus, with only minimal information before it about the family— certainly less than would have been available in a compact colonial community as a matter of common knowledge—the court revoked the parents' natural guardianship.

The *Ex parte* Crouse opinion also spoke indirectly to another institutional innovation in which the government had a considerably larger investment, emotional as well as financial: public schools.[13] A few years before the decision the city of Philadelphia, after a difficult political struggle, had placed its schools on a sound financial basis.[14] Leaders of the public school movement—many of whom, it is important to note, also served as managers of the reformatory—looked forward to a period of unexampled growth.[15] At this critical juncture an adverse judicial opinion on the constitutionality of government-financed reformatories would surely have been unwelcome; it would inevitably have tarnished the reformers' larger educational mission and the benevolent assumptions which underlay it. Perhaps with these considerations in mind, the managers met the issue head-on. They urged the judges to place both types of facility, public school and reformatory, under the safeguard of the *parens patriae* doctrine, and to establish once and for all time that the state's provision of education for the poor was a legitimate exercise of its police powers.[16]

The court agreed entirely with the managers' point of view. The reformatory, it insisted, was nothing but a residential school for underprivileged children, a horizontal expansion of the fledgling public school system. A reformatory was "not a prison but a school." Its objectives were in the broadest sense educational: to train children in industry, morality, the means to earn a living, and most importantly, to isolate them from the "corrupting influences of improper associates." The court went on: "As to the abridgement of indefeasible rights by confinement of the person, it is no more than what is borne, to a greater or less extent, in every school; and we know of no natural right to exemption from restraints which conduce to an infant's welfare." In sum, the court concluded, the government's right to incarcerate children who had not committed criminal acts was neither capricious nor vindictive, for the house of refuge was nothing but a residential public school for unfortunate youth.[17]

Not until 1870 did any state court dispute the two key assertions in *Crouse:* the unlimited power of government to disrupt natural family relations and incarcerate children considered to

be potentially criminal, and the analogy between houses of
refuge and public schools. But challenge did come in 1870 in an
Illinois case, *People* v. *Turner*, one of the most remarkable, and
atypical, cases in American constitutional history.[18]

On the charge of "misfortune," Daniel O'Connell was arrested
and committed on an indeterminate sentence to the Chicago
Reform School. Daniel had become liable under an 1867 statute,
notable even by loose nineteenth-century standards for vagueness, which authorized apprehension of "any boy or girl, within
the ages of six and sixteen years, who . . . is a vagrant, or is
destitute of proper parental care, or is growing up in mendi-
cancy, ignorance, idleness or vice."[19] Shortly after the arrest,
Daniel's father petitioned for a writ of habeas corpus, contend-
ing that his son had committed no discernible crime. To this
petition the Illinois appellate court, unlike dozens of others faced
with similar cases in the nineteenth century, responded affirmatively and ordered Daniel's immediate release.

The appellate court had no evidence before it on the quality of
treatment at the reform school; hence it claimed to base its
decision on constitutional issues alone. In truth, however, the
court enunciated general philosophic principles only marginally
related to the Bill of Rights. First, the judges disputed the
analogy between reformatories and public schools. By its very
nature, they affirmed, imprisonment was punitive. The prosecution's contention that incarceration in a reform school did not
constitute imprisonment defied reason. Deprived of parental
care, denied freedom of movement, committed to the will of
others for an indeterminate period, Daniel correctly felt, according to the court, that he was a slave. "Nothing could more
contribute to paralyze the youthful energies, crush all noble
aspirations, and unfit him for the duties of adulthood."

Second, the court questioned previous interpretations of
parens patriae, largely by appealing to Higher Law (although it
tended to confuse separate traditions of divine and natural
law).[20] Cutting quickly to the heart of statutory imprecision, it
admonished the State to show greater compassion for parental
failings and more tolerance for different styles of child rearing.
Even the best and kindest parents often disagreed on proper
methods of child care, the court observed. "What is the standard
to be? What extent of enlightenment, what amount of industry,

what degree of virtue, will save from the threatened imprisonment?" Moreover, the statute in question was so vague as to cast all parental rights in doubt. Indeed, the court concluded, "there is not a child in the land who could not be proved by two or more witnesses to be in this sad condition."

Third, the court held that children had inviolable legal rights, especially children of the poor who were the nominal beneficiaries of various schemes of "benevolence." When children were imprisoned for the "good of society," whether or not they had committed criminal offenses, the legitimacy of the State itself was brought into question. "The disability of minors does not make slaves or criminals of them," the court advised would-be philanthropists. "The principle of the absorption of the child in, and its complete subjection to the despotism of, the State, is wholly inadmissible in the modern civilized world."

Fourth, and equally contrary to traditional views, was the court's delineation of parental rights. The court was no ideologue on the matter; parental rights were not absolute. Still, it insisted, the government should not "disturb this relation, except for the strongest reasons." In the present case governmental interference was unwarranted, for Daniel's father had been declared negligent on the flimsiest of evidence. The breakup of the O'Connell family under these circumstances, the court held, was both unconstitutional and unethical. Parenthood emanated "from God, and every attempt to infringe upon it, except from dire necessity, should be resisted in all well governed States."

Finally, the court asked a rhetorical question which threatened the legitimacy not only of the juvenile justice system but of all "preventive" governmental efforts in education and child welfare. "Can the State, as *parens patriae*, exceed the power of the natural parent, except in punishing crime?" However useful and desirable a rationale for new social policies, the court affirmed, *parens patriae* must give way when it conflicted with constitutional or Higher Law.

As a wide-ranging, contentious, and idiosyncratic inquiry into the legal and philosophical meaning of *parens patriae*, the case of *People* v. *Turner* was unexcelled, from that day to this. Even recent decisions challenging various components of the juvenile justice system—like *In re* Gault (1967), which called for the reintroduction of selective due process for children, or still more

recent "right to treatment" cases, which argue that *parens
patriae* is invalid unless effective rehabilitation accompanies
imprisonment—fail to raise underlying issues as forthrightly.[21]

By and large, though, *Turner* was a dead letter,[22] even though
renegade state courts occasionally confirmed one or another of
its arguments. For example, in 1897 a California court ruled it
unconstitutional to imprison youngsters on indefinite sentences
without trial.[23] The case concerned Josie Becknell, who was
charged with burglary, and the failure of his parents to convince
the presiding judge to assemble a jury. The appeals court based
its decision on an unusually narrow interpretation of *parens
patriae*. The parents, argued the court, could not have their
natural guardianship voided "except by a proceeding to which
they are made parties, and in which it is shown that they are
unfit or unwilling or unable to perform their parental duties."

But more representative of nineteenth-century legal opinion
was the decision of another set of Illinois judges (post-*Turner*) in
the 1882 case of *Petition of Alexander Ferrier*.[24] The case centered on the custody of nine-year-old Winifred Breen, whom the
Chicago police had spotted parading the streets at night on
numerous occasions. Winifred's mother was, according to the
prosecutor, divorced and "at times insane," having once attempted to hang her daughter and then herself. Winifred will-
ingly testified in court that she was afraid of her mother, and
that she would consent to a committal to a private reformatory
for girls in Evanston. Obviously, then, the prima facie case in
Petition of Alexander Ferrier was very different from that in
Turner.

The appellate judges, however, were apparently waiting for a
chance to override *Turner*—it evidently had caused them considerable embarrassment in the legal world—and seized the opportunity.[25] Their rationale for annulling *Turner* amounted to
nothing more than a restatement of the two key ideas in the
earlier *Crouse* decision: reformatories were residential public
schools, and the doctrine of *parens patriae* legitimated incarceration of noncriminal youth. Responding directly to the view that
imprisonment, by its very nature, constituted a deprivation of
liberty, the court, recalling Blackstone's distinction between
natural and civil liberty, declared that due process protected
only the latter. On both moral and legal grounds, the State was

bound to intervene when children became victims of their natural liberty. "There are restrictions imposed upon personal liberty which spring from the helpless or dependent condition of individuals in the various relations of life. . . . There are legal and just restraints upon personal liberty which the welfare of society demands, and which, where there is no abuse, entirely consists with the constitutional guaranty of liberty."

Rather than dispute the view that reformatories by any other name were still prisons for children, the court simply affirmed the opposite. Remarkably enough, it relied entirely on the word of institutional officials to determine the effectiveness of treatment and to substantiate the traditional analogy to public schools. "This institution is not a prison, but it is a school. . . . We perceive hardly any more restraint of liberty than is found in any well regulated school." This barely updated version of the 1838 *Crouse* opinion served as the principal constitutional bastion for expanded use of reformatories in the late nineteenth century. *Turner* caused hardly a constitutional ripple.

Parens Patriae and the Juvenile Court

As noted earlier, reformers in the early twentieth century generally argued that the opening of juvenile courts introduced a wholly new set of legal principles into the operation of American juvenile justice. Although some recognized that *parens patriae* had provided the legal foundation of reformatories, they nonetheless insisted that the doctrine acquired very different meanings in the practice of juvenile courts. This latter contention has some merit, as I shall demonstrate in chapter four. Suffice it to observe now that very little of a substantive nature was added to the law of juvenile justice in the Progressive era.[26]

The seminal decision on the constitutionality of juvenile courts occurred in 1905 in *Commonwealth* v. *Fisher*.[27] The case involved Frank Fisher, who was committed to the same house of refuge in Philadelphia which had been involved in the *Crouse* decision nearly seventy years earlier. Fisher's counsel argued three basic points: first, Frank had not been taken into court by due process of law; second, although arrested for a felony, he had never been granted the option of a jury trial on that charge; and third, the juvenile court had discriminated against Frank due to his age by committing him to a reformatory on an indeterminate sentence.

The appellate court in Pennsylvania did not take Frank's counsel seriously, however. It dismissed the first contention almost without argument, affirming that how a child was brought into court was irrelevant if the government's intentions were benevolent. The latter two points offered little more difficulty. Frank's case did not require a jury because "There was no trial for any crime here. . . . The very purpose of the act is to prevent trial." As to the charge of discrimination according to age, the appellate judges simply invoked the doctrine of *parens patriae* and the traditionally benign legal view of reformatories. "The act is but an exercise by the state of its supreme power over the welfare of its children, a power under which it can take a child from its father, and let it go where it will. . . . The design is not punishment, nor the restraint imprisonment, any more than is the wholesome restraint which a parent exercises over his child." Clearly, then, the legal foundations of the juvenile court were consistent with those of nineteenth-century juvenile justice.

The rare exceptions to *Commonwealth* v. *Fisher* highlighted judicial consensus in the Progressive period. No appellate court contested the constitutionality of juvenile courts as vigorously as *Turner* had challenged reformatories.[28] The case of *Mill* v. *Brown* in 1907 typified the infrequent instances where a committal from a juvenile court was overturned on appeal.[29] Thirteen-year-old Albert Mill was sent to a reformatory by a juvenile judge in Salt Lake City for stealing a box of cigars. His counsel offered a varied defense, concentrating on the issues of due process and infringement of parental rights. To all appearances, the father won his appeal. The appellate judges ruled that before juvenile courts could break up natural families, two additional hearings were necessary. First, with or without parental testimony, the child must formally be declared delinquent. Second, the parents must then be charged in criminal court with neglect, abuse, or incompetency and be accorded due process of law. Seemingly in the spirit of *Turner* the judges argued that some of the acts defined as delinquency were "so trivial in themselves that any thoughtless boy might commit them and be adjudged delinquent, and by a careless judge be sent to the industrial school when the parent was not only willing, but most competent, to have control of the child, and would offer it better surroundings and training than the state at best could give or afford." There was a critical legal distinction, concluded the court, between showing that a child was headed for moral ruin and demonstrating that a parent was so derelict or incompetent as to forfeit "his natural and legal right to continue the relation." Thus Albert Mill was released—but only until, and if, his father was properly and convincingly charged.

Despite these pointed comments, the appellate judges had few reservations about the procedures and goals of the juvenile court.[30] They refused, for example, to consider the complaint that Albert had been denied specific due process safeguards such as the right to trial by jury, to arraignment and plea, to suspension of sentence, to not being a witness against himself, and so forth. Instead they merely cited *Fisher* and a host of nineteenth-century cases which presumably had settled the issue. Mills's reliance on the *Turner* decision as precedent received only derision: after all, argued the appellate judges, the case was very old and its reasoning by and large was irrational. Thus, while the appellate court rescinded Albert's committal, the decision marked no new judicial stand. The judges even invoked the traditional analogy between reformatories and public schools: "No school can continue without discipline, and it is this discipline which is denominated restraint in schools such as are provided for juvenile offenders." Such, in short, remained the conventional wisdom in the Progressive era as in the early nineteenth century—even among the few judges who sustained constitutional objections to the juvenile court.[31]

Conclusion

This brief analysis of appellate court decisions underscores a more general point about the development of juvenile law. The courts' role was mainly symbolic: judges legitimated inventive legislative programs designed both to advance and ameliorate social change. Thus the evolution of juvenile law fits into the larger framework of legal development suggested by such historians as Willard Hurst, Morton Horwitz, Stanley Kutler, and Lawrence Friedman. As in the realm of economic policy, judges facilitated social innovation by reconciling legislative initiatives

with ancient common law principles which might prove re-
strictive.[32]

In this context it was little wonder that a singular decision like
People v. *Turner* earned its authors derision, for the opinion
went wholly against the grain of nineteenth-century social and
legal thought, which was nothing if not expansive.[33] The great
majority of Americans, judges included, believed that universal
education was a social panacea; that children, especially children of the poor, had few legal rights; that impoverished parents
lacked moral character and were incapable of providing healthy
conditions for child rearing; and that anything which the
government could do to instill their children with proper values
was for the better.[34] In affirming the constitutionality of reformatories and juvenile courts, the judiciary simply gave legal
expression to these conventional beliefs.[35]

That these beliefs continue to figure heavily in educational
and welfare policy in the 1970s is, of course, vivid testimony to
their earlier vitality.[36] But their persistence also points up the
necessity of understanding the law of juvenile justice more in
terms of conscious social policy than obscure legal precedents.[37]
In the remaining chapters I shall therefore pay scant attention to
juvenile law, and instead concentrate on vibrant social forces,
ideologies, institutional designs, and pedagogical theories which
more directly shaped our correctional past.

2

Juvenile Justice in the Age of Jackson

As is often true in the development of new fields of knowledge, scholars focus first on points of origin. The historical treatment of American juvenile justice is no exception: in the several studies completed in the last decade by such authors as Robert Pickett, Robert Mennel, Joseph Hawes, David Rothman, and Sanford Fox, the nation's premier reformatory, the New York House of Refuge, has attracted a disproportionate share of interest. With attention centered on the Jacksonian period, it is easy to forget that the juvenile reformatory did not gain a firm foundation throughout the country until the 1850s and 1860s, and that the middle years of the century were also seminal in correctional thought and design.[1]

I do not wish to belabor well-known points about the earlier period here: the impact of Enlightenment and Utilitarian philosophy on correctional theory; the importance of the trans-Atlantic connection in early nineteenth-century penal reform movements (especially between the United States and Britain); the transformation of New York City from a rather compact, homogeneous colonial market town to a polyglot commercial metropolis; the upper-class, Quaker sponsorship

An earlier version of this chapter appeared in *Teachers College Record* 76 (September 1974): 119–33. © 1974 Teachers College, Columbia University.

of penal innovations; and the patronizing views of the poor which underlay new conceptions of benevolence and stirred optimism in the possibilities of rehabilitation.[2] Rather, I would like to focus on the New York House of Refuge as a particular kind of organizational model which, although abandoned fairly early as an ideal, exerted enormous influence over the next century and a half of correctional practice.

Uplift and Correction:
The Genesis of Reform

As a prominent member of the New York Free School Society wrote in 1809, four years after he and several dozen of the city's most distinguished residents had established a permanent fund for the support of charity schools:[3]

> To remedy the important evils, which vice and ignorance have disseminated, and which find the most congenial soil, where there exists the greatest concentration of wealth and population, requires a foundation no less solid than a well conducted system of education for the poor of the rising generation, on such a plan as shall embrace for the objects of its tuition all the children of the unfortunate, improvident, or abandoned.[3]

Several historians have demonstrated convincingly that these men, all members of the city's pious upper-crust, were drawn together by a set of related fears and missionary drives centering on the changing nature of urban education. Recognizing with alarm many recent alterations in the city's physical structure and demography, they regarded traditional educational agencies as anachronistic. Residential segregation hampered access to and supervision of the child-rearing practices of the poor. Inexpensive pay schools could no longer be trusted to provide the bulk of low income youth with a modicum of work skills. Protestant churches were increasingly class-bound. And, the city's commercial and religious elite observed that, as a threatening consequence of these several developments, deference by the lower classes was decidedly on the decline.[4]

These fears about urban education acquired greater urgency as the cessation of the Napoleonic Wars induced hundreds of poor British and European families to migrate to America, the bulk of them arriving at the port of New York.[5] While the charity schools received much praise for doing yeoman duty, the dissipation of lower-class children and families seemed to continue unabated. To buttress the city's educational armaments further, several members of the Free School Society joined in 1816 to create the Sunday School Union, hoping thereby to reach youngsters whose parents refused to send them to weekday charity schools. Sunday schools, they believed, would serve indirectly to uplift lower-class parents through the moral precepts instilled in their youngsters. One good weekly dose of religion and personal contact between rich and poor, the union believed, would preserve the city's moral reputation, maintain traditional social hierarchies, and preserve order. Thus, under the assumption that it would be good for everyone if the poor were virtuous, the city's elite chose schooling, in one form or another, to uplift, correct, and establish surveillance over the lower-class family.[6]

Successive waves of immigration in the 1820s, and the development of a bitter religious rivalry among competing denominations for public funds, impelled the Free School Society to centralize, streamline, and expand its educational efforts.[7] Under a new governmental charter, they re-formed as the New York Public School Society in 1825, with exclusive control over city and state education monies.[8] Petty religious rivalries would no longer be tolerated, they admonished, for nearly twenty thousand children of the poor had escaped the grasp of either charity (now public) or Sunday schools. "Our schools are the very foundation, upon which rest the peace, good order, and prosperity of society."[9] The Sunday School Union had put the same line of thought more forcefully. "We are supporting our own welfare, our own happiness, our own character. We are guarding our prison door from being crowded with offenders, our streets from being polluted with additional crime, our dearest interests from being invaded."[10] In this spirit of resolve checkered with fear, the mid-1820s thus witnessed both a culmination and a new beginning for advocates of public education.

Similarly, penal reformers in the mid-1820s saw a new beginning for their own continuing efforts to establish more rational methods of prison discipline and rehabilitation. The historian W. David Lewis has recounted the extravagant expectations, bitter disappointments, and renewed exaggerated predictions of success centering on a variety of penal experiments begun in the 1790s. Thomas Eddy, the noted Quaker philanthropist, exemplified this alternating pattern of hope and despair. Soon after the legislature opened the state's first penitentiary at Newgate in 1801, Eddy predicted that it would "become a durable monument of the wisdom, justice, and humanity of its legislators, more glorious than the most splendid achievements of conquerors of kings; and be remembered when the magnificent structures of folly and pride, with their founders, are alike exterminated and forgotten."[11] Newgate would indeed be remembered, but not for the reasons Eddy prophesied. The penitentiary deteriorated rapidly into a hellhole for men unfortunate enough to be consigned there. Though he remained confident that a rational scheme for the correction of adult offenders could still be devised, even Eddy had to admit in 1825 that Newgate was "so badly conceived that it can never be successfully used as a Penitentiary."[12]

As atrocities in Newgate became public, the legislature authorized the erection of another penitentiary in western New York, at Auburn. Upon its opening in 1817, the institution's administrators took a hard-line position toward recalcitrant inmates by making extensive use of solitary confinements. This step carried significant ideological overtones, for New York had previously rejected the solitary or cellular system of prison discipline employed in Pennsylvania.[13] As in Pennsylvania, the lengthy solitary confinements soon drove many inmates at Auburn insane and broke down their resistance to disease. After legislative inquiry revealed the disastrous results, New York's experiment in solitary confinements ended in 1825.[14]

These legislative investigations, though, did lead to a series of recommendations, embodied in the famous Yates report, which inspired yet another era of hope among penal reformers that their ideas would be faithfully implemented. Undaunted by repeated failures, the reformers sensed an important shift in public sentiment in the aftermath of the Yates inquiries and growing support for a rehabilitative program relying less on punishment and isolation than on discipline, religion, and hard labor. These optimistic expectations extended to the new penal facility then under construction at Mount Pleasant on the Hudson, popularly known as Sing-Sing. The legislature had authorized its erection in 1825 to replace Newgate as primary receiving station for the city's convicts. Even Elam Lynds, the superintendent of Sing-Sing and later a nationwide symbol of the hard-line position, appeared in the beginning to support a less coercive program.[15] Thus, as with the reorganization of public schools, the mid-1820s saw both a culmination and a new start in reformers' attempts to educate a more virtuous citizenry.[16]

A Prison and a School: The New York House of Refuge

In the midst of these developments the House of Refuge for juvenile offenders opened in 1825. Sponsored and managed by many of the same people instrumental in penal and educational reform, notably Eddy and the Quaker chemist and educator John Griscom, the institution emerged after two years of careful planning and fund raising.[17] The managers predicted that the Refuge would play an important intermediary role in the city's ongoing reform enterprises. Indeed, they contended, early rehabilitative achievements of the penitentiaries owed much to their imitating the Refuge's mode of treatment. Similarly, the Refuge itself was a correctional success because it took the city's public schools as exemplars. Employing the same basic educational technique in both the reformatory and public schools—Lancaster's system of mutual instruction—the managers carried over into the reformatory their faith in emulation as a substitute for force in instructing and disciplining youth.[18] Despite the criminal backgrounds of many inmates, the managers referred to them simply as "scholars," and spoke of them as if they were students at the public schools. Referring to the inmates, they wrote: "The minds of children, naturally pliant, can by early instruction, be formed and moulded to our wishes.... The tender mind can be easily made to love all that is excellent in virtue itself, and to perceive the advantages which will be obtained from observing its dictates."[19]

No simple analogies sufficed to describe the nature or functions of the Refuge. At one time or another the managers compared it to a factory, a workhouse, a prison, a public school, a nursery, a hospital, a boarding school, a poorhouse, and an orphanage. That they were in a quandary is not surprising; the Refuge was any and all of these at the same time.[20] Still they grappled again and again with the difficult matter of self-definition in annual reports to the legislature, anxious on the one hand to boast of the institution's originality, fearful on the other to let anyone think they were coddling confirmed lawbreakers.[21] They explored questions that might easily have been ignored.[22] How uniquely American was the Refuge, and how much simply a combination of the best features of various foreign examples? How much did the Refuge spring from new ideas in philanthropy, and how much from the mere necessity of assigning someplace, anyplace, to confine the growing numbers of offenders? And, most frequently, how much was the Refuge a school and how much a prison?

Of one thing its founders were certain: the House of Refuge was a full-time residence for dependent, delinquent, and neglected youth. No theme emerged with greater clarity in the correctional thought of the period than the dangers of housing children with adult offenders. Despite attempts by the wardens of the city's Bridewell and Bellevue Prison to provide separate quarters and instruction for young inmates, there was universal agreement that these efforts were inadequate and that segregated facilities for juveniles, before and after trial, were essential. Before all else, the House of Refuge was the institutional embodiment of this line of argument.[23]

Most commentators on juvenile crime, from judges to lawyers to educators to ministers, believed that a segregated facility for children was only a first and partial step. This was natural: having insisted all along that the danger of housing children in prison was that adults taught them to become criminals, the commentators understandably were skeptical about any institution which failed to separate criminal youth from those merely impoverished, ill, or orphaned. In fact, because children were likely to take their peers as role models, it was even more necessary to separate the relatively innocent from the relatively hardened. "They may not, indeed, receive from each other, such profound lessons in the science of crime, nor hear from the lips of their equals, observations which will tend so effectually to blast every germ of compunctive feeling, and establish the guilty soul in the principles of infidelity and misanthropy, but with associates of their own cast, they will more readily assimilate, and their initiation in depravity may prove the more certain."[24]

However difficult to implement in practice, segregation and classification of inmates were simple enough principles to guide correctional strategy. They only begin, though, to explain the range of social functions which the Refuge was expected to serve and to suggest the heady educational ends to which its founders aspired.

The managers were very frank in discussing the Refuge as an instrument for compelling lower-class children to conform to middle-class standards of behavior.[25] The very existence of the Refuge, they contended, would deter crime by alerting the "neglected and misguided portion of our juvenile community" to the dangers of misbehavior. In fact, they said, the facility would reinforce the crumbling authority of impoverished parents overburdened with the demands of daily life, giving them a potent symbol of fear with which to scare "ungracious and disobedient" children into humility and quiescence.[26]

Furthermore, the Refuge promised judges, juries, police, and disgusted or overwhelmed parents an alternative to committing children to local jails or prisons. Many commentators alleged that the practice of juvenile justice had brought sacred principles of jurisprudence into disrespect. Placed before the bar of justice with irrefutable evidence against them, accused youth were often set free by sympathetic juries. "Even when guilty," the managers lamented, "jurors have strained their consciences to find some ground for their acquittal. Their youth, their helpless situation, and a heartfelt repugnance to consign them over to the common herd of malefactors, has often pleaded powerfully in their behalf, when truth and justice exacted their conviction."[27] Hugh Maxwell, the city's energetic district attorney, protested that many citizens exercised a misplaced humanitarianism by refusing to press charges against children detected committing crimes. These sins of omission, Maxwell charged, had led inevitably to sins of commission by encouraging "depraved parents to send very young children to depredate on the community,—if detected they knew no punishment would follow." Thankfully, Maxwell observed in 1826, the recent opening of the Refuge had "removed all objections to convictions in cases of guilt," thereby buttressing the waning respect for criminal law throughout the community.[28]

These claims presumably did much to elicit community interest and legislative financing for the new facility. Whether effective or not in rehabilitating inmates, the Refuge doubtless pleased most New Yorkers by guaranteeing that children of the poor would no longer be free to commit crimes with impunity. But the managers' yearly statements also indicated that the Refuge, like the public schools, was not conceived simply as an agent of control, and that its managers were genuinely ambivalent about its nature, purposes, and methods.

Joining themes from the Enlightenment and Utilitarian philosophers, the ideas of Montesquieu and Bentham, the managers boasted that the Refuge embodied the spirit of a new age of Reason and Improvement. In the early nineteenth century penitentiaries, public schools, and reformatories signaled a willingness to take control and shape human destiny, to use law, religion, and science as instruments of social amelioration. A major shift in attitudes toward the past had occurred, partially reflected, as Morton Horwitz has shown, in the way lower court judges now responded to the dictates of the common law. Law now came to be understood more "as an instrument of policy" than as a set of sacrosanct precedents, more "as a body of prudential regulations framed . . . from the perspective of enlarged and liberal views of policy" than "as an eternal set of principles expressed in custom and derived from natural law."[29] This emphasis encouraged experimentation and a willingness to use government in new ways.[30]

To the sponsors of penal and educational reform in Jacksonian New York City, there was never a doubt that each step they took brought them one closer to the enthronement of true Christian benevolence as the arbiter of human affairs. "When generations to come look back to trace the amelioration of their species, they will find among the first grades our Infant and Public Schools, the reformation of Juvenile Delinquents, and our merciful penitentiary code. . . . It is a step in the improvement of mankind, which it is so obvious Providence is permitting."[31]

The attempt to use law to improve human conduct and consciously advance social progress was one of the most striking features of social thought in the new century. To be sure, as Horwitz has argued, changing attitudes toward the law reflected new policy concerns. "Judges often explain in functional terms why they are free to disregard the authority of prior cases . . .

[and] formulate legal doctrine with the self-conscious goal of bringing about social change."[32] Officials of the Refuge, though, looked backward as well as forward in time for a conception of law which seemed to them both pragmatic and enlightened. Like ancient Roman jurists, they insisted that law was an educational instrument that shaped national character as it dispensed justice, that the moral fiber of a civilization was written largely in its lawbooks. In the fashion of the philosophes, they studied the histories of nations in search of reasons for past social advancement. No conclusion seemed more obvious than that "the meliorations which are visible from time to time in the criminal code of nations" provided the truest indices to "the progress of refinement, and the growth of enlightened feeling." Societies which allowed the emotion of vengeance to sway dispensation of justice were, in the managers' view, in a "savage and barbarous state."[33] Deterrence, not revenge, inspired the criminal codes of the past which they took as models for the future.

Though children were generally not at the center of attention in late eighteenth-century penal theory, general admonitions against revenge were assumed to apply with even greater force to them.[34] Indeed, by the Jacksonian period it was already becoming axiomatic, in both legal doctrine and popular educational thought, that children were unique beings requiring special indulgence and not merely miniature adults.[35] The traditional common law rulings on criminal responsibility were inappropriate; Blackstone's dictum that children over seven were criminally culpable ignored the peculiar psychology of the young, their susceptibility to suggestion and improvement if instructed diligently in moral principles. "Never let them be made victims of the Law," pleaded the managers, "their years and their inexperience forbid the idea of making them the subjects of retributive justice. The vengeance of the law, when inflicted upon them as a terror to others, is altogether misplaced, and has neither vindication for its practice, nor apology for its severity." Surely, they asserted, "every child may demand of its parent, of being well instructed in the nature of its duties, before it is punished for the breach of their observance."[36]

The inclusiveness of the Refuge's legal mandate provided another example of the managers' desire to use law, in Horwitz's term, "instrumentally," and was also probably the single best indicator of their faith in education as a social panacea. The institution received not only convicted lawbreakers, but dependent, neglected, and recalcitrant youth committed by their parents for incorrigibility. Technically almost no child in New York City was beyond the managers' guardianship. Children of the poor, of course, were expected to form the principal clientele; they came under "the influence of bad example" far more often than did wealthier youth. But the Refuge could—and, its sponsors liked to point out, occasionally did—receive well-to-do youngsters either detected committing crimes or incarcerated by disgusted parents.[37]

The managers' plenary authority clarified the nature of the Refuge by distinguishing it from all previous experiments in "child-saving" (to use a phrase which became popular in the Progressive era) at home and abroad. Massachusetts had long possessed a law to compel neglectful parents to surrender their children to state care, but the legislature had never provided special facilities for their confinement and instruction. Similarly, while England and several European countries could claim to have opened houses of refuge prior to 1825, these were, in the view of the managers, "mere penitentiaries" for punishing criminal youth. The latter facilities lacked authority to detain children not formally convicted of crimes, and also lost control over them after their sentences expired.[38] The New York House of Refuge, on the contrary, received all variety of impoverished and criminal children, and sentences to it were indeterminate, the inmates to be released only at the managers' discretion (unless they turned twenty-one first).[39] In 1829 the managers gloated: "Parents or guardians, from the time it is legally sentenced to the Refuge, lose all control over its person. . . . it is in this sense that we may say in truth, that the New-York House of Refuge was the first of its kind ever established."[40]

The Nature of Treatment

However enlightened the new laws of juvenile justice, they were only means to ends. The nature of treatment, not the liberality of a legal mandate, provided a firmer basis for evaluating the sponsors' intent.

It was precisely on this issue, though, that the managers were most equivocal. They insisted, on the one hand, that the Refuge was an educational enterprise meriting comparison with public schools, designed especially for children whose miserable home situations hampered their ability to attend classes daily. Its employees were teachers; inmates were scholars; confinement was a pedagogical necessity, not a punishment for misdeeds. The Refuge, in sum, was a boarding school for children of the poor, reminiscent of Pestalozzi's school in Yverdun and Fellenberg's in Hofwyl.[41] But the managers also affirmed that the Refuge was a "juvenile penitentiary," a prison scaled down to children's size and abilities. Of necessity, its officers were caretakers forced to regard inmates as potentially dangerous criminals with vicious habits requiring thorough eradication. The dual nature of the New York House of Refuge was thus not simply reflected in the institution's loose "entrance requirement," it was part of the founders' ambivalent aspirations for uplifting the children of the poor.

In their various public statements, the managers tied the social aims and pedagogical means of the Refuge inextricably to those of the public schools. A full-time residential school was essential only because of the inmates' perverse home environments. "Have not they the most emphatic claim to the charity of public instruction who have the misfortune to be drawn into the vortex of crime, by the force of inevitable suffering, by the urgency of guilty parents, by the excitement of wicked associates?" From this general proposition, the managers reasoned that imprisonment was nothing more than an educational necessity. "But how are the peculiar objects of your bounty to be educated, unless they are entirely withdrawn from the purlieus of wickedness?"[42] Incarceration, in their view, constituted neither punishment nor even deprivation of liberty. It was simply a matter of protection, of preserving the native innocence of children and segregating them from evil associates. Whether a child should be imprisoned depended in good measure upon the quality of his parents, his home, his community: his social status as much as his behavior was at issue.[43]

Inmates spent only four hours a day in classrooms—two for moral indoctrination and two for mental improvement—compared to eight at labor. Still, the managers expressed little concern that their intellectual attainments would lag behind those of public school students. Indeed they suggested a rather ingenious explanation for the educational achievements of inmates, combining popular social thought with an elementary transference theory of learning. Most delinquents, they argued, were precocious because they had been forced to exercise their mental faculties earlier than their wealthier peers. "The frauds or tricks he has practised to provide for his sustenance, or for the gratification of his vicious propensities, have obliged him to exercise thought, reflection, and ingenuity." Moreover, life on the city streets made delinquents more independent and self-reliant, qualities which could be turned to benefit in the Refuge—or so the managers believed. "An early self-dependence prepares these children to receive instruction, and when their minds are rightly directed, that ability which would have made ingenious rogues, renders them apt scholars."[44] Whether valid or spurious as either psychological theory or actual educational experience in the Refuge, the explanation did, at least, provide cause for optimism.

Consistent with their critique of vengeance and with their educational mission, the managers claimed to rely primarily on persuasive modes of discipline.[45] Beatings and whippings, they felt, were inhumane and also ineffective as inducements to learning. All children were teachable without resort to force if instructors capitalized upon their native impressionability and budding capacity to reason. "An appeal to the understanding and affections will generally awaken feelings that soften the mind and elevate the character; no human being ever gave himself credit for doing right from fear, but everyone feels a self-respect, when he is conscious that he does right from reason." The managers concluded, in anticipation of the movement later in the century to abolish corporal punishment in all educational enterprises: "It requires much less capacity, much less knowledge of human nature, to govern a child by his corporal, than by his mental feelings."[46]

In addition to asserting that inmates received as good an education as students in public schools, the managers alleged that they also better learned the meaning of virtue. Casting the Refuge as an embodiment of Jacksonian egalitarian ideology, the managers described it as a miniature democratic community where character, merit, and a willingness to help others counted for recognition and reward. Inmates were awarded "badges of distinction" for performing routine chores without complaint and for showing the right attitude, that is, accepting imprisonment as an opportunity to eliminate bad habits and become virtuous. The managers claimed also to be teaching inmates the rules of success in the outside world; not only would they suffer no stigma from imprisonment, but they would actually be better able to adapt to worldly demands. "You have had experience that must teach you, that if you are good you may be happy, if you are bad you must be miserable. . . . If your life be hereafter exemplary, the errors of your infancy will be forgiven or forgotten. In our happy country, every honest man may claim the reward he merits."[47]

In practice the New York House of Refuge, like its counterparts in Philadelphia and Boston, did not abandon physical coercion in favor of emulation, did not treat children as unique beings who thrived on indulgence, and did not provide inmates with the skills and attitudes necessary to achieve success in Jacksonian society.[48] None of this is surprising. More to the point, however, is that the managers were in fact hesitant from the beginning to waive traditional views of the criminal responsibility of children, to scrap punishment for a wholly educational solution to juvenile crime. As often as they insisted that the Refuge was a school, they insisted that it was—and was meant to be—a prison.[49] While the managers perceived no inherent conflict between these two organizational models, they did employ two different pedagogical schemes, one drawn primarily from the public schools (emulation) and the other from the state penitentiaries (strict regimen, hard labor, physical punishment).

Thus the daily routine at the Refuge was similar to that at Auburn and Sing-Sing, with an emphasis on order, firm discipline, and elaborately detailed work schedules. Far from instilling inmates with a success ethos, the managers emphasized the traditional expectations for a lower-class citizenry: duty, self-denial, probity, submission to legitimate authority.[50] By having inmates conform to the exacting demands of a uniform schedule, they hoped to teach not only the necessity but the habitual practice of orderly, meek existence.[51] The "curriculum" of the Refuge was contained in the precise organization of activities as much as in any particular set of skills or attitudes actually taught.[52]

The managers also shaped the Refuge to look, architecturally, more and more like a penitentiary. When it opened in 1825 the institution was makeshift, composed of wooden barracks used by the federal government for an arsenal in the War of 1812. It appeared nothing like the massive stone structure at Auburn or the buildings then under construction for Sing-Sing. Within just a few years, though, the managers built a high surrounding wall and erected several large stone buildings with individual cells.[53] The cells, they granted, were built with the same intent as in penitentiaries. "It is in the silence of night, in solitude, and within the naked walls of a cell, that the mind is obliged to turn upon itself, and that reflection is awakened." By these means, they predicted, the "House of Refuge for Juvenile Delinquents may become *a true penitentiary.*"[54]

Finally, the Refuge relied on common prison punishments to enforce discipline, although, as a rule, such punishments were used less frequently and for shorter periods. Inmates were regularly whipped or placed in solitary confinement for failing to conform to the daily regimen; some were punished because their labor productivity was low. The managers could hardly be considered sloppy sentimentalists about the utility of harsh discipline in treatment, as they demonstrated in defending Superintendent Nathaniel Hart, who had come under public scrutiny for the severity of his punishments. Nonsense, replied the managers: "There are some natures who can be made to feel only through their corporal senses; and the managers have not been willing to suffer these to be sacrificed to notions of ultra-philanthropy which would abolish all punishments."[55]

Inmates might not be considered as culpable for misdeeds as adults, but the managers were unwilling to allow past sins, real or suspected, to go unpunished. Ignoring the fact that many children in the institution had not been tried for specific criminal acts, the managers nonetheless made it clear that all would "be treated as that they may not forget that they are placed here for their misdeeds. . . . that they are offenders against the laws of our country, that they are in a place of punishment, and that that punishment is confinement and labor."[56] Lest the analogy between reformatories and schools be pushed too far, they cautioned: "[We] cannot think that these inmates are to be treated exactly as they would be if they were the innocent inmates of a college. Were they to be treated as those deserve who are pure and innocent, they might be led to think, that vice was not odious to mankind, and that the stain of crime was too easily obliterated."[57] And, as if to remind themselves once again of the dangers of "ultra-philanthropy," the managers concluded: "It must not be forgotten, that the House of Refuge is in fact a prison for children."[58] It was unlikely, indeed, that the children would forget.

Conclusion

The founders of the New York House of Refuge offered no single explanation of the nature of their institution. It was a product of both "enlightened" penal theory and expediency; of new intellectual perspectives on the instrumental uses of law, and a pragmatic desire to open some facility for criminal youth so that juries would not hesitate to convict them. It was both a prison and a school, a place to punish as well as to teach. Whatever their difficulties in explaining why and what they had created, there was one organizational model which the managers rarely invoked: the human family.[59] By mid-century a small but growing body of educationists and charity workers with little stake in the existing institutional arrangements concluded that the only reformatory worth having was one modeled, architecturally and pedagogically, on the family, and that the Jacksonian refuge was already an anachronism.

3

Domesticating the House of Refuge: The Family Reform School in Victorian America

That the Jacksonian house of refuge triumphed in America is readily apparent to anyone who visits the numerous facilities in every state for the care and treatment of juvenile offenders. Most reformatories appear to be nothing more than prisons for children.[1] The obvious exceptions, like the forestry camps (which receive inordinate publicity despite their limited role), are more than offset by the jail-like detention facilities which often do not even appear in official accounts of how many children are incarcerated.[2]

The triumph of the congregate reformatory did not always seem inevitable. In the middle decades of the nineteenth century and periodically for the next hundred years, a new alternative appeared which, its proponents felt, better comported with the expressed goal of rehabilitating delinquents without primary reliance on force or the threat of force. The alternative was the cottage or family reform school (I prefer the latter term) which can be found scattered throughout the countrysides of various states today.

The latter half of the nineteenth century was the age of the American reformatory, as most states opened their first separate facilities for delinquent, dependent, and neglected youth.[3] Frequently located in rural settings, most of these facilities were modeled on the New York House of Refuge. For treatment they relied mainly on regimen, religion, elementary academics, and manual labor—more often in factories than on farms—all within the congregate prison design.[4]

Not all states adopted the congregate organizational model. Several, notably Massachusetts, Ohio, Wisconsin, Illinois (Chicago), and Indiana, chose in the 1850s and 1860s to experiment with the family reform school,[5] which was then receiving considerable publicity in England from such respected penal reformers as Sydney Turner, Matthew Davenport Hill, and Mary Carpenter.[6]

Analysis of the family reform school is complicated by the sentimental rhetoric so characteristic of the Victorian era. Most obstacles can be overcome, though, by distinguishing carefully between the language and the substance of purported correctional innovations. From the 1850s onward, reformatories of all shapes, sizes, and rehabilitative methods were hailed in domestic metaphors as homes, cottages, and families appealing to children through love and affection. The analytical problems presented by this rhetorical style were obvious in an 1855 report to the New Hampshire legislature by a group of gentlemen appointed to design an institution for juvenile offenders. Though they proclaimed the virtues of European family reform schools, the architectural plan they submitted belied their ostensible endorsement.[7] What they proposed, in fact, was merely a new set of verbal justifications for the older Jacksonian model. In this they were typical of numerous correctional reformers throughout the country: theirs would be a conventional house of refuge permeated by a family spirit, a family atmosphere.[8]

Rhetorical sleights of hand like these, though bothersome, also aid analysis. In particular, as I shall argue toward the end of the chapter, they point up several subtle changes in value which tied the growing appeal of the family reform school to broader intellectual currents in Victorian America.

The Jacksonian Refuge under Attack

By mid-century the inability of the Jacksonian house of refuge to rehabilitate or even maintain order was becoming, at least in charity circles, a frequent topic of conversation. Even the most tradition-bound had good reason to doubt the optimistic front presented by entrenched correctional administrators.[9]

In the halcyon early days, at least through the 1830s, the houses of refuge in New York and Philadelphia were widely heralded for their humane treatment of inmates, their remarkable rehabilitative achievements (from seventy-five to ninety-five percent of the inmates were reported as being rehabilitated), and even for the quality of academic instruction. (The early history of Boston's House of Reformation was more tumultuous and received a wider range of commentary.) At home and abroad these houses of refuge were acclaimed as additional evidence of America's undisputed leadership in things penological and educational, worthy counterparts to her prisons and public schools.[10]

But around mid-century the nature of daily life within the institutions began to come under more careful scrutiny, particularly after a series of fires, legislative investigations, unkind remarks by foreign visitors, and exposés revealed a wide gap between public claims of administrators and actual practices. It became increasingly clear, for example, that many staff members were cruel, even sadistic, and were more concerned about maintaining order than about caring for inmates. Contrary to common belief, physical coercion was an instrument of first resort and was frequently as severe as in prisons. A former assistant superintendent at the New York House of Refuge, Elijah Devoe, reported: "Corporal punishments are usually inflicted with the cat or a rattan. The latter punishment is applied in a great variety of places, such as the palm and back of the hands, top and bottom of the feet, and lastly, but not rarely or sparingly, to the posteriors over the clothes, and also on the naked skin." Instruments of physical coercion, he concluded, were "liable to be used everywhere at all times of the day."[11]

Other charges were both startling and disappointing. Educational achievements were minimal; rehabilitative accomplishments were exaggerated; corruption was rife; political considerations intruded into the appointment process and inflated expenses; active proselytizing of Catholic inmates was pursued against the wishes of their parents; hardened and relatively innocent offenders mingled at will, negating the original purpose of the institution to prevent "contamination"; sex segregation developed homosexual tendencies, encouraged sexual exploitation, and exacerbated emotional problems; vocational training programs amounted to no more than busywork or worse still, exploitation of cheap child labor for private profit; and finally, incarceration provided a perfect setting for mutual instruction and reinforcement of the norms and techniques of criminal behavior.[12]

Americans began to develop in the antebellum period what might be termed, paraphrasing Richard Hofstadter, a standard "reformatory jeremiad," invoked every so often to vent collective frustration, confusion, and guilt about this tenacious institution.[13] The New York House of Refuge, wrote DeVoe, employed "a stern, brutal, coercive government and discipline, entirely the opposite of that paternal establishment so amiable and ingeniously pictured in the 'annual reports.'"[14] One group of investigators captured the tone of mid-century criticism when it remarked of the Boston House of Reformation: it was "too much of a prison, too little an institution of instruction, too much the residence of law and punishment, too little an institution of grace and culture."[15]

Foreign Influences: The Rauhe Haus and Colonie Agricole

As noted in chapter two, it is impossible to understand the genesis of American juvenile corrections—its goals, institutional formats, and pedagogical techniques—without reference to the trans-Atlantic context of early nineteenth-century penal and educational reform.[16] The communications in the Jacksonian period between reformers in the United States and Britain expanded during the next several decades to include the Continent, especially Germany and France.[17] With lessening hesitation Americans in the 1850s and 1860s entered an ongoing trans-European dialogue on the theory and practice of juvenile corrections which far surpassed their own in levels of enthusiasm and sophistication (much to the surprise of many who had tended to assume the perennial leadership of the United States). "There is hardly, perhaps, a subject, the Crimean war excepted, which occupies a larger share of attention at the present time, than Reformatory Schools," reported the *London Quarterly* in 1856. "To use a familiar expression, they are becoming all the rage."[18]

As Americans soon learned, the congregate house of refuge was considered passé in Europe; a new organizational model, the family reform school, was in vogue. Although family reform schools differed widely, Americans usually focused on the two pioneering ones: Johann Wichern's Rauhe Haus, in Horn, near Hamburg, Germany, and Frederic DeMetz's Colonie Agricole, in Mettray, France.[19] Though a few Americans, notably Horace Mann, had been very much aware of these institutions since the 1840s,[20] the foreign reform schools first gained nationwide attention as a result of two child welfare conferences held in New York City in 1857 and 1859.[21]

The conventions provided forums for a variety of rehabilitative ideas, new and old, indigenous and foreign. Defenders of the house of refuge were out in force, insisting upon the viability and benevolence of the original Jacksonian design. For example, the superintendent of the House of Refuge at Rochester, New York decried the excessive attention being paid to the separation of confirmed and relatively inexperienced lawbreakers. Careful classification of inmates was unnecessary, he argued, because it was a positive good to have them mix indiscriminately. "It seems to be one of the arrangements of Providence that in society the virtuous and vicious should in some respects be together.... I do not think it wise to separate boys and girls from temptation. God has not so ordered it."[22]

The prevailing sentiment at the conventions was otherwise, however.[23] The nation's best-known charity and penal reformers came out strongly in favor of the family design in all new institutions.[24] Connecticut's famous educationist and expert on reformatories, Henry Barnard, drummed home the point: most Europeans no longer looked to America for guidance because they considered the house of refuge anachronistic.[25] Once a world leader in penological circles, America had lost its pre-eminence. Instead of slavishly aping the New York House of Refuge, Barnard urged, Americans should abandon prison vestiges entirely and erect reformatories with a less forbidding architectural plan and a more humane set of rehabilitative principles. Though insistent in recommending improvements for older congregate facilities, Barnard and others clearly preferred to place their bets on the future and on the new.[26]

The discussion of foreign family reform schools by Americans tended to be highly selective. As the contemporary critic Bradford Peirce pointed out, Americans saw mainly what they wanted to see. Less attractive or reproducible features, as well as more costly ones, tended to be left out of their comments.[27]

Americans portrayed the reformatories at Horn and Mettray as "anti-institutional institutions," in stark contrast to the highly formalistic houses of refuge.[28] On the one hand, the foreign institutions accepted the need for structure, for a carefully designed and self-contained setting in which to carry out treatment. On the other hand, they introduced new residential arrangements in order to break down structural barriers to the natural interaction of staff and inmates. Advocates of the family reform school intended to introduce a human element missing from the refuge routine, to make personal contact and communication the essence of the rehabilitative effort. Appealing to children's native capacity to love and be loved as the most effective spur to moral regeneration, they emphasized the cultivation of the emotions.[29] Their stress, in modern terms, was not on curriculum content but on increasing the frequency and enhancing the quality of empathetic interpersonal relations.[30]

To Americans the essence of the family design was a format whereby anywhere from one to three dozen inmates with similar personality traits were placed in separate small homes or cottages under the supervision, ideally, of a surrogate father and mother. Each family lived, worked, and attended school together, meeting with other inmates only on infrequent ceremonial occasions. This residential arrangement contrasted sharply with the Jacksonian refuge, where children of different ages and dispositions slept in cells or barracks-like dormitories, performed identical tasks according to a uniform schedule, and possessed no close authority figure to appeal to for personal assistance or comfort.[31]

By providing each child with a pair of exemplary parent substitutes and a secure environment, it was expected that the child would learn to look to and respect adult authority, savor the joys of sure employment and domestic bliss, emulate their betters, and provide mutual assistance in the elimination of bad

habits. Inmates would develop such strong emotional attachments to their surrogate parents that withdrawal of "familial"
affection would substitute effectively for punishment. More than
in the Jacksonian period, the emphasis, ideally, at mid-century
and after was on the manipulation and evocation of children's
native emotional resources. Treatment, in modern terminology,
was to focus on the affects.[32]

The impact of these ideas on American correctional practice
was apparent first in Massachusetts.[33] The Massachusetts experience, I hasten to add, was far from typical. But the willingness
of the Bay State, traditionally in the vanguard of educational
reform movements, to experiment with the new ideas helped
legitimate and popularize these ideas, and also provided working models of their viability. What follows is a brief analysis of
how optimism engendered by the family design affected the
correctional history of the state, revitalizing the faltering faith of
legislators in the ability of institutions per se to rehabilitate.

In the wake of several exposés of the horrid conditions for
children in the Boston House of Reformation, especially their
frequent intermingling with abject and corrupt adults, the
Massachusetts legislature opened the nation's first state-spon-
sored reformatory in 1848.[34] Financed partially by the state and
partially by a large donation left by Theodore Lyman, the
institution epitomized the Jacksonian house of refuge. Massive,
built like a prison, its correctional strategy reflected the
characteristic ambivalence of the Jacksonians: "The institution
should be considered a place of punishment as well as a place for
reform."[35] Thus, despite a glowing report from Horace Mann on
the virtues of foreign family reform schools, the legislators opted
to build American. They evidently considered it more urgent—
and less problematic—simply to separate child from adult
offenders than to experiment with new correctional ideas.[36]

Lyman had expected the institution never to house more than
three hundred inmates.[37] A "liberal" admissions policy, facilitated by an unregulated commitment procedure, soon rendered
that ideal illusory, however; within a few years local magistrates
and overseers of the poor filled the reformatory to capacity. In
order to prevent overcrowding and its inevitable concomitant,
disease, the legislature authorized an addition to the structure,

which doubled the inmate capacity. By 1858 the Massachusetts State Reform School, with six hundred and thirty-nine inmates, was not far behind the fantastic number of one thousand lodged in the New York House of Refuge (which had recently been removed from Manhattan to Randall's Island).[38]

The legislature had also voted in 1854 to create a separate institution for female delinquents, the first of its kind in the nation. Prodded by critics of the State Reform School like Samuel Gridley Howe, who from the first considered the Jacksonian design anachronistic and ill-advised,[39] and by numerous others who shared the common belief that the physical and emotional make-up of girls was inherently more delicate than boys', they agreed to experiment with the new family format. There was an intimate relation, explained Governor George Boutwell, between the architectural design and rehabilitative program of the institution. Each girl was housed with twenty-nine others, a matron, and an assistant, in a building intentionally made to appear like a normal middle-class family dwelling. "Each family," the governor observed, "is to be by itself,—to have peculiar and special relations to its head, and to be no further connected with any of its neighbors, and maintain no more intimate intercourse with them ... than is seen to exist in common life between families that reside near each other." Employed in the sundry occupations of a family, the girls would learn to "receive and reciprocate the affectionate love, the careful discipline, and the wholesome instructions that the members of a family should always receive and reciprocate."[40]

The trustees of the institution elaborated the governor's sentiments and further differentiated the aims and methods of a family reform school from a house of refuge.

> It is to be a *home.* Each house is to be a *family*, under the sole direction and control of the matron, who is to be the *mother* of the family. The government and discipline are strictly parental. It is the design to give a home interest, a home feeling and attachment, to the whole family; to make these homeless, parentless, or worse than parentless, wanderers and outcasts, feel that there is, at least, one place on earth in which they have an interest, and which has an interest in them; that there is one affectionate, motherly ear, into which they can whisper their wants and afflictions, with confidence and sympathy;

one heart which beats in union with their own, and to which
they can appeal for kindness, for guidance and support, and
around which their affections may cluster, with the assurance
of a kind and affectionate response. It is to educate, to teach
them, industry, self-reliance, morality and religion, and prepare them to go forth qualified to become useful and respect-
able members of society. All this is to be done, without stone
walls, bars or bolts, but by the more sure and effective re-
straining power—*the cords of love.*[41]

The reputation of the Massachusetts Industrial School for
Girls spread quickly. As the nation's first completed family
reform school, it attracted much attention at the previously
mentioned charity conferences held in 1857 and 1859. Here was
living proof, it was argued, that the ideas of Wichern and
DeMetz were practicable.[42] Within the state of Massachusetts,
moreover, the burgeoning fame of the Industrial School cast a
pall on the reformatory for boys. Not only caustic critics like
Howe but other prominent citizens began to acknowledge
reluctantly that in creating a Jacksonian style reformatory, the
state had uncharacteristically taken a giant step backward.[43]
Late in 1858—to some it seemed by divine agency—Westborough was set ablaze. It was, remarked the prominent
reformer Franklin Sanborn, "a most fortunate conflagration."[44]
The fire destroyed the entire addition, reducing the facility to the
original building sponsored by Theodore Lyman. More than a
decade later Sanborn, secretary of the Board of State Charities
(the first supervisory agency of its kind),[45] asserted that legislators contemplated tearing down the whole institution in the
fire's aftermath. This, however, was probably an expression of
momentary frustration;[46] in any case, they soon reconsidered,
choosing instead to retain the original structure but to limit
inmate population to two hundred. More significantly, the
legislature authorized construction of five small buildings on the
family design, each to house thirty youngsters just as at the girls'
reformatory. The cottages were soon in operation and gained
enthusiastic approval from the staff, particularly after the
removal of the old superintendent and several trustees "who
were supposed to be less friendly to the family system than
public opinion demanded."[47]

The Massachusetts State Reform School was thus transformed

into a curious combination of older Jacksonian and newer Victorian motifs, a large central building surrounded by small family cottages. By 1865 Sanborn reported that throughout the state the family design had revitalized faith in the ability of reformatories to stem the growth of delinquency. Inmates at the institution exhibited a more positive attitude than had previously been true, the bulk regarding it as their one true home; sorry to leave, they returned in later years with pleasurable memories. Sanborn made explicit the comparison with DeMetz's Colonie Agricole. "'When I see the clock-tower of Mettrai,' said a pupil of that school, 'walking don't answer; I must run.' The boys at Westborough have the same affection for the place of their education."[48] No doubt this represented a degree of wishful thinking on Sanborn's part, but it also provided undeniable testimony to the impact of the foreign experiments on the correctional history of Massachusetts.

Pressures at Home:
The Anti-Institutionalists

The apparent decline of the house of refuge and the ready availability of an alternative correctional model joined with another set of strategic concerns in the 1850s to enhance the appeal of the family reform school. The period witnessed the rise of a sustained and highly vocal critique of most forms of long-term institutional care, especially reformatories.[49]

The criticism was two-pronged. Primary reliance on reformatories, it was argued, though perhaps appropriate to the needs of the 1820s, was inadequate for the more heterogeneous, populous, industrializing cities around mid-century. The rapid acceleration of social and demographic changes had rendered the reformatory marginal to modern urban conditions.[50] But there was more to the anti-institutional critique than this. Undergirding it was a set of values and pedagogic principles unique to and characteristic of Victorian America.[51] These can best be appreciated through the writings of the two leading anti-institutionalists, Charles Loring Brace of New York and Samuel Gridley Howe of Massachusetts.[52]

The ideas of Brace and Howe, though similar in many respects, were also subtly different and require separate exposition. Brace's ideas on corrections were intimately tied to his evangelism. An ordained Congregationalist minister, he saw the mid-century ferment in juvenile justice as part of a nationwide, indeed a worldwide revival of religion and philanthropy. The driving force behind the revival, he believed, was that religion should be "practical" and concentrate on the building up of God's kingdom on this earth. Most religionists, he believed, had gone to one of two unfortunate extremes, becoming either too intellectual or too emotional.[53] To counter these trends, Brace espoused the principle of voluntarism, and argued for it force-fully in a popular book entitled *Home Life in Germany*.

Brace gave vigorous support to Germany's Inner Mission, an "immense popular movement" geared to root out the enervating forces of Rationalism in religion.[54] The Inner Mission em-phasized ardent confessions of faith coupled with charitable work. Most German principalities, however, opposed the Inner Mission, requiring citizens to profess conformity to the state religion with a government-sponsored confession of faith and to obtain confirmation from a pastor. Brace objected strongly to these practices. The acid test of religion, he affirmed, was its ability to inspire works of benevolence, and this kind of religion could come only through voluntary conversion. Compulsory religion, he felt, led inevitably to indifference, as detrimental to public mores as skepticism or atheism. According to Brace, the German middle classes, "the most influential portion of a People, who stamp especially its social character," had come to look upon the profession of faith as they did tax paying or military drill, deeds performed only because compelled by the threat of force.[55] The result, he said, was the moral deterioration of the nation.

These observations on religion led Brace to formulate general principles of behavior which he applied to the treatment of juvenile delinquents. In his indifference and duplicity, Brace argued, the German Bauer was akin to the inmate of a reforma-tory. The latter's much-touted reformation was superficial. At best inmates were little more than disciplined robots unable to cope with temptations in the real world. Obeisant inmates, Brace warned, made the best display pieces; visitors to institu-tions like the New York House of Refuge should not confuse compliant behavior with true inner conviction. Time and again he returned to the theme of real versus assumed virtue. "The virtues must not be drill-virtues; they must spring from the heart, and be exposed to the strain of temptation. A mere treadmill goodness, which has gone through a daily round of observances, under the pressure of force, is of little worth for every-day life."[56]

Even worse, Brace said, was the hypocritical inmate. All reformatories, he pointed out, "come to have their model wicked-reformed children, who listen year after year to the tale of their former wickedness and their present piety, until they arrive at a condition, if possible, worse than their first sensualism and bold sinfulness—a conscious, canting, hypocritical state."[57] In Brace's view, then, a truly rehabilitated delinquent, just like a truly pious Bauer, expressed his faith voluntarily and through good works, not through shibboleths in order to avoid punishment.

As an evangelist, Brace believed that children were immortal beings who one day would have to answer for their worldly hypocrisies. Yet there was more to his critique of reformatories than a heartfelt belief in the afterlife and a hatred of religious deception. At the core of his evangelism was a belief in children's native innocence and God-given individuality.[58] Reformatories, Brace observed, attempted to submerge rather than develop personalities; they treated inmates as if all were alike, forgetting that each suffered a "separate moral malady."[59] This unfortunate attitude seemed to be an occupational hazard: "All who deal with the poor and semi-criminal are so much inclined to treat them in mass, or to consider each child as a number or a name not a person, that personal influence comes to be forgotten."[60] "Each poor, deserted, unfortunate little creature in the streets is an *individual* like no other being whom God has created," he insisted. "The pledge of his immortality, is his individuality . . . which makes it impossible ever absolutely to include him within the machinery of a system."[61] In sum, Brace attacked reformatories for training inmates to be either robots or hypocrites, for failing to prepare them for real life, and for ignoring individual sensibilities.

In the nuclear family, particularly the western farm family, Brace found the antithesis to the refuge system (and also, happily, a less expensive way to cope with growing urban delinquency).[62] Under his direction the Children's Aid Society sent several thousand children each year to live and work with farmers, to become part of their families in spirit if not by formal adoption.[63] His reasoning, which reflected the attitudes R. Richard Wohl has described as the "country boy myth," was straightforward: the nuclear family was the most natural and therefore the best setting in which to reshape character and instill piety. It was "God's reformatory," the one and only institution which could induce the delinquent's voluntary adherence to a new moral code.[64] The stark contrast Brace drew between the treatment of city youth in reformatories and farm families integrates the several components of his thinking on juvenile corrections.

> The poor vagabond boy, or the child whom misfortune has made wretched and homeless, goes to a quiet country home. He is not under a system, he is not put up by name as a vagrant, he is not mingling with others who are as miserable, and perhaps more unprincipled than himself. He does not feel himself the member of an Asylum, where at best, under the kindest officers, the care can only be general and public. He is one of a little Christian family. He sits at the same table with the farmer's family, and goes to school with his children; his habits are closely watched by them, and he watches theirs.... he learns what they think to be proper and right.... the poor lad remembering the dirty cellars, and the alleys piled with garbage and the filthy holes of the great city, wonders with delight at the orchards and lilacs and the green grass and the pure air of his new home. Soon, perhaps for the first time in his life, Love begins to enter the little castaway, and he feels at length, there is somebody in the world who cares for him.[65]

By mid-century Samuel Gridley Howe had earned an international reputation for his innovative work with the deaf, blind, and mute as well as for his heralded exploits in the Greek war for independence. Now an elder statesman in the field of charities and correction, his mind remained as nimble, experimental, and as open to new ideas as ever. Though he, like Brace, was an anti-institutionalist (at least when it came to juvenile corrections), his ideas developed out of a different philosophical framework.[66]

Howe's critique of reformatories evolved naturally from his

larger complaint against governmental over-involvement in philanthropy. "Our people have rather a passion for institutions," he remarked in a vein similar to his transcendentalist friend Emerson.[67] What many regarded as benevolence on the part of the state, Howe judged destructive of an intangible spirit of place and brotherhood. He criticized, for example, the growing reliance on almshouses as a solution to housing for the poor. "The place for the poor in a Christian community is the home of those who are not poor," he argued. Since that typically colonial arrangement no longer seemed possible—if only due to matters of scale—the most humane alternative was not the isolated almshouse but the creation of homes "in the *midst of our own and as near like our own as may be. We should not sever* social ties, be they ever so feeble, nor break local attachments, but let the poor live on where the lines have fallen to them."[68]

Thus Howe (with a logic not dissimilar to that underlying the community action programs of the 1960s)[69] conceived of philanthropy as a secular crusade to raise the moral tone of whole communities. The magic of place held almost religious significance for him: to send social misfits to central institutions was to remove from localities a powerful stimulus to holiness. Rightly conceived, philanthropy was a species of social revivalism—but only if carried on by the people themselves.[70]

Unlike Brace, therefore, Howe proposed to keep juvenile offenders in their hometowns, to use them, as it were, to incite feelings of social sympathy which he believed had characterized colonial Puritan villages. "Each citizen should be led not only to sympathize with all of whatever class, but to show sympathy by action."[71] Juvenile reformatories, like the state almshouses, he said, had unwittingly plugged up outlets for the evocation and expression of sympathy, and consequently for the dampening of social tensions.

Just as Howe was troubled by the impact of governmental philanthropy on traditional notions of Christian brotherhood, he was similarly concerned about the detrimental effects of large reformatories on youth. Americans, he suggested, tended to draw false analogies between "material and moral forces" and to judge the beneficence of reformatories by their size; Americans not only had a passion for institutions but for big institutions.[72] "We see the effect of organization, discipline, and combined effort for any material enterprise, and infer that it is necessary for reformation. Congregation in numbers, order, discipline, absolute powers of officers and entire submission of soldiers, are essential to the efficiency of any army; but the object of armies is to make machines; in reformatories, it is to make men."[73]

Howe denied the frequently startling claims of rehabilitative success by proponents of the houses of refuge, insisting that no one had the slightest idea how many inmates had reformed. Indeed, given the broad legal mandate refuges enjoyed, the odds were that most of the purported successes should never have been imprisoned. They probably had become good citizens "in spite of, rather than by reason of, the influence of the reformatory."[74]

To Howe as to Brace, the upright nuclear family had been ordained by God to rear children. Delinquents placed in virtuous families, Howe affirmed, could not help succumbing to their subtle pressures to reform. Child psychology and social constraints worked hand in hand: "As new faculties, feelings, and emotions are brought into play, those formerly too active subside, and he begins to get into sympathy with the public feeling of the household."[75]

In the 1860s Howe translated these ideas into a program for juvenile corrections. At first he wanted only to break up reformatories and under the supervision of rural Massachusetts families, to lease small farms for delinquents to "colonize."[76] But he soon expanded his ideas considerably and began to advocate that the state "renounce the attempt to instruct and train the children for any length of time in the reformatory" and place them instead either with righteous families or local private benevolent societies.[77] Instead of maintaining expensive permanent institutions, he wanted the state to pay a stipend to individual families who agreed to rear delinquents until the age of twenty-one. Howe recognized that additional problems might arise under this arrangement, but considered any reasonable alternative preferable to incarceration of children.

At its core, Howe contended, the anti-institutionalist position reduced to plain common sense. "Let every man put the question to himself,—if he were poor and dying, and had to leave his little child, or his wayward son or daughter, at a public charge, would he prefer that it should be in a State almshouse, or a reformatory, or would he take the chance of such treatment as might be expected in any one of a thousand families of whom he knew nothing, except that they were ordinary New England families, and deemed worthy of trust by the constituted authorities?"[78] When in doubt, Howe believed, choose human nature over elaborate human contrivance.

Not surprisingly, then, he opposed all institutions for delinquents, whether on the new family or the old congregate design. To be sure, he was no ideologue: "We shall find in our public institutions, that, other things being equal, the nearer they approach to the family system the better, and the contrary."[79] Still he insisted that an institution by any other name was still an institution, not a "family" or a "home." In 1854 he jeopardized the proposed Massachusetts Industrial School for Girls by refusing to endorse the family idea. However benevolently conceived or designed, he said, inmates would invariably carry the stigma of imprisonment the rest of their lives. Call them family reform schools if you will, Howe concluded in resignation, but anyone who took their domestic pretensions literally was either a cynic or a fool. "The family must grow; it cannot be made in a day, nor be put together by rules and compass. . . . We have, at best, a make-believe society, a make-believe family, and, too often, a make-believe virtue."[80]

Evaluation of the ultimate impact of anti-institutionalism on nineteenth-century juvenile corrections is difficult and fraught with conceptual and methodological problems. Joseph Hawes's attempt to tie Brace's work to the later establishment of juvenile courts, for example, is teleological and supports a Whiggish interpretation of historical evolution.[81] Still, I would suggest that the anti-institutional critique had a relatively immediate, if indirect, influence, which boosted the appeal of the family reform school in ante- and postbellum correctional circles.

Brace and Howe were two of the most famous and respected philanthropists of the century; their opinions could not be easily ignored. While neither managed to halt the financing of large congregate institutions, their prestige within the charities and correction field did place members of the reformatory establishment on the defensive. Thus, it was not surprising that some correctional administrators began to look approvingly on the ideas of Wichern and DeMetz. Brace and Howe, quite unintentionally, thrust forward the family reform school as a new middle ground in mid-nineteenth-century corrections, an intellectually and politically disarming compromise between the Jacksonian house of refuge and no institution at all.[82] By the force of their critique they helped generate what might be termed a new liberal consensus on a modified version of the status quo, a new "sensible" position around which members of the institutional establishment could rally to defeat the radicals and at the same time support change. Together with the other developments examined in this chapter, the anti-institutionalist critique further helped legitimate the family reform school and bolster its appeal. By the end of the nineteenth century it became the conventional wisdom in American correctional ideology.[83]

The Cult of Domesticity and the Family
Reform School

To specify each of the diverse intellectual currents in the early and mid-nineteenth century that impinged directly and indirectly on correctional theories would be to write a brief intellectual history of the period, so intimate is the tie between the criminal justice system and the deeper values and beliefs of a society.[84] The phrenological psychology which became popular in the 1840s and 1850s, for instance, influenced thinking on the rehabilitation of delinquents as much as other reformist efforts in public education, temperance, and care of the insane.[85] Similarly, the gradual displacement of liturgical by evangelical types of religious expression, especially after the triumphs of Charles Grandison Finney, lent a pietistic flavor to mid-century correctional discussion which had earlier been absent.[86] Still, the individual impact of phrenology, evangelism, romanticism, naturalism, and so forth, is generally difficult to isolate.

However difficult, it is essential to specify one intellectual development that was critical in providing a conceptual framework for the legitimation and popularization of the family reform school. Several historians have argued convincingly that the antebellum period witnessed a subtle shift in popular opinions on proper techniques of child nurture.[87] The shift did not include rejection of a Calvinistic for a Romantic conception of child nature.[88] Rather, the changes all occurred within the framework of Lockean epistemology and modified Calvinist theology. They led less to a view of children as innately good than to an emphasis on native emotional resources which suffusive parental love could bring to the surface and then direct toward good citizenship. As in earlier periods, the ultimate aim of child rearing was to cultivate obedience and instill an unwavering moral sense. But now the motivational techniques were to be different: the stress was on persuasion, kindness, empathy— what I term affectional discipline—rather than on breaking a child's will through force. Shame, guilt, and above all, love were to substitute for physical punishments.

In this context, I would suggest, the appeal of the foreign reformatory experiments becomes more understandable. What correctional reformers increasingly recommended for reha- bilitating delinquents was in accord with the disciplinary tech- niques practiced—or at least advocated—in their own domi- ciles.[89] Though a foreign import, the family reform school meshed nicely with this emerging American "cult of domesticity."[90]

Rather than being embodied in statutes, sermons, and biblical precepts, as in the colonial period, the newer views on child rearing were conveyed in popular printed form, through dozens of books and several widely read magazines.[91] A key article of faith was that the child's moral development and ultimate salva- tion were entirely the products of parental effort, or, as Horace Bushnell immortalized the notion, of "Christian nurture."[92] Writers around mid-century urged that the reception of grace was less a matter of spontaneous conversion than of persistent ethical upbringing. The future of a child's soul, they wrote, lay almost entirely in the hands of his parents, over whom, presumably, God obsessively watched. Not to inculcate correct scriptural precepts, but to provide the child with perfect behavioral examples was the parents' main religious function.[93]

Antebellum authors portrayed childhood as a distinct stage of human development, thereby fostering greater tolerance for the moral and intellectual limitations of children qua children. Since children were to be weaned into salvation, they could no longer be viewed for religious purposes as miniature adults subject at death to the same eternal punishment as their elders. Children required a toned-down religious message suitable to their tender years and immature understanding (as provided in the rapidly expanding system of Sunday schools for middle-class youth),[94] not the hell-fire and brimstone scare techniques still commonplace, especially in rural communities.[95]

Schoolroom procedures embodied and reflected the newer views of childhood. Corporal punishments for misbehaving students declined dramatically, as the rod came to be considered inefficient for teaching discipline. Expurgated editions of literary classics like *Tom Jones*, used freely in late eighteenth-century classrooms, were replaced by a special brand of juvenile literature better suited, it was thought, to children's moral needs. Homework assignments for students were also substantially reduced, often to no more than a half-hour, to accord with children's limited physical and mental stamina. And, perhaps most tellingly, precocity of any sort in children came to be seriously frowned upon. Precocity, it was felt, was a sure indication that a child was headed for trouble by overreaching innate limitations and seeking the prerogatives of adult status too soon.[96]

With the popularization of phrenological psychology, it became common to refer to the affections and emotions as if each occupied specific, identifiable parts—faculties—of the brain. The writers on domesticity frequently discussed new methods of discipline in phrenological jargon.[97] They assumed that in normal growth the affections developed first, long before the diverse faculties of intellect and reason. From this perspective, the tendency of parents in the colonial period to dwell on a young child's capacity to reason appeared unnatural, unscientific, inefficient, and probably harmful. At best, the theory went, it would lead to superficial obedience, at worst to positive dissimulation. It might also encourage unhealthy precocity. On the other hand, and a source of great optimism, was the theory that the manipulation of innate "benevolent affections" would assure the child's normal physical, emotional, and mental maturation and lead naturally to filial obedience.[98]

Although their ideas were relatively new and untested, the antebellum authors remained confident that affectional discipline would inculcate parental and social controls more effectively than repressive techniques. To Lydia Maria Child the result was an "invisible restraint" of lifetime duration.[99] Even to Heman Humphrey, who upheld many Calvinistic views on the corrupt nature of children long after most domestic advisers had discarded them, "affectional persuasion" was "the grand instrument to be employed in family government. . . . The child is too young, indeed, to know why it yields, but not too young to feel the power by which its heart is so sweetly captivated."[100]

The application of affectional discipline was, to say the least, a full-time concern. Indeed it was as much a product of the overall household environment—its moral ambience—as of direct parental teachings. Gentle manipulation of children's affectional faculties required constant tranquility within the domicile. A parent's every smile conditioned character, awakening and elevating "the noble affections and pure sympathies of infancy," whereas uncontrolled displays of anger or of any passion might forever unbalance a child's moral gyroscope.[101] In the domesticity literature, consistency of affection was as necessary as affection itself; parents had consciously to submerge disagreements and emotional displays.[102]

In contrast to the preeminence of the father in the colonial period, the paramount role of the mother was at the center of attention in the antebellum literature. Writers waxed eloquent about the innate ability of women to cultivate the affectional faculties. According to George Ackerly: "What love and understanding can equal that existing in the mother for her offspring!"[103] Lydia Sigourney, an ardent foe of the early women's rights movement, insisted that nurturing was an inherent characteristic in women: "My friend, in becoming a mother you have reached the climax of your happiness."[104] And Washington Irving exclaimed, no doubt with a sigh: "Oh! There is an enduring tenderness in the love of a mother to a son that transcends all other affections of the heart."[105]

By the 1850s some writers had gone beyond the merely sentimental, stressing the prenatal determinants of children's character. The moral potential of a child, it was argued, was fixed at the time of conception in accordance with the mother's attitude toward intercourse. If conceived in lust, a child would forever bear his mother's moral onus; whereas if conceived in a morally rarefied passion—a "Love Child"—his righteous character development was more certain.[106]

Finally, the writers on domesticity insisted upon isolated residential settings. They saw an intimate relation between home ownership and the possibilities for moral education and cultivated, in both a physical and psychological sense, the sacredness of exclusivity. The more isolated a household, they affirmed, the more easily parents could pursue Christian nurture without interference. The ideal home was a sanctuary which "shut out whatever of bitterness or strife may be found in the open highway of the world."[107] In short, the successful application of affectional discipline required a special milieu in which the home was conceived as a world unto itself.

The prescriptive parent education literature of the Victorian period, then, reflected a major transformation in the pedagogy of obedience.[108] Emphasis on persuasion and manipulation of children's native emotional resources, especially their capacity to receive and reciprocate affection; on strong maternal influence; on close, frequent, and informal relationships between youngsters and exemplary authority figures; on isolated domestic settings in order to avoid perverse worldly influences: this was affectional discipline, whether in the home or correctional institution. Though the clienteles were different—a factor with enormous implications for practice—the spokespersons for the Victorian middle-class household and the family reform school were speaking the same language, proceeding upon similar assumptions about the nature and needs of children and expecting equally effective results. At least in the realm of theory, the antebellum domesticity literature further helped legitimate the family reform school and domesticate the Jacksonian house of refuge.

Conclusion

Fed by influences indigenous and foreign, the theory of juvenile justice in the mid-nineteenth century thus embodied a broad reorientation in values. In the Victorian period, affect (in the psychological meaning) became the moral and pedagogical axis around which, ideally, religion, literature, architecture, education, child nurture, and juvenile corrections revolved. A characteristically new approach to the power of sentiment and emotion in human affairs had been enshrined.[109] Though no single American was as readily identified with the family reform school as Horace Bushnell was with religion, Lydia Sigourney with polite literature, Andrew Jackson Downing with design, Catharine

Beecher with child rearing, or Elizabeth Peabody with education,[110] the new correctional ideals nonetheless ran parallel to new trends in mainstream culture.

4

Love on the Move: The Juvenile Court Movement in Progressive America

Historians and social workers have lavished so much attention on the Progressive era as the critical stage in the development of modern juvenile justice that it is uncommonly difficult to separate myth from reality.[1] Even those hostile to the Progressive reformers have perpetuated the conventional myths; Anthony Platt, for example, argued that the Progressive period witnessed "the invention of delinquency."[2] Plainly this view is misleading: it distorts the attitudes and policies of the nineteenth century and provides no context for asking what, if anything, was unique about Progressive juvenile justice.[3]

The Progressive era, I believe, was indeed a seminal one, although for reasons different from many of those customarily given by both sympathizers and detractors of the juvenile court movement. To understand what was new, it is essential to view the court and probation as part of a continuing stream of social thought and institutional experimentation that had been developing in response to juvenile delinquency for nearly a century.

Most problematic in any attempt to characterize the juvenile court movement as a whole was the role of Denver's Judge

Ben Lindsey, by far the court's most famous and prolific booster.[4] Lindsey's engaging tales of delinquents who responded positively to his counsel, who confided intimate secrets to him, who after appearing in court obeyed parents they had previously scorned, and who attended school, worked steadily, and reported regularly to probation officers provided a glowing commentary on the achievements of one early juvenile court. If one is to believe Lindsey—and there is little solid evidence to challenge his view—neglected, dependent, and delinquent children in Denver received more solicitous treatment than would have been possible in a city where stricter rules of evidence and procedure applied. Lindsey appears to have wielded his enormous power with discretion, humanity, and shrewdness. By taking familial, social, and economic factors into account—and adding a dose of his remarkable intuition—Lindsey mediated constructively between an impersonal criminal code and the distinctive problems of children. Despite the seeming contradiction, he ruled as a benevolent judicial despot.[5]

Although Lindsey's methods were uniquely his, especially his active role in probation, he became the acknowledged spokesperson for the court movement throughout the country.[6] Through dozens of books and articles on his Denver experiences, extended trips and speeches in support of the institution, and his prominent political and social connections, Lindsey more than anyone legitimated and popularized the mission of the court. While other judges, probation officers, and charity workers spoke and wrote about their experiences, none provided nearly as much detail and insight into the decision-making process of the court as he did. Lindsey came close to dictating the form and content of contemporary opinion on the subject for at least two decades, especially through his artful renditions of didactic sentimental stories.[7]

Lindsey stood in relation to the court movement much as John Dewey did to progressive education and Jane Addams did to social settlements.[8] All were popularly acknowledged as leaders of their respective institutions, yet all differed considerably from the rank and file of reformers who identified with them. Just as Dewey's grasp of the educational needs of an industrial democracy and Addams's insight into the psychological and cultural mainsprings of immigrant behavior far surpassed their followers' understanding of the issues in both sensitivity and sophistication,[9] so Lindsey's understanding of the possibilities and limitations of the court was more profound than that of most partisans.

Yet at the same time Lindsey, like Dewey and Addams, shared many of the aspirations and cultural appreciations of his reform colleagues.[10] It was not merely fortuitous that all three came to be identified as leaders, for the quality of their writings enabled the rank and file to comprehend general statements of purpose and action even while failing to penetrate their more subtle meanings.[11] Lindsey's writings remain central to any examination of what the court movement was all about, especially in its early phases.

The Juvenile Court Movement:
An Overview

The efforts to establish juvenile courts and probation departments in the early twentieth century were part of a broader social movement to accommodate urban institutions to an increasingly industrial base and a predominantly immigrant population; to introduce control and planning into diverse aspects of city life previously monopolized by entrepreneurs; and to apply recent discoveries in psychology, sociology, medicine, and business management to the education of children.[12] The juvenile court also played a special, if unplanned-for, symbolic role. The court inevitably became the ultimate proving ground for many other reform measures, such as child labor laws, industrial education, compulsory school attendance, visiting nurses and teachers, the establishment of kindergartens, and so forth.[13] Whenever a child was brought into court for reprimand or punishment, it was apparent either that these reforms were not reaching him—the most generous and typical explanation of the reformers—or that reform measures were not having the desired salutary effect.[14]

The juvenile court served not only as a symbolic proving ground but as a literal dumping ground. It was the place where children and parents landed who could not, despite much institutional revamping in their behalf, perform in the larger society on terms the reformers considered acceptable. In practice the juvenile court functioned as a public arena where the dependent status of children was verified and reinforced and where the incapacities of lower-class immigrant parents were, in a sense, certified. The juvenile court flunked parents just as the public school flunked children; in both instances the lower-class immigrant was the principal victim.[15] While offering assistance and guidance, the court also gave its imprimatur to failure, societal and individual.[16]

The juvenile court movement was more diverse in practice than in theory. Nearly all commentators, including Ben Lindsey, subscribed to common goals and methods.[17] To be sure, a charismatic figure like Lindsey ran his court differently from a legal systematizer like Julian Mack in Chicago; procedural flexibility was much greater in Indianapolis than in New York City; investments in detention facilities and probation staffs varied widely from place to place.[18] Yet the movement cohered nonetheless; a consensus existed on what constituted an ideal juvenile court.

But what was unique to the Progressive era about this consensus? What distinguished the court movement from the innovations in theory and practice of the Jacksonian and Victorian periods? What made the juvenile court movement sui generis?

First and most celebrated of juvenile court reforms was the introduction of preventive and diagnostic purposes into judicial proceedings. In the nineteenth century one of three things had probably happened to children under the age of sixteen brought into court on criminal charges (a scarcity of information makes it impossible to be certain).[19] After pleading guilty or hiring a lawyer to dispute alleged facts, these children were either (1) convicted by judge, jury, or both and committed to an institution, (2) truthfully found innocent and released, or (3) falsely declared innocent by sympathetic judges and juries who simply refused to commit them to available penal facilities.[20] Although (as earlier discussed) a child did not have to be guilty of a crime to be committed to an institution, the main object of judicial hearings was to determine, using many traditional procedures of criminal law, the truth of formal charges.

In theory the creation of juvenile courts altered the nature and purpose of courtroom appearances for children.[21] Indeed, if possible, the child was to be kept out of court entirely. The ideal

procedure was to have a probation officer, after being notified
by petition, complaint, or arrest of an alleged dependent,
neglected, or delinquent child, investigate the home situation to
determine whether judicial intervention was warranted. The
probation officer, it was expected, would obviate judicial intervention by resolving many difficulties with the personal advice
and services he offered, and by mediating between the child's
family and available health, recreation, financial, and other
resources in the community. But if this option did not work to
the probation officer's satisfaction, or if the probation officer
decided it was inappropriate to the problems at hand, the child
and his family—the two were always considered together—
would be brought into court.

Once in court the child was to be treated very differently from
the adult criminal, especially in the area of procedure. Ideally,
the juvenile court would employ varying degrees of procedural
informality in order to assess the causes of delinquency—not
what the child had done, but why he had done it.[22] Relying
heavily on reports by probation officers, the judges would attempt to elicit additional information from the child, his parents,
social workers, and anyone else who had pertinent information.
Medical analogies were frequently used to describe the aims and
methods of these investigations. The object of judicial and probationary inquiries, and the basis of the disposition, was to be
the child's "condition" rather than specific offenses which
brought him to the court's attention in the first place. Though
proponents of the court occasionally recognized that abuses of
power might result from these unregulated procedures, they
generally sanctioned without reservation a benevolent judicial
despotism.

The second unique feature of the court movement was the
creation of separate detention facilities for children accused or
suspected of crime, dependency, or neglect.[23] In the nineteenth
century, children had generally awaited trial in sordid jails,
where they commingled with adults and where they often returned if found guilty and unable to pay a fine. In the early
twentieth century these practices were gradually phased out, at
least in large cities. The necessity of detention was now argued
on three grounds: diagnostic, educational, and punitive.[24] While
in detention youngsters were to be carefully observed and in-

spected by doctors and other supervisory personnel to determine what was distinctive about their physical and mental make-up that might assist in later disposition. They were also to receive academic and moral instruction to help them keep apace of schoolwork (in the Progressive era, even those who had taken out working papers were expected to attend continuation schools). A final argument, though one less frequently articulated, was that the detention centers would serve a new penal function: judges and probation officers could employ them as sanitized jails for children who, in their judgment (with or without a formal hearing or determination in court), required short-term chastening instead of long-term commitment.

A third innovation, least frequently enacted and even less frequently enforced, was the adult delinquency statute. The sponsors of the juvenile court intended to raise standards of child rearing throughout the country by holding neglectful or malicious adults criminally liable for juvenile delinquencies. At the very least, the sponsors hoped to eliminate the most egregious examples of bad parenting.[25]

In the nineteenth century the responsibility of parents for their children's delinquencies was, at one and the same time, taken for granted and considered irrelevant for the disposition of a case involving the child.[26] In the juvenile court of the Progressive era, though, parent and child were on trial together. The parents' ability to provide future care for the child lay at the heart of the court's decision-making process. Under most adult delinquency statutes, parental liability had to be proven in a separate legal proceeding.[27] Parents or others considered responsible for a child's delinquencies (barkeepers or prostitutes, for example) could be fined, assessed a fee to support the child in a reformatory, or even imprisoned themselves. Given the wide jurisdiction over parental behavior in many juvenile courts, domestic relations or family courts began to evolve from them before the First World War.[28]

The fourth and most significant—though least strictly new—feature of the juvenile court was probation.[29] Rehabilitation of delinquents in their own homes, as contrasted with the nineteenth-century preference for quick removal of problem youth to reformatories, was the primary goal of Progressive juvenile justice.[30]

To be sure, the sponsors of the court considered commitment of dependent, neglected, and delinquent youth to be necessary and viable dispositional options. They could hardly be termed anti-institutionalists in the same sense as Charles Loring Brace or Samuel Gridley Howe.[31] Still, they saw no good reason to institutionalize most delinquents, especially first offenders.[32] By definition, they argued, an institution was an artificial arrangement for the rearing of children; no institution could replace the affectional ties between most natural parents and their offspring. Instead of relying on the institution, the court's sponsors focused on the offender's home as the center of treatment and the probation officer as the key remedial agent. In the Progressive era rehabilitation was to be family-, and not merely child-oriented.

Prominent advocates of the juvenile court conceded that its fate rested on the quality of probationary care. As Charles Heusiler put it: "The probation system is not only desirable, and is not only needed as an adjunct, but it is *absolutely impossible* to do the work without it, and without it the laws had better be repealed."[33] Spokespersons for the court asserted that probation alone could transform the juvenile court into an educational mission to impoverished children and adults. While the role of the judge was important, explained Harvey Hurd, "even more will depend upon the probation officer. He (or she) it is who comes in personal contact with the child, and in the majority of cases with the parents and associates, where practical good common sense goes for so much."[34]

Probation officers were to be educationists in the broadest sense imaginable: at least in theory, nothing in a child's home, school, occupation, or peer group relations was beyond their purview. "The work," insisted Heusiler, "must be carried into the homes and the heart of the boy and his people. Not the offense alone must pass under the observation of the court, but the temptation, the lack of opportunity, the bad examples, all the inducing causes of the offense must be discovered, and when discovered rooted out."[35] Delegated broad powers of surveillance and intervention, probation officers embodied the progressive educationist ideal of ministering to the whole child perhaps better than any other group of "educators" in the era.

The probation officer was less a legal official than a family tutor. He was expected to instruct children and parents in reciprocal obligations, preach moral and religious verities, teach techniques of child care and household management, and reprimand when "lessons" went incomplete. "Loving, patient, personal service," argued Frederic Almy, provided the "antiseptic which will make the contagions of daily life harmless."[36] The emotional bonds established with children and parents were both the means and the ends of the probation officer's rehabilitative effort. "The youth must be ruled by kindness and suggestions," wrote Heusiler. "The voice of pity and compassion must reach him in his home, and reach his parents also in his home. Down to the very depths of that home must it go—the probation system must recognize that in the moral as in the material world the rain and the sunshine of pity and compassion is for the roots of the plant as well as its flowers."[37]

The unique features of the juvenile court movement, then, were four: informal courtroom procedures for preventive and diagnostic purposes; age-segregated detention facilities; penal sanctions for neglectful or malicious adults; and treatment focused on the child's home and family. The latter was the critical shift, the truly distinguishing characteristic of Progressive juvenile justice.[38] The single most important question which any inquiry into the ideological origins of the juvenile court movement must address, then, is this: why the new interest and reliance on the home as the center for treatment?

Economic Necessities and Institutional Precedents

In retrospect, the juvenile court and probation appear to have been inevitable responses to a changing society. After all, the very factors to which delinquency had long been attributed— especially the instability of home, family, and community life among the urban immigrant poor—were exacerbated in the late nineteenth century by mass immigration, rapid industrialization, long periods of economic depression, and the worsening of urban housing conditions. The unfeasibility of keeping institutional expansion apace of demographic and social changes became obvious, and the economic advantages of noninstitutional care increasingly clear.[39]

Frederic Almy noted, for example, that "the economy of probation greatly reinforces the support of the system on ethical grounds. It is not often that a measure of social reform makes an immediate appeal to the taxpayer, but probation relieves him from the public maintenance of many delinquents who under this plan are maintained at home at their parents' charge."[40] Charles Heusiler confirmed this view: "There is a double appeal to us all in the creation and maintenance of the children's courts. They call for the display of all the boundless wealth of our aggregated and personal charity—and they appeal to the economic side of our financial nature."[41] Thus the probation system carried the dual promise of being both cheaper and pedagogically more effective than the reformatory system.[42] In this sense, an economic determinist explanation for the rise of the juvenile court has much to commend it.[43]

Spokespersons for the court, however, did not see themselves bound by economic and demographic constraints to seek new institutional arrangements, even though they readily admitted the financial advantages of probation. Rather, in support of new correctional ideas they pointed most frequently to a few, isolated judicial and charitable experiments which had earned solid reputations. Two examples were most important. The first involved several judges in different parts of the country who had begun to conduct separate hearings for child offenders as early as the 1880s.[44] The judges' justification for this tactic was simple. It merely applied to judicial proceedings what had long been said of common jails, namely, that children were corrupted by frequent contact with confirmed adult criminals. The introduction of segregated court appearances for children carried the principle of segregation to a logical conclusion; there was nothing distinctively Progressive about it.[45]

The lengthy experiment with a crude probation system in Massachusetts was the second and more frequently noted precedent. Probation had begun in the 1840s due to the efforts of a kindly Boston shoemaker, John Augustus, who convinced local magistrates to entrust first offenders to him for supervision or, if necessary, for placement in foster families. In 1869, building upon Augustus's example, the legislature created the position of Visiting Agent within the Board of State Charities to investigate the social and family backgrounds of juveniles accused of crimes and to receive them for supervision and placement after trial. By 1880 the agents had investigated 17,136 cases and received 4,392 children for supervision. Limited at first to the Boston area, probation was gradually extended throughout the state. If nothing else, the experience of Massachusetts demonstrated to reformers in other states that probation was cheaper than the creation of new institutions and that it was not, at least in an obvious way, a catalyst of crime.[46]

If separate hearings for children in New York and the evolution of probation in Massachusetts provided working models for juvenile corrections reform, more careful scrutiny of correctional facilities also encouraged a search for judicial alternatives to institutionalization. A prefatory word is necessary here. It is, admittedly, all too easy to develop what amounts to a cyclical explanation of correctional reform movements, where reform appears as a logical and necessary response to prior institutional failures.[47] At the same time, however, it is impossible to ignore the growing awareness of and publicity on institutional liabilities in the Progressive period. By the 1890s criticism of correctional facilities had increased dramatically.[48] By itself this would explain little, but when considered in concert with new Progressive thinking on related educational and welfare issues, it contributes to a more complete understanding of why alternate methods of rehabilitation were increasingly discussed.

Homer Folks, head of the Pennsylvania Children's Aid Society and later a prominent proponent of New York's juvenile court and probation program, voiced the new critical consensus in a speech at the National Conference of Charities and Correction in 1891.[49] Despite the "untiring zeal and noble devotion" of personnel in reformatories, he contended with a bow to the institutional status quo, "certain evils seemed inherent in the reformatory system." First, the plethora of public facilities had tempted many parents "to throw off their most sacred responsibilities" and commit children voluntarily to institutions without sufficient cause. Second, Folks said, the great majority of reformatories still mixed criminal and relatively innocent youth, thereby facilitating "the contaminating influence of association" and turning reformatories into schools of crime. Third, despite the benevolent intentions of those who created reformatories, a stigma invariably attached to all ex-inmates just as if they had been sent to adult prisons. Fourth, even the best of institutions was incapable of individualizing treatment: "moral infirmities require as careful diagnosis as physical, and to treat all practically alike seems to us as valid as for a physician to prescribe one sort of medicine for all diseases." And fifth, he concluded, reformatories had provided inmates with a poor preparation for real life; indeed in many instances they had incapacitated inmates for later adjustments.[50]

Like most critics of the reformatory from the mid-nineteenth century onward, Folks was not an anti-institutionalist. He placed great confidence in probation to stem the growth of juvenile crime, but never doubted that institutions would always remain necessary. The proper classification and affectional care of children in reformatories remained a central concern of his. Rather than dealing with anti-institutionalism, the thrust of Folks's recommendations dealt with assuring "parental" attention at every stage of juvenile criminal proceedings—before, during, and after trial.[51]

Withal, by the turn of the century keepers of reformatories were more on the defensive than ever before, as the superintendent of a Missouri facility, L. D. Drake, revealed in trying to turn the tide of public opinion. Two erroneous popular ideas, he argued, stood in the way of success for ex-inmates of reformatories. One was that the institution was nothing but a prison, the other "that it is a place of idleness and pleasure, where ne'er-do-wells go to become no better than they were." Both views, he said, were mistaken. "There are upon inmates no badges of disgrace and felony. There are no walls encompassing them about. There are no guards with loaded guns to keep them within bounds. Children that enter these institutions are given every advantage possible." In short, Drake pleaded, he and the thousands of individuals "spending their lives in the upbuilding of humanity" had been treated unfairly. More careful inspection of what actually took place in reformatories, he contended, would alter the common false impressions.[52]

Unfortunately for Drake, of course, that is precisely what was being done in the Progressive era. His aggressive defense served mainly to indicate the extent of pessimism regarding institutional care and the effectiveness of the reformers' attacks in molding opinion. The increasingly publicized failure of reformatories to rehabilitate contributed to a growing willingness to develop less coercive, less formal, and less expensive modes of treatment.[53]

Intellectual Backdrop: Tempting but False Issues

While each of the foregoing developments helps to make the juvenile court movement comprehensible, none adequately conveys the movement's strength and positive thrust. The juvenile court, after all, was one of the most popular innovations in an era renowned for its solicitous attention to children.[54] It could only have taken hold across the country so quickly by synchronizing diverse but congruent elements in Progressive social life and thought. In brief, the juvenile court must be understood as a cultural artifact and not simply an economic expedient or an inevitable response to institutional deterioration. Its attraction lay in the realm of popular ideas as much as in the realm of public finance.[55] The question remains: of the sundry new intellectual developments in the Progressive period, which most directly shaped the rehabilitative mission of the juvenile court?

Charity and correctional workers frequently cited three sets of ideas to explain why the court came into existence: (1) shifting attitudes toward child nature and nurture, (2) the emergence of naturalistic theories of delinquent behavior, and (3) changing judgments on the causes of poverty. Each of these intellectual developments, numerous historians have argued, lay at the core of one or another reform measure in education and social welfare in the Progressive era.[56] In my judgment, however, none of these ideas was actually decisive in reorienting public policy toward juvenile delinquents. Together the ideas contribute little to differentiating the intellectual underpinnings of Progressive, Victorian, and Jacksonian juvenile justice.

Having determined earlier that a relatively benign attitude toward original sin and a preference for affectional discipline matured in the middle decades of the nineteenth century, the first issue, that of shifting attitudes toward child nature and nurture, can be treated with dispatch. True, scientific perspectives on the mental make-up of children increasingly came to dominate the prescriptive literature of parent education in the late nineteenth century and largely replaced earlier debates on whether children were innately good or bad. Differences of opinion on child rearing were now argued more within a framework of nascent developmental psychology than within the moral philosophy framework employed in the early part of the century.[57] Still, the end result of the scientific approach to raising children was mainly to extend Victorian lines of thought and action: on the one hand reinforcing the moral responsibility of parents for whatever their children became, on the other stressing more insistently that the painless path to childhood obedience was via the cultivation of the affections. As Bernard Wishy has argued, "The new knowledge from the scientists . . . made parenthood ever more serious work, with mothers, fathers, and trained observers now working together to preserve or purify the race and speed the progress of evolution."[58] The Progressive years (as suggested earlier) were not the first to witness a "soft pedagogy" approach to child rearing.[59] The message of developmental psychologists to rely less on force than trained parental love had long since been ingrained, at least in the prescriptive literature.

The fate of naturalistic theories of delinquent behavior requires a somewhat different explanation. These theories owed much to the isolation of adolescence as a distinct developmental stage by the famed psychologist and president of Clark University, G. Stanley Hall.[60] Hall's key idea, the recapitulation theory, hypothesized that in his personal growth, every individual passed through all stages in the evolution of the race (thus Hall's nickname as the "Darwin of the mind"). The recapitulation theory led Hall to formulate pedagogical imperatives: for every race stage in the individual life cycle, an appropriate disciplinary and instructional technique was essential.

At first glance Hall's theories appeared to suggest radical departures from the traditional emphasis on bad family and environment as the key causal factors in delinquency. Hall and his many followers, after all, accepted the formation and activities of youth gangs as natural phenomena, indeed as defining characteristics of adolescence. To them adolescence was a period of "unselfing," an age when the gregarious and social instincts bloomed.[61] Writers inspired by Hall argued that the adjective "gangy" should no longer be considered a term of opprobrium, since there was "a gang-forming instinct in the soul of everyone's boyhood." Boys entered gangs because nature impelled them to: "The boy in his earliest formative years is passively self-centered. Gradually he evolves away from his shell. As he grows older his social instincts desire free play: when his instincts crave further development, the boy seeks the gang."[62]

Yet the differences between those in the Progressive era who explained delinquent behavior within a Hallian framework and those in the Jacksonian era who had done so within a Lockean framework were more apparent than real. True, reformers like Jane Addams dutifully incorporated Hallian jargon into their analyses of delinquency causation.[63] Still, most of these reformers concluded by blaming delinquency primarily on parental and environmental faults, just as had been the case for the past one hundred years at least.[64] Hall's contribution to a new theory of delinquency causation was thus far from revolutionary. Most reformers still conceived of juvenile delinquents as impoverished immigrant youngsters victimized by ignorant or malicious parents who neither shielded their children from perverse influences nor provided for their developmental needs. If anything, Hall's ideas led logically to a greater emphasis on the need to separate children from impoverished or unfit parents, not in the direction of support for probationary supervision.

The acceptance of environmentalist explanations of poverty and, as a corollary, the emergence of new interest in delinquency prevention have long been standard themes in histories of Progressive welfare policy,[65] but several trends in recent scholarship tend to challenge these accepted views. First, it is clear that individualistic and moralistic explanations of poverty persisted, and coexisted, with environmentalist perspectives throughout the Progressive period. The degree to which one or the other viewpoint predominated is still debatable, but the reformers themselves and later historians have usually exaggerated the extent of the transformation.[66] Second, welfare reformers in the Progressive era were a diverse group who might draw together to sponsor particular pieces of legislation, but who differed greatly in the depth of their understanding of social and cultural phenomena. The best known and most frequently cited publicists, such as Jane Addams, Robert Hunter, and Lillian Wald, belonged to a select group whose insights into the causes of poverty and human psychology surpassed by far those of the majority of their reformist colleagues.[67] And third, many reformers were quite sympathetic to hereditarian explanations of poverty. In fact, their active support of eugenic measures fitted nicely into their social thought and policy formulations.[68] The traditional interpretation can even be turned on its head: the advent of probation may have seemed essential to free public monies for large-scale custodial facilities to house the "unfit" persons whom eugenicists identified for permanent segregation.[69]

Furthermore, even if the traditional interpretation is accepted—just for the sake of argument—would a significantly new explanation of the relation between poverty and delinquency necessarily follow? The answer, as previously suggested, is no. The conventional wisdom had long attributed juvenile crime to environmental causes; delinquent children (up to age sixteen) had generally not been considered responsible for their errant conduct. Curious though it may appear in retrospect, throughout most of American history popular views on why adults remained poor or became criminal rarely determined explanations of why children became delinquent.[70] Continuity rather than change best characterizes American thinking on the subject of delinquency causation.

In historical perspective, then, these features of Progressive social thought were less salient than they might at first appear in accounting for widespread endorsement of noninstitutional treatment for the great majority of problem youth.

Ally as Well as Enemy: The Poor Family and Probation

In addition to the important economic considerations discussed earlier, the best way to understand the rise of the juvenile court movement is through a contextual rather than a causal argument. The rehabilitative methods of the juvenile court were one manifestation of a newly heightened sensitivity in the Progressive period to the emotional bonds and educational possibilities inherent in all families, even those in fairly dismal straits. To be sure, this argument must be advanced cautiously. No more than their nineteenth-century forebears did child welfare workers in the Progressive era romanticize the nature of lower-class immigrant family life. If they generally did not lump all poor people into the category of the "dangerous classes," they often described ghetto life in ghastly, Hobbesian terms. Buttressed by the racist beliefs associated with the eugenics movement, the stereotype of an all-enveloping "culture of poverty" remained part of the Progressive imagination.[71]

Still, there was change. However biased and shortsighted the early twentieth-century reformers may appear from a modern vantage point, they were more optimistic about the possibility of redeeming lower-class parents than were their nineteenth-century counterparts. To be sure, most Progressive-era commentators on the poor were not nearly as compassionate or sensitive as writers like Addams, Wald, and Hunter. Nonetheless, as Robert Bremner has argued, in the Progressive period societal recognition of the involuntary causes of poverty grew appreciably. The common nineteenth-century caricatures of the poor as degraded creatures inhabiting a nether world gradually gave way to believable portraits of the poor as human beings suffering hardship and pain. The utter hatred and scorn for the adult poor in the nineteenth century, evident even in the writings of a reformer as discriminating as Charles Loring Brace, became much less frequent in the Progressive era. Not a revolution but a subtle change in traditional views of the immigrant poor had occurred; the widespread appeal of probation was one indication of this larger change.[72]

While proponents of the juvenile court continued, in nineteenth-century fashion, to ascribe delinquency to bad environment and poor upbringing, they developed at the same time a set of counter-justifications for preserving natural family units among the poor whenever feasible. The aim of probation, Frederic Almy wrote, was "the retention of natural conditions, in the home, if it is at all fit."[73] Ambivalence replaced outright condemnation. Much more than in the writings of earlier charity and correctional reformers, the possibility of teaching inept parents to mend their ways was seriously entertained.[74]

Proponents of the juvenile court drew ideas and language freely from the Social Gospel, insisting that the capacity to love and be loved was not class-bound. Like religious salvation, the moral uplift of offending juveniles would be a family affair.[75]

Thus, rather than define their task in terms of disruption and removal, reformers like Homer Folks, Ben Lindsey, and Julian Mack defined it mainly in terms of mediation and reconciliation. Like the creators of the Sunday school a hundred years earlier, these reformers expected to regenerate lower-class family life principally through the agency of the child.[76]

The juvenile court movement captured that peculiar blend of sentimentality and practicality, realism and boundless hope that characterized the myriad reforms of the Progressive era. But perhaps because most historians have concentrated on the child as the axis around which the reformers' faith revolved, the family orientation of many policy innovations has been obscured.[77] A few examples will suggest the importance of this theme and its obvious relation to the rehabilitative mission of the juvenile court.

One of the most persistent topics in late nineteenth- and early twentieth-century social commentary was the changing functions and future viability of the family in an industrial society. The writings of scholars such as John Dewey, Edward Ross, Arthur Calhoun, Elsie Parsons, and Willystine Goodsell are perhaps most familiar, but the concern permeated all levels of reformist thinking.[78]

For instance, Joseph Lee, a prominent advocate of playground construction, was typical in asking whether the family could survive industrialization and the expansion of governmental initiatives in education.[79] Stating a commonplace of the day, he argued that the industrial revolution had eliminated the home as a productive unit. Reinforcing this trend, Lee asserted, was the recent vogue of apartment living, which had further hampered the practice of the traditional domestic arts. Lee, as others, was deeply troubled by both of these developments, for he considered the family to be an irreplaceable bulwark of social order and public morality.[80]

Even more troublesome, if ironic, he said, was the fact that the expansive curriculum of the public schools had contributed, in the name of democratic political theory, to the ongoing erosion of family functions. To make schools serve better as equalizers of opportunity, American educationists, Lee believed, had unwittingly undermined one type of school—the family—in favor of another. Children now looked almost exclusively to public institutions for occupational training, domestic instruction, medical care, and recreational opportunities. While Lee recognized these developments as inevitable and considered many of them beneficial, he had grave doubts about their implications for the future of the family. The family, he pleaded, was "the mother of the affections, the first school and the best." It would be cruel irony indeed if in their "fight to save the child" reformers impaired or allowed to decay "that institution in relation to which, more than in all else, his life is to be found." By all means let government play an active role in ameliorating miserable conditions and enhancing the quality of urban life, Lee concluded, but let government also do everything possible "to foster and preserve" the family.[81]

Lee remained ambivalent about whether public schools could or should retreat from the areas he saw as already usurped. But according to him, the feeding of children in school, a relatively new proposal at the time he was writing, was definitely the educational straw that would break the family's back, leaving it with nothing to claim the allegiance of youth. Emotionally he argued: "I believe that we should draw the line here if we are to draw it anywhere; that we must oppose the general policy of school feeding if we intend to preserve the family at all. Outlying territory we can abandon, but here our citadel is reached. If we cannot defend this wall we might as well surrender."[82] The wall crumbled, of course, leaving Lee and many others—whatever their opinion on the single issue of school feeding—to worry about how the family could survive without a material or educational base.[83]

This Progressive era anxiety about the future of the family was also evident in voluminous writings on the subject of divorce. Divorce rates were on the rise in the early twentieth century perhaps because, as David Kennedy has suggested, of the "intensified emotional demand of family life" after the displacement of "economic partnership from the matrix of marriage."[84] Whatever the causes, the frequency of divorce stimulated lively and prolonged debate about its implications and fierce exchanges between die-hard opponents (who seem to have been in the majority), pragmatic acceptors, and a few gloating enthusiasts.[85] As Kennedy and William O'Neill have observed, however, these debates shed more spark than light on underlying issues: all assumed that the traditional nuclear family was the only effective setting for child rearing. "Practically everyone agreed on the paramount importance of the family in human life. . . . There were really no radical opinions on the family. Even the Socialist critics of marriage wanted only those changes that would 'make it possible for every mother to devote herself to the care of her children.' From that goal virtually no one dissented."[86]

The arguments over divorce, of course, went beyond the subject of crime prevention among juveniles to the larger issue of women's rights.[87] Inevitably, though, the debates brought the role of the family and the threats to its survival more sharply into focus as issues of public concern. This heightened interest both reflected and carried over into broader policy discussions on the welfare of children.[88]

Another indication of the growing interest in preserving family functions and forms among the poor was the mothers' pension. An early stage in the evolution of Aid for Dependent Children (ADC), the mothers' pension swept the country in the 1910s, despite some lingering opposition from older charity organizations.[89] Advocates for the pension drew upon the general Progressive hostility toward public residential facilities, orphanages as well as reformatories. "By the turn of the century," Mark Leff has written, "dissatisfaction with the 'products' of orphanages, combined with objections to institutional regimentation, artificiality, and inability to dispense individual care, elicited substantial popular opposition. 'Even a poor home,' it was said, 'offers a better chance for a child's development than an excellent institution.' "[90]

Pension advocates contended that any woman whose husband had died or abandoned his family should be assisted by the government to remain at home, thus enabling her to devote her full energies to child care. No woman, said pension advocates, could be both breadwinner and homemaker; to do both would be to menace the physical and moral well-being of the child. "Aid to prevent this disintegration," Leff has astutely remarked, "was distinguished from other relief because it buttressed traditional family roles."[91] In short, the mothers' pension, like probation, was a new mechanism for upbuilding traditional family forms.[92] Whereas reformers in the Age of Jackson and afterward had idealized orphanages as models of family organization, those in the Progressive era sought to preserve whatever remnants remained of natural family units.[93]

Equally revealing of new perspectives on the utility of preserving lower-class family life was the day nursery or day-care movement. Charity investigators believed that lower-class mothers entered the work force only because economic survival impelled them to, and that for lack of alternatives they had to leave their children at home alone for as long as fourteen hours per day (not to mention parents desperate enough to leave children at orphanage doorsteps or to patronize the baby farms). Day nurseries served the dual purpose of helping lower-class mothers to make financial ends meet and preventing bodily damage to unsupervised toddlers. Educational and developmental goals were minimized in favor of safe baby-sitting. Some reformers considered day care a temporary expedient which would become unnecessary with the expansion of public welfare. "The Day Nursery is only a make-shift. The great issue is the family, and the proper place for development is the home. Any system that permits the breaking up of home surroundings must be make-shift."[94] But most advocates of day care, as Margaret Steinfels has argued, regarded the preservation of the home as their first principle and assumed that long after mothers' pensions were established day nurseries would still be necessary.[95]

Still another group of reformers expressed its concern for the integrity of lower-class family life by organizing to teach poor wives to become efficient, scientific housewives. The home economics movement, which gained nationwide attention from women's and civic organizations, public schools and colleges, and various governmental agencies, derived from a commonly held if oversimplified view that lower-class husbands frequented saloons and deserted their homes because their wives failed to keep house properly.[96] However naive the justification, the movement inspired the formation of mothers' clubs throughout the country, devoted to the creed that efficient home management kept husbands at home, families together, and children in line.[97]

The founder and high priestess of home economics, Ellen Richards, believed that the data of "sanitary science" were so extensive that their dissemination, especially to the lower classes, would revolutionize the quality of home life.[98] Though she believed that all women could assimilate the new knowledge, Richards insisted upon the certification of trained experts to verify that proper instruction would be available to all. "Eternal vigilance," she admonished, "is the price of safety in sanitary as well as in military affairs."[99] She viewed household management as being doubly valuable: it was preventive rather than remedial (the same argument used to justify probation), and was, unlike the women's suffrage movement, a conservative and hence broadly appealing method of assuring women's influence in social reform. Home economics, Richards felt confident, would make women content by teaching them to appreciate the challenge of traditional domestic chores; content women would have little difficulty keeping their husbands at home and their children under control.[100]

Thus Richards advanced a relatively new reformist strategy which, like the mothers' pensions, focused public policy on the home and reinforced belief in the potential of poor families to improve themselves with outside assistance. Domestic science, like probation, served as a wedge into the homes of lower-class children and a lever for uplifting them.

A final example of how child and family together assumed the spotlight in Progressive welfare policy was the municipal mothering campaign. The role of women in the suffrage fight and social settlements has overshadowed this intriguing, popular, and characteristically Progressive movement.[101] Led by educated, though not usually college-educated, urban middle-class women from all over the country, the campaign acquired permanent form in 1897 with the organization of the National Congress of Mothers (forerunner of the PTA).[102] The philosophy of social action these women advanced was remarkably eclectic. Of special interest was their manner of adapting recent social scientific knowledge, especially the ideas of G. Stanley Hall and Ellen Richards, to traditional feminine roles and to older methods of charity distribution.

Representatives at the annual congresses were careful to distinguish their aims from those of the larger women's rights movement, or at least to state their priorities plainly. For example, Mrs. Theodore W. Birney, president of the National Congress of Mothers in its early years, cast a skeptical eye upon the clamor of women for admission to college: "Much has been said and written in these latter days about woman's higher education and her extended opportunities, so much that we have failed to hear the small voice appealing to us in behalf of childhood. . . . The higher branches of book learning are well enough for the girl or woman who has the inclination or time for them, but they should be secondary in her education to the knowledge which shall fit her for motherhood."[103] Another delegate, Mrs. Mary Lowe Dickinson, president of the National Council of Women, expressed less hesitation about higher education for women, as long as it prepared them to meet their traditional responsibilities. "It is the one thing of universal interest to the present, of universal importance to the future of the individual, of the nation, that the women of to-day accept, as their divine responsibility, the childhood of to-day." Higher education in these women's views, then, was invaluable insofar as it paved the way to enlightened motherhood by convincing women to "become students of childhood and students of every system, scheme, plan, and practice for the development of the body, mind, and character of the child."[104]

Other delegates maintained that the new sciences of developmental psychology and household management had literally turned youth into natural resources, subject to supervision and control by experts. Like Ellen Richards, Mrs. A. Jennesse Miller believed that "sanitary science" would revolutionize public health: "I believe the time is coming when it will be considered a crime to say, 'I am ill.' " Mrs. Miller's faith in dietetics as a reformist tool was emphatic, and was clearly (if illogically) tied to the aim of crime prevention: "I am in favor, first and foremost, of scientific feeding—of feeding men into heaven and children into morality."[105] The consensus of the National Congress of Mothers on direct intervention into impoverished households was most succinctly captured by Miss Frances Newton, who proclaimed: "Your children belong to me, to the neighbors, to everybody else, to every one with whom they come in touch. You can not keep them to yourself. . . . They are only lent to you to care for, to help, until they can stand on their own feet and live their own lives independently of you."[106]

A speech entitled "Mothers of the Submerged World" by Mrs.

Lucy Bainbridge embodied the municipal mothering campaign's overall strategy toward crime prevention. To Mrs. Bainbridge, the family life of the poor represented the antithesis of everything the National Congress of Mothers stood for. She classified common domestic problems under the "nine D's"—darkness, dirt, disease, dress, debt, distress, drink, disaster, and death—and affirmed that the best way to correct them was to send middle-class women to the poor as moral missionaries. "Some people say that the first need of the submerged world is better tenements. But it seems to me that we must first elevate the woman herself, and then she will be capable of using a better tenement. The woman, the mother, must be helped by other women."[107]

What distinguished Mrs. Bainbridge's advice from that of the charity agent, however, was her emphasis on science, especially the new sciences of child psychology and household management, as much as on moral uplift. The true cause of human misery, she argued, was not poverty per se but ignorance of up-to-date domestic skills. Homes that were poor in material things did not have to be poor in spirit if mothers learned "the ABC of home-keeping." Instruct mothers of the poor in "how to cook and what to buy and what to do with their old bread and how to manage a day's wage," urged Mrs. Bainbridge, and you would guarantee the self-sufficiency of the most impoverished household.[108]

Equally necessary, according to Bainbridge, was instruction of the poor in the latest child-rearing theories. Lower-class mothers, she insisted, must learn to amuse their children just as middle-class mothers did, for child psychologists had clearly demonstrated the centrality of healthy recreation to normal childhood development. Instead of permitting ghetto children to roam their joyless neighborhoods at will and to model themselves on sordid street characters, Bainbridge said, mothers of the poor should confine their youngsters at home and teach them to imitate doctors and nurses in planned play activities suited to their developmental needs.[109]

Finally, warned Mrs. Bainbridge, children must be disciplined through affection rather than by the rod; to do otherwise was to increase the possibility of social unrest. "The great trouble in our large cities," she wrote, "and one which leads to the anarchism, socialism or any other 'ism,' is that the mothers lose the hold they have upon their children, and the child ceases to obey or respect her. The boy who scoffs at mother's authority will soon defy the law of the land." Fortunately, she felt, mothers of the poor were ready to learn to do better, if only their more knowledgeable social betters would recognize their duty to aid the poor. "These mothers are willing to learn how to cultivate respect for themselves in their children, but they do not know how. They need to be told of a better way to make a child obedient than slapping the child on the hand or screaming at it."[110]

"Mothers of the Submerged World" revealed the tendency of charity workers in the Progressive era, like their forebears, to trace the causes of juvenile misconduct to poor upbringing. But, equally important and different from earlier assumptions, was the speech's emphasis on a new faith in the ability of trained middle-class women to befriend mothers of the poor, teach them modern child-rearing and household-management techniques, and thereby eliminate home conditions which generated delinquency.[111] In the municipal mothering campaign, as in the several other reform efforts examined, the family had begun to replace the institution as the ideal center of correction and uplift. The juvenile court movement shared this new policy orientation. The poor family had become an ally as well as an enemy in the crusade against juvenile crime.

2

The Practice of "Progressive" Juvenile Justice

Introduction to Part 2

Historians in the past decade have increasingly recognized and attempted to demonstrate discrepancies between promise and performance in a variety of large-scale efforts at "behavior modification" (to apply the term more comprehensively than is usual) in public schools, prisons, mental hospitals, utopian communities, universities,. professional organizations, military installations, and political movements, to give just a few examples.[1] Their principal method has been the case study, or intensive analysis, of single institutions whose histories suggest patterns of development elsewhere. There are obvious pitfalls to this type of research, most centering on the criteria of selection. Since the case studies that follow deal with only two institutions (both in Wisconsin) when they might well have dealt with numerous others, the reader is entitled to know in advance what I hope to demonstrate by telling their stories.

My theme to this point has been the genesis and transformation of the "progressive" viewpoint in nineteenth- and early twentieth-century juvenile justice. Having examined the intellectual origins of this viewpoint and its varied expression in the Victorian and Progressive periods, a natural question is: did it make any difference in the treatment of delinquents? Stated another way: what was the relation between the theory and practice of "progressive" juvenile justice?

There are a number of ways to examine these questions. Most obvious, perhaps, would be to look at those correctional facilities generally identified with the "progressive" ideas. In the case of Victorian juvenile justice, this would mean focusing on the nation's first family reform school for boys, opened in Ohio in 1857. In the case of Progressive juvenile justice, it would mean focusing on one of the two juvenile courts (in Chicago and Denver) which claimed to be "first" (both opened in 1899). Surprisingly enough, these institutions have been studied little despite all the attention given them as pioneers.[2]

But for several reasons I have decided to concentrate elsewhere. Most important of these reasons is that to focus on seminal institutions would invariably give a distorted impression of the fate of "progressive" correctional ideas in public policy. What was most conspicuous in the late nineteenth and early twentieth centuries, and remains so to this day, was the wide gap between generally approved theory and actual policy in the treatment of delinquents. Indeed, with the passage of time and the gradual popularization of the "progressive" viewpoint, the gap between what was being said and what was being done grew even wider. Thus, to concentrate on instances where "progressive" theory first took root would seriously undermine the utility of the case studies for purposes of generalization.

The Wisconsin institutions, on the other hand—though inevitably idiosyncratic in many respects—present a more representative picture of the fate of "progressive" correctional ideas. The Wisconsin State Reform School exemplified the superficial way most states experimented with the foreign reformatory models. Similarly, the Milwaukee Juvenile Court exemplified the sloppy way most cities inaugurated programs of noninstitutional treatment and the persistence of harsh attitudes toward the lower-class immigrant family. In both institutions "progressive" theory generally obscured more than it revealed about actual correctional practices and helped foster an illusion that punishment had been eliminated from the juvenile justice system.

In sum, the story of the Wisconsin institutions illuminates general trends in the evolution of policy that are as apparent today as they were then, and it also generates firmly grounded guidelines for future empirical investigation in other localities. Before beginning, however, two conceptual points must be made because they intentionally limit the scope of the analysis.

First, I have not tried to evaluate the success or failure of treatment with any precision, and think it is generally imprudent for historians to attempt to do so.[3] What does it mean, after all, to say that an inmate of a reformatory or a client of a juvenile court is "reformed" or "rehabilitated"? Without delving into all the complexities, suffice it to say that the question occasions vigorous debate in the field of corrections today, the criteria of assessment remain remarkably imprecise, and the data for reaching reliable judgments are generally shoddy or inconsistent.[4] For obvious reasons, problems of evaluation in historical analysis are even greater. In my estimation the question is better ignored than explored. In Wisconsin, especially, it would be difficult to reach an evaluation, since the data are frequently less complete than in other states.[5]

Second, my attention will be mainly on the process of implementation, the area most amenable to empirical analysis. That I concentrate on implementation, however, should not at all be interpreted to mean that I wish "progressive" correctional ideas had been better understood or more faithfully applied.[6] In fact, as will become clear shortly, I have serious doubts about the wisdom and workability of "progressive" theories. But that is entirely another issue and, in my judgment, best reserved for later.

5

The Victorian Reform School: A False Start

There are many individuals in the correctional system of Wisconsin today who believe that until the 1960s, the goal of juvenile justice was merely to punish delinquents as if they were adult criminals. The celebrated opening in 1962 of the Kettle Moraine School for Boys, located in the lovely rolling hills just west of Sheboygan, and the closing and rapid destruction of the old "industrial school" in Waukesha, epitomized to them the emergence of brand new rehabilitative ideas.[1]

In the Kettle Moraine School, it was predicted, inmates would be treated as individuals and would become part of small, intimate surrogate families. Rather than relying on laborious work programs or the threat of the whip, surrogate parents in each cottage would emphasize personal intervention as a discipline technique and provide the care, warmth, and love inmates presumably were denied in their natural families. Educational opportunities would be many in order to prepare inmates for reentry into public schools after their "sentences" expired (technically, after they had been declared rehabilitated by the superintendent). Manual labor would be confined to vocational education classes and simple maintenance and gardening tasks.[2]

With allowance for the passage of time—and for the use of drugs and isolation cells for recalcitrants—the Kettle Moraine School for Boys seemed much like an updated, Victorian family reform school.[3] Its goals, expressed in the modern language of behavior modification, stressed the manipulation of children's emotional capacities into socially acceptable channels, a process thought to be facilitated by quasi-familial living quarters. No one connected with the facility seemed in the least aware that approximately a century earlier the state had opened a highly touted "progressive" reform school. Instead, most of those involved were intent on the achievements awaiting them now that the state had torn down the old industrial school and provided a modern, beautifully located institution.[4] Little marred their vision of the future, least of all an accurate understanding of the fate of "progressive" correctional ideas in the past.

Initial Frustration

Serious concern over the numbers and treatment of juvenile offenders first surfaced in Wisconsin in the 1850s, especially in Milwaukee. The lakeside metropolis was still in its infancy, but leading residents predicted rapid urban growth and a future population larger than its arch-competitor, Chicago. Aware of the social problems attending the rise of eastern metropolises, and of the various steps taken there to insure order, control deviant populations, and fend off impending "crises," they hoped to spare Milwaukee the plethora of ragamuffins who infested the streets in other cities. Vigilance was considered essential to control of the problem, and despite a relatively small population (just over 20,000), leading residents urged Milwaukeeans to anticipate a burgeoning crime rate and adopt, as a "preventive" measure, a city-financed reformatory for delinquents.[5]

Ethnic diversity helped stimulate the fears of the city's native-born, Protestant social elite. In the 1850s Milwaukee exhibited sharp cultural divisions and corresponding antagonisms. Though transplanted New Yorkers and New Englanders predominated among native-born residents, foreigners accounted for two-thirds of the population. Germans were the largest ethnic group, with 38 percent, although a sizable Irish population

(14 percent) wielded political influence far greater than its voting strength. Every ethnic group, Bayrd Still has written, tended to form isolated, "self-contained and self-conscious" subsocieties.[6]

Native-born residents, skeptical about the child-rearing goals and capacities of many immigrants, generally expressed their fears indirectly. Incoming foreigners were singled out as perpetuating gross immorality and irreverence. Germans and Irish bore the brunt of the attack, especially for their frequent Sabbath-breaking, day-long drinking, and easy profanity. In the view of native-born residents, the foreigners' reluctance to send their children to public schools also cast doubt on their willingness to assimilate conventional Protestant standards of morality and behavior. Moreover, these cultural conflicts had political counterparts. As in antebellum Boston and New York, a widespread disgust with Irish drinking habits and German profanation of the Sabbath combined with a growing antagonism to immigrants' allegiance to Democratic politics to fashion a strong nativist campaign in municipal elections.[7] Though Milwaukee produced no equivalent to the burning of the Ursuline convent in Boston or the sporadic riots in Philadelphia and New York, these ethnic rivalries still produced considerable tension and focused attention on potential sources of juvenile delinquency in the city.

Milwaukee newspapers paid close heed to the growth of juvenile crime, yet referred only occasionally to individuals who took active responsibility for curtailing it. No doubt, as in the Northeast, ministers, educationists, and popular lecturers sounded frequent warnings about the growing menace, but their remarks were never published.[8] It is thus difficult to trace the origins of Wisconsin's first reformatory with precision, although the little information available sheds considerable light on later correctional developments.

The staunchest advocates of a new public policy to deal with delinquents in Milwaukee were not charity workers and educationists in touch with the latest European ideas and penal experiments, but criminal justice officials and newspapermen engrossed by and seeking a pragmatic solution to a local problem.[9] When they first expressed interest in the early 1850s, their main objective was to respond in the cheapest way possible to the plight of children in Milwaukee jails. According to contemporaries, five key individuals aroused initial concern about the jail problem and led campaigns to establish segregated facilities for young lawbreakers. Clinton Walworth, for nine years police justice of the city; A. R. R. Butler, county district attorney; and Edward P. O'Neill, a leading Democratic legislator and later four-term mayor, worked for a decade within the governmental structure to convince the city council to appropriate funds. As their jobs suggest, these men were not disinterested philanthropists. Rather they were experienced police and legislative officials who learned firsthand that it was self-defeating to confine children with adult criminals in county and city jails.[10]

More vocal than Walworth, Butler, or O'Neill were two newspapermen: John Hinton, a free-lance reporter, and Rufus King, the distinguished editor of the Republican *Milwaukee Sentinel.* King's views were especially interesting, for they confirmed the common tendency of Milwaukeeans to compare their own problems to those of older, more populous urban centers. "In every city," King warned, "there congregate in the dark recesses and slums these social rats. They have human forms, but ... have no aims but the satisfying of animal passions.... They are outcasts, hardened, irredeemable." Policemen alone knew the extent of this aberrant class in Milwaukee, which King, like Robert Hartley and Charles Loring Brace in New York, equated with fixed castes in India and China. How shocking for middle-class sensibilities when "boys young in years, but old in sin, with strange, precocious faces, are dragged into the light."[11]

Like charity reformers in the East from the early nineteenth century onward, King and Hinton minimized distinctions between children who committed criminal acts and children who were merely poor. Rare were the cases, Hinton argued, where "poverty and virtue maintain a continued and noble struggle." Far better, therefore, to treat alike the "children of the poor and of the erring.... to arrest the incorrigible in his incipient steps, than be compelled to deal with him as a confirmed criminal." Hinton dramatically summarized this traditional belief in the value and legality of incarcerating noncriminal youth: "snatch up these neglected ones, teach them, reclaim them, convert them, civilize them, Christianize them, turn them out fitted for the duties of an American citizen."[12] Despite all the efforts of King, Hinton, and others, however, these early attempts to create a city-financed reformatory failed. The local jail remained

integral to the administration of Milwaukee juvenile justice well
into the early twentieth century.[13]

Sensing defeat on the local level, King, Hinton, and the others
turned their lobbying efforts toward Madison, the state capital,
in 1857. The legislators (with what degree of conflict it is impossible to say) quickly approved the idea of a state-funded reformatory and authorized $20,000 to begin its construction.[14]
Shortly thereafter Governor John Randall chose three commissioners, charging them with picking a site and designing an
architectural layout. Alerted to the forthcoming convention of
charity and correctional officials in New York City, the legislature was also persuaded to allot travel monies so that the commissioners could attend.

The three commissioners were a motley group; none had had
the least experience with charitable or educational endeavors.[15]
Martin Mitchell of Winnebago was a former writer for the
Oshkosh Democrat and a one-time congressional candidate. At
the time of his appointment as commissioner he was apparently
out of work. Edwin Palmer, a prominent Milwaukee Republican, was a carpenter by trade and the most logical appointee
because of his architectural talents. He had designed one of the
city's finest edifices, Plymouth Church. Winchell D. Bacon, the
wealthiest and largest landowner in Waukesha County (about
fifteen miles west of Milwaukee), was a Republican state
senator.[16] Because the position of commissioner carried with it
an indefinite term of office, paid daily salaries, expense allotments, and travel fees, it was a political plum for party regulars.
In choosing two Republicans and one Democrat, Governor Randall followed the customary distribution of patronage in Republican Wisconsin.

Before leaving for New York, the commissioners selected a
location for the proposed facility. As with earlier state-
sponsored enterprises, like the prison at Waupun and the mental
hospital at Delavan, the legislators assumed that interested communities would cede land in order to make their bids more
enticing.[17] Under the prodding of Commissioner Bacon, the
village of Waukesha raised $6,000 to purchase grounds for the
reformatory and easily won the bidding.[18]

Various reasons accounted for the village's interest in the
reformatory's location. First, numerous businessmen anticipated

direct economic benefits from the institution. Waukesha's abundant supply of limestone would be used in construction and probably for future building expansion. Small merchants in Waukesha would supply daily institutional needs. Town boosters also expected to draw statewide attention to other local attractions, notably Bethesda Springs which were reputed to have marvelous healing capacities. Most important, perhaps, Commissioner Bacon owned a timber mill and a share of a stone quarry which would supply construction needs. Bacon, it was widely believed, dictated local Republican policies and easily swayed party allies to go along with his wishes.[19]

En route to New York, the commissioners were only vaguely aware of the growing interest in family reform schools (whether they even knew that Ohio had approved one the previous year is unclear). At the convention, though, they became active learners, questioning advocates of different correctional philosophies and evaluating details of design and finance. Notwithstanding the political nature of their appointments, they appeared to become genuinely absorbed in their mission. Though the consensus at the convention was for the family reform school, the commissioners wanted to see for themselves whether the ideas of Wichern and DeMetz were functional and whether the older houses of refuge were as outmoded as detractors claimed. They visited several institutions in the New York City area, in upstate New York, New Jersey, Maine, Massachusetts, and Illinois. Upon returning to Wisconsin, they were unanimous in their support of the family design and in short order completed a full-scale layout calling for three family buildings. Thus, Wisconsin seemed ready to embark on an experiment in juvenile corrections which would place it in the vanguard of American penal reform.[20]

For all their practical experience before becoming commissioners, Messrs. Mitchell, Palmer, and Bacon were naive about the politics of social innovation. They anticipated few difficulties in translating their own enthusiasm for the European correctional ideas into institutional reality. Events proved them mistaken.

Construction of the reform school began in summer of 1857, the contract stipulating that the first building be completed by August, 1858. The estimated cost of the proposed structure was

$40,000, twice the original appropriation, but the commissioners assumed the legislature would make up the difference. "Nothing has been done for mere ornament," they assured legislators, "but care has been taken ... to combine beauty with usefulness."[21] Work proceeded on schedule and by the following spring the basement was complete and the lowest tier of timbers laid.[22]

In June, though, construction was halted as the Republican legislature, responding to the onset of economic recession, refused to allocate funds for completion of the structure. Disagreements over priorities in economic policy split Republicans into "House of Refuge" and "Anti-House of Refuge" factions. Commissioner Bacon urged that the facility be completed before hard times had the predicted effect of increasing rates of juvenile crime and dependency, but the Republican majority, now under strong attack for corruption and mismanagement from a rapidly growing Democratic minority, felt compelled to abandon the reformatory in addition to several other state projects.[23] It became obvious that political factionalism and economic recession, quite as much as new correctional theory, would determine the pace and shape of penal reform.

With political alignments sharpening during the recession (which coincided with ripening party divisions prior to the Civil War), the reform school became little more than a political football. The wavering allegiances of Waukesha Democrats revealed this clearly. First they attacked the legislature for withholding funds, charging that nothing better could be expected from the Republican "Shanghais." Within two months, though, the Democrats changed sides. Holding several political rallies to encourage fellow townsmen to rescind the tax voted the previous year to provide $6,000 for the purchase of reformatory grounds, they became bitter opponents of the reformatory. By the spring of 1859, however, as they anticipated a Democratic victory in the forthcoming election, they again began waving the reform school banner.[24]

Construction was at a standstill in 1858 when Democrats began a personal attack on Commissioner Bacon. The Democrats, claiming to represent "industrious farmers, mechanics, and laborers," found the politically powerful, pseudo-aristocrat Bacon easy game. Bacon, charged the Democrats, had spent extravagantly, collecting fees for services he never performed and letting contracts to party affiliates who overcharged for their work. Bacon and the reformatory were alleged to epitomize Republican profligacy and economic irresponsibility in the recession politics of the late 1850s.[25]

A new political stratagem emerged in the fluid political situation of 1859, as both sides began to sponsor state philanthropic projects in order to boost their public images. Early that year, Republicans and Democrats joined forces in appropriating $10,000 to advance construction of the reformatory. But political wranglings did not abate. Bacon now answered his critics by claiming that the cost of his services far exceeded what he charged the state for them. The Republican press in Wisconsin rallied to his support and then launched its own attack by charging the secretary of state, a Democrat, with illegally withholding the $10,000 appropriation for reasons that, according to the Republican papers, were obviously partisan. "His object was doubtless to prevent the work from going any further under the present Commissioners, and in this he was backed by Mr. Elmore [a leading Democrat] ... who, perhaps, anticipated a change of administration next fall, and was desirous that the handling of this amount of money should be confided to them."[26] Accusation and counteraccusation continued, but in early summer the money was disbursed and construction proceeded slowly. After a Republican sweep in the fall elections, two bipartisan legislative committees absolved the commissioners of financial wrongdoing. This eliminated a major bone of political contention and in effect removed the reform school from the field of partisan rivalries (at least for the moment).[27]

On the eve of the Civil War, Wisconsin could at last boast a segregated institution for juvenile delinquents. But was it a family reform school, as the commissioners had originally promised? The answer was clearly no. Instead of three buildings there was only one, and it was considerably larger than the family cottages in France, Germany, Massachusetts, and Ohio. Although the decision to abandon the original design was never made public, economic recession and incessant political squabbling had presumably undermined it. Against the commissioners' wishes, the legislature had chosen a cheaper path to state benevolence.[28] Still, considering the unavoidable financial shortages and the political bickering, most commentators seemed relieved that Wisconsin finally had someplace other than common jail cells to house juvenile offenders.[29]

A Victorian in Power: Moses Barrett

The opening of the Wisconsin State Reform School in July 1860 was a gala affair attended by prominent Republicans and Democrats and marked by a lovely picnic on the facility's uncultivated farm. Judge J. B. D. Cogswell of Milwaukee welcomed visitors with an informative talk on the status of correctional theory and practice in different states and countries. The earlier an offender was identified, Cogswell argued, "the better for his own good and that of others; and the longer the period of his commitment, the greater is the chance of his permanent reform."[30] The method of treatment was equally germane, and Cogswell expounded on it in typical Victorian fashion. "It is agreed by all who have experience, that the boy is to be softened through his feelings. Uniform and long-continued kindness satisfy him at last that there is such a thing as disinterestedness and unselfishness."[31] Despite its Jacksonian design, in other words, Wisconsinites could expect their reform school to apply the precepts of affectional discipline.

Even the fanfare of opening ceremonies, however, could not hide keen disappointments felt by many of those involved with the institution. Most obvious were potential health dangers of the site. In Wisconsin as elsewhere, the administrators of large institutions were troubled by the awful possibility of epidemic; the state's recent bout with cholera reinforced those apprehensions. It was no secret, of course, that pork-barrel considerations influenced locations of state institutions, but the case of the reformatory was a particularly glaring example of the practice.[32] Located just outside Waukesha's town limits, adjacent to a fetid swamp, the reformatory's water supply could easily become contaminated.

There were also structural problems. Unlike some reformatories of the congregate design, the Wisconsin institution housed inmates in individual cells. This security measure presented an ominous fire hazard.[33]

Finally, there were legal difficulties, at least for those who accepted Cogswell's argument that the longer the sentence, the better the chance for rehabilitation. At the last minute the legislature had rejected the commissioners' plea for indeterminate sentencing. The nature of the new facility was not properly understood, complained the commissioners. It was not simply a segregated jail for children, or even a house of refuge, but a *reform* school. Inmate cooperation was essential to the goal of rehabilitation; treatment would be undermined if inmates knew their date of release in advance. Nonetheless the first inmates were committed for brief, predetermined time periods and released upon expiration of sentence, whether or not they had "reformed."[34]

In addition to these disappointments, the institution opened with the solitary building incomplete, forcing inmates and staff to devote the entire summer to construction work. A new board of managers appointed by the governor to supervise operations excoriated the commissioners for keeping secret the unfinished state of the building.[35] The fault was not theirs, rebutted the commissioners, for contractors had refused to accept legislative appropriations in scrip (especially after the state reneged on several issues of scrip). The ultimate blame in this area as in many others, the commissioners charged, lay with an impecunious legislature insensitive to the needs of delinquent youth.[36] Mutual recriminations continued, but the board of managers soon settled into more pressing administrative tasks.

The governor had taken three years to complete selection of the nine-member board. His choices revealed both partisanship and a determination to select a few highly regarded individuals who would have leisure to visit the institution, and who would arouse interest in the community and command the attention of legislators. Obvious political choices were Thomas Reynolds and Henry Williams.[37] The former, a Republican army colonel from Madison well-known for inebriety and for consorting with prostitutes, was sentenced to prison for larceny a year after his appointment. Williams had frequently been arrested for drunk and disorderly conduct.

Neither Reynolds nor Williams, however, served on the executive committee, which exercised the real power and leadership of the board. Board members Isaac Lain, Talbot Dousman, and Cicero Comstock were highly respected and talented members of their local communities, but the most prominent member was Andrew Elmore, a pioneer settler of Wisconsin and later a founder of the National Conference of Charities and Correction.[38] As secretary to the managers, Elmore's role was much like Horace Mann's in Massachusetts.[39] Though not a full-time employee, Elmore penned lengthy reports revealing a missionary fervor, a familiarity with the latest ideas in other states and countries, and a precise understanding of administrative minutiae. An effective lobbyist in his private business concerns, he pleaded the cause of the reform school wherever in the state he happened to be. Records of the managers' deliberations have not been preserved, but it seems probable that by force of his personality and by his proximity to the institution (he lived in Muckwonago, in Waukesha County), Elmore set the tone and direction of board meetings.

The managers searched several months for a superintendent. After several interviews they chose Moses Barrett, a physician and close friend of *Sentinel* editor Rufus King. King was especially pleased with the appointment and remarked, "Dr. Barrett possesses the ability, the sagacity, the prudence of making a faithful officer. He is a thoroughly educated physician and will bring much scientific knowledge to his aid in the duties of his office."[40]

Self-righteous and convinced his was an annointed mission, Moses Barrett was a lay revivalist who believed religious salvation resulted from benevolent acts of practical piety. An active churchman, he had taught weekly lessons at Milwaukee's YMCA and also lectured on the relations between religion and science. Barrett's optimism concerning the reform school knew few bounds. He predicted permanent rehabilitation of 90 percent of the inmates, provided they were imprisoned before acquiring "the controlling force of matured passions." The superintendent felt nothing but scorn for citizens indifferent to the institution's mission. "Public sentiment is slow in advancing to the high position of enlightened Christian Benevolence upon which Reform Schools are founded. The great truth seems hardly to have dawned upon society, that its greatest security depends more upon the *reformation* of the offender than upon his *punishment*."[41]

Whenever Barrett discussed the conditions of child rearing in large cities—and in his writings, as in the writings of Rufus King, obvious differences between a city the size of New York and one the size of Milwaukee tended to get blurred—he was a thorough-going environmentalist. He viewed cities as being perverse edu-cators of the young, titillating them with a range of experiences whose moral worth they were unprepared to evaluate. Unless shielded, indeed smothered by protective parents, Barrett saw little hope for urban youth. At least for the purposes of child care, evil and the city were synonymous. The opposite side of this coin, for Barrett as for the great majority of Americans, was the idealization of rural life and values; country living was no less than heaven on earth. Farm life was inherently uplifting: it improved a child's physical health, allowed him to remain out of doors, and magically imbued him with everlasting moral virtue. To Barrett these commonplace ideas acquired special urgency, for they emphasized how thoroughly the behavior and value system of urban delinquents had to be transformed.[42]

Barrett's views led him in two different pedagogical directions. On the one hand, he had much in common with charity spokes-men of the Jacksonian period like Thomas Eddy and John Gris-com. Taunting "idle, vicious parents" who provided lackadaisi-cal supervision, the superintendent promised that all "vicious indulgence" would be suppressed. Kept well or kept ill, to para-phrase Carl Kaestle's description of apprentices in the eighteenth century, the inmates would certainly be kept busy, leaving no time for daydreaming or sexual promiscuity.[43] As in the older houses of refuge, disrespectful children would learn to kneel before legitimate authority, to display, in a common nineteenth-century phrase, "habits of subordination."[44]

But Barrett's sensibilities were of the Victorian period as much as of the early nineteenth century. He often spoke the affectional discipline language of the domesticity literature and in the main advocated a method of rehabilitating delinquents which con-formed to it. Unlike the founders of the New York House of Refuge, for instance, Barrett did not place faith in regimen or hard work alone as remedies for delinquent behavior. Nor did he feel it was enough to cleanse a living environment of moral impurities in the expectation that inmates would become habitu-ated to upright conduct. True rehabilitation, he believed, de-pended more upon the evocation of kind sentiments than upon the use of force; the avenue to the will was through the affections, not the body. To Barrett, what was wrong with older methods of rehabilitating delinquents was analogous to what was wrong with contemporary religion: it was overly formal and made little appeal to the emotions. Thus Barrett, at the same time he was an environmentalist, also believed children retained an inborn potential for good which affection, persuasion, contact with nature, and evangelical religion could draw out. In religion, ethics, views on child nature and nurture, and correctional strategy, he was a Victorian's Victorian.[45]

Barrett was understandably disappointed with the reformatory's congregate layout, since it hampered the application of affectional discipline. He pleaded with legislators to construct small family cottages like those at the Ohio Reform School to facilitate close and frequent interaction between staff and inmates. Though a patient man, he could not fathom the seeming indifference of legislators to the pressing needs of delinquent youth or to the necessity of making a sharp break with the penal policies of the past.[46]

Still, he was no pessimist. Despite the inappropriate Jacksonian setting, he vowed to incorporate a "family spirit" in the reformatory by his daily labors. Central to this effort were his wife and two teenage daughters, who served respectively as matron and teachers. Through them Barrett hoped to recreate the moral presence of a righteous middle-class family. Every evening he would bring inmates, his wife, and daughters together for what he termed a "family" conference, combining prayer, confession, ethical instruction, and, most importantly, sympathetic listening. He encouraged contacts between inmates and the women of his family to accustom them to true "mother love." Forget former associates and parents, the superintendent implored arriving inmates, and adopt the Barretts as foster parents and the reform school as your first real "home."

The superintendent also counseled his small staff in the art of affectional discipline. Inmates, he instructed them, were not criminals but erring and misguided youth. If approached with understanding and given proper training in the institution, they would learn to obey constituted authority gladly. Even more insistently than Jacksonian reformers, the superintendent held that the reasons for a boy's incarceration were irrelevant. In most instances such reasons provided only circumstantial evidence of his character and potential for good. Rapists, larcenists, orphans: all were innocent, educable, and redeemable in the eyes of God. Naturally enough, then, Barrett applauded vague statutory definitions of delinquency in order to widen the range of children who could be placed in the reformatory for their own good.[47]

What Wisconsin's correctional history might have been with a man like Barrett in charge of a genuine family reform school is an intriguing, if ahistorical, question. Still, there was more to the early history of the institution than having the right man in the wrong place. No individual or group of individuals could have divorced the reformatory from shifting economic and political tides; prevented police, judicial, and legislative officials from manipulating it to serve their self-interests; or persuaded the community at large that affectional discipline and farming were adequate responses to the growth of juvenile crime. Less for what he achieved than for the ambivalences in correctional theory and policy which his career inevitably highlighted, Moses Barrett's fate at the reformatory merits study.

A Mixture of Motifs

The reformatory in its early years was underpopulated. With cell space for 108, the total number of inmates was forty after six months and, after some fluctuations, only forty-one three years later. Moses Barrett was understandably ambivalent about this unexpected development. On the one hand, underpopulation meant that there was a reasonable number of inmates for the practice of affectional discipline; on the other it lessened the potential impact of the reformatory on juvenile crime. The managers attributed underpopulation in part to a general confusion about the institution's purpose and entrance requirements. But the most serious problem behind underpopulation was legislative interference, particularly from upstate legislators.

The institution had been sponsored mainly for Milwaukee's use; it therefore was not surprising that of the first year's inmates, 62 percent came from Milwaukee.[48] Nonetheless, representatives from upstate exploited this fact to justify a bill charging each county a weekly fee of one dollar per inmate. Not unexpectedly, the judiciary in Milwaukee (most of whom were popularly elected) responded to pressures to curb municipal costs by cutting commitments to the reformatory. By 1865 the percentage of youngsters at Waukesha sent from Milwaukee had declined to less than a fifth of the total. Most Milwaukee children arrested for crime or vagrancy were either released with a stern warning or put in local jails.

The county tax confused and confounded Moses Barrett. It inhibited judicial discretion and discriminated against the very city most needing the institution's services, he complained. Upstate legislators had no right to remain aloof from Milwaukee's problems, he added, because the city actually lured mischievous and uncared-for boys from all over the state. Angered that magistrates in Milwaukee were again placing numerous young offenders in jails, the managers issued a strong warning: "We hesitate not to say that unless the law is changed the institution must prove a failure, and the expense of carrying it on should be saved to the State by abandoning it altogether."[49]

But the objections of Barrett and the managers were to no avail, and the county tax remained. Thus the city of Milwaukee, which had seemingly shifted primary responsibility for juvenile corrections onto the state in the late 1850s, found itself again faced with the problem of segregating juvenile from adult offenders. And, as had been recognized for several decades, the response of judges and juries to this problem of age segregation would doubtless be to let many delinquents go free rather than imprison them with adults. From Milwaukee's point of view, then, the creation of a state reformatory left many long-standing issues and grievances unresolved.

The legislature's initial refusal to bind judges to indeterminate sentencing nettled the managers as much as did the county tax. The managers soon overcame the legislative opposition, however; thereafter the policy was that every inmate, whatever his "offense"—larceny, burglary, stubbornness, and so on—would stay at the reformatory until age twenty-one unless released at the managers' discretion. As noted earlier, Barrett vigorously supported this position. If forced to meet arbitrary time schedules, he felt, his efforts would be in vain. "We possess no power of exorcism.... Angry passions and vicious propensities will not down at our bidding. We can only resort to human instrumentalities, and watch with patience the slow progress of intellectual and moral development."[50]

To his dismay the superintendent learned rather early that some legislators considered his approach to rehabilitation sentimental, naive, and unduly expensive. All they wanted was a segregated prison for children, where inmates would repay the state for upkeep by working in shops managed by outside contractors. The superintendent was certainly no opponent of manual labor, but he insisted that to serve rehabilitative ends labor must awaken mental and moral as well as physical energies. In practice this distinction ruled out most traditional forms of remunerative contract labor. Barrett asked legislators to show less concern for making unfortunate children pay for upkeep and more for offering them the same educational opportunities as students in public schools.[51] In part because he defended his position with vigor, and in part because the reformatory's farm produced crops which sold well in local markets and supplied institutional needs, Barrett successfully fended off attempts to introduce large-scale contract labor.

Barrett's opposition was intellectually well grounded. He did not, like many mid-century reformers influenced by resurgent revivalism, reify the traditional distinction between mind and heart. As a physician he had learned to respect attainments that were chiefly intellectual. The complementary nature of reason and ethics was manifest: "moral truths will be awakened only as intellectual perceptions are awakened."[52]

Rebuffing economy-minded legislators who wanted to limit academic instruction to evenings so inmates could produce marketable goods during daylight hours, he asserted: "the advantages for intellectual and moral culture should not be sacrificed to the desire for mere productive labor."[53] Affirming the central role of education in the reformatory's rehabilitative program, Barrett concluded: "The period usually passed at the reformatory is the most important in life for educational purposes, and it is folly to contend that evening schools, after the physical system is exhausted by ten hours labor, will meet the wants of these immortal natures. There is no power on earth compared to the elevating source of sound mental culture."[54]

Legislators were not the only ones to criticize Barrett's administration. Judging from the expression of public opinion in the newspapers, the community at large appeared about equally divided in its opinion of the superintendent's abilities. A reaction typical of many of the favorable ones came from a visitor whom Barrett had taken on a tour of the institution. "The manner in which Superintendent Barrett is conducting affairs at the State Reform School cannot fail to win golden opinions from all." However trustworthy as description, the visitor's comments nicely captured Barrett's own point of view. "Dr. Barrett's discipline of those confined to his care, is exercised through kindness, and at the same time firm and decisive. He seeks to reach the heart of his pupils (as we may term them) rather by love and moral suasion, than by the rod. So far his efforts are being crowned with success."[55]

Other commentators, however, were less sanguine. In addition to several parents who unsuccessfully tried to remove their children from the institution on habeas corpus grounds, there were many more who criticized health and disciplinary standards. Several inmates died during Barrett's tenure. The managers explained the deaths by charging that the inmates had been ill prior to their admission, and excoriated local magistrates for sending to the reformatory children who rightly belonged in hospitals. The outbreak of twenty-five cases of typhoid in 1863 brought the health issue to a climax. Waiting several months until the last boy had recovered before daring to enter, a legislative investigating committee found conditions in the reformatory appalling. The inmates appeared slovenly, filthy, and susceptible to communicable disease. Locating the real source of present health hazards in the politics of Building Commissioner Bacon, members of the committee affirmed that they could not "but feel surprised at the ignorance, stupidity, or something worse that caused this building to be built upon its present site." Situated adjacent to a fetid pond, hampered by a poorly constructed sewer, the building stank of swamp effluvia. The committee recommended detailed improvements but concluded that "as long as the present location is adhered to, disease in an epidemic form will be a frequent visitor."[56] Fortunately no further outbreaks of typhoid occurred during Barrett's administration.

A more fundamental criticism cut to the heart of Barrett's Victorian correctional ideas. The superintendent early gained a reputation for lax discipline and a nonchalant attitude toward escapes. Inmates ran away frequently, generally heading for Milwaukee by train. With a depot only three-quarters of a mile from the institution, they could jump the train unnoticed before it gained speed. Milwaukeeans soon became accustomed to spotting inmates of the reformatory on the streets.[57]

Rufus King of the *Sentinel* gently chastened his friend for leniency: "These escapes have become quite frequent, and while we have no desire to censure the Superintendent, who is certainly a most humane man, we would suggest a little more care to prevent escapes."[58] The issue flared with the arrest of four members of an Irish gang called the Bunker Boys, whose sentences at the reform school had recently expired. The claim of the gang's fifteen-year-old leader that he had escaped from the institution several times and could do so again in forty-eight hours triggered numerous responses from irate citizens, several of whom called for the superintendent's removal.[59]

Barrett responded quickly to the public indictment. He pointed out that not only had most escapees been recaptured (unlike the case in the Chicago reformatory), but the escape rate at Waukesha was comparatively low. Barrett could have let his defense rest on this statistical argument. But the charge of undue leniency struck at the core of his approach to corrections, so he took the opportunity to address the community on the special mission of a reform school. "Isolation and seclusion are incompatible with juvenile reformation," he argued. "It is the policy of Reform Schools to impose the least possible degree of physical restraint, and to throw the inmate upon responsibilities and trusts." Moreover, he held that a benignly fatalistic attitude toward escapes was essential to the institution's vocational program. "To fit them to become 'farmer boys,' which is of vastly more consequence than any trade learned under confinement in shops, it is necessary to give them more or less liberty, and there are always some who will take advantage of it."[60]

Though the newspapers continued to print complaints about Barrett from irate citizens, the superintendent's decision that no solution was the best solution held sway. He successfully fended off attempts to surround the facility with barbed wire; any inmate who had the inclination could easily run away. Whatever the structural disadvantages of the institution, Barrett asserted that he would do his best to incorporate the "spirit" of affectional discipline.

Critics notwithstanding, Barrett was certain his methods were effective. Though reliable data were scarce, he claimed that only a handful of inmates committed on indeterminate sentences had been released unregenerate; most had gone into farming or continued their education in public schools. When rumors circulated that there were more "graduates" in state prison than schools, Barrett found solace in letters from boys doing well—that is, children who were both religious and out of jail. "I am trying to do the best I can," wrote one youngster, "and I find my help in God. I never shall forget what kind of care I had when I was sick. My happiest days have been spent in the Reform School, and I want you to tell the boys so."[61] A former inmate, a soldier in the Union Army, penned a more revealing letter highlighting the institution's devotional tone and providing an unintentionally amusing commentary on the limits of moral suasion.

> I received your letter the other night and was very glad to hear from you. I received the Testament also, and was very glad to read it, and I will read it every day. I am trying to be a good boy, but it is pretty hard to be a good boy in the army, but I will try to do the best I can. I learnt a great deal when I was in the Reform School, and I did not like to leave when my time was up. You wrote to me that I should not use any intoxicating drinks. I never used any intoxicating drinks yet, *nor I never will.* But there are some of the boys who get drunk almost every day, and they are trying to get me drunk, but I tell them I would not do it. Please write soon.[62]

By 1865 Barrett's strenuous efforts had broken his health. The last two years of his administration were especially perplexing, due to the impact of the Civil War on juvenile vagrancy and criminality. Dozens of fatherless boys, observed Rufus King, were roaming the streets of Milwaukee at will. "Probably at no time have there been so many children in the State who are proper objects of the fostering care of the School."[63]

If the streets were filled with children in need of care, so was the reformatory. Inmate population soared to 175, forcing many youngsters to double up in cell beds. To be sure, many children had been committed on false pretenses. The managers lamented that magistrates (especially from rural areas with no established welfare machinery) were violating "the spirit of the law, if not the letter, in sending children here for no apparent reason, except to relieve the county of their support."[64] But the managers' request to screen admissions was rejected by upstate legislators. Thereupon the managers, intent on preventing chaos and the outbreak of disease, resorted to their one alternative: wholesale parole. Without suggesting that most inmates were rehabilitated, they sent them home en masse. Paroling first those boys whose parents were alive and employed, they transformed the institution for a short period into a holding station for children whose main crime was that their parents were dead.

Barrett's parting thoughts captured his disillusionment. No longer was he optimistic that the reformatory could play a major role in stemming juvenile crime, or more importantly, that the community at large possessed the willpower to make the effort. "It has become a very grave question, what shall be done with the large class of children in our cities and large towns, who will not avail themselves of the ample provisions made for their education, but who are growing to manhood in ignorance and under the blind guidance of vicious passions and depraved appetites," he observed. "The problem will be solved, if not by a wise and liberal policy, for their intellectual and moral culture, by riot and arson, by the upheaving of an infuriated and degenerate populace."[65]

In less than a decade, Wisconsin had repeated (on a smaller scale) the discouraging histories of most eastern reformatories. The Wisconsin experience had also demonstrated the difficulties of implementing Victorian correctional ideas in an inappropriate structure and under public auspices. To all appearances the institution had gone the same route as had the Massachusetts State Reform School in 1859, when, as Franklin Sanborn later reported, "a most fortunate conflagration" had leveled it and provided an unexpected opportunity to introduce the family design.

The Heyday of the Family Reform School?

At midnight on January 10, 1866, the fire bells of the Wisconsin State Reform School tolled loudly, but a thick fog prevented local townsfolk from determining the exact nature of the blaze. By the time Waukesha residents arrived at the scene, the main building had been consumed by flames. It was later learned that only the alert response of the morning guard, who had unlocked or broken down all the cell doors in just a few minutes, had saved the institution from a grave tragedy.[1]

The confusion surrounding the fire provided a perfect opportunity for inmates to escape. One-quarter of them fled the facility, and although the two arsonists were apprehended, less than half of the others were recaptured. Rumors abounded as to the arsonists' motives. Many claimed that they were retaliating for being placed in solitary confinement and locked in ball and chain. Others hypothesized that they could not face the prospect of imprisonment until age twenty-one and therefore began the fire in order to obtain transfers and shorter sentences at the state prison. Whatever the boys' motives, they drew stiff sentences. Charles, age eight, received a one-year term in the Waukesha County Jail, while

Malcolm, age fifteen, drew a ten-year sentence at Waupun Prison.[2]

A delegation of legislators investigated the ruins and concluded there was little left of the reformatory that was worth salvaging. Recalling the previous outbreak of typhoid and future toxic dangers presented by the adjacent swamp, the delegation recommended that the institution be relocated on more elevated land. There were more immediate needs, however, notably the erection of temporary living quarters for staff and inmates. Assisted by sympathetic townsfolk, the inmates built makeshift shelters. Meanwhile negotiations for a new site proceeded slowly. Escapes occurred daily, and all who remained suffered hardships. In early summer, after negotiations had broken down, the managers purchased a 120-acre farm only a half mile from the old site.[3]

Like Franklin Sanborn in Massachusetts, the managers of the Wisconsin State Reform School were anything but despondent about the fire. They had always regretted the substitution of congregate for family design, made while the building was under construction in the late 1850s, and were elated by the unexpected opportunity to plan a new layout. Though some legislators carped at the idea of erecting small, separate, and necessarily more expensive cottages, the managers concluded without regret: "The burnt building was not well adapted to the wants of such an institution, and was in our opinion very defective for the purposes intended."[4]

Since the Chicago Reform School had recently adopted a modified family plan, the managers traveled to Chicago to see it.[5] They also obtained reports from a convention of correctional workers held in Boston the previous year which had endorsed the family design in all future reformatories.[6] After purchasing the new site, the managers contracted for three cottages, each to house forty inmates, and each modeled quite explicitly on Frederic DeMetz's Colonie Agricole. A new era in public policy toward juvenile delinquents had begun, the managers declared triumphantly.[7] Nine years after its initial endorsement, the Victorian reform school had come to Wisconsin.

The "Progressive" Facade

When Moses Barrett resigned late in 1865 (apparently for reasons of health), the managers hired a former public school administrator, A. D. Hendrickson, as superintendent of the reformatory. Well-regarded throughout the state, Hendrickson seemed like just the man to carry forward his predecessor's mode of treatment, this time in a suitable structural setting. But it soon became clear—at least in retrospect—that Hendrickson's approach to rehabilitation differed subtly from Barrett's and that the state had adopted the facade rather than the substance of Victorian correctional ideals.[8] It also became clear that when divorced from Victorian theoretical premises, the family reform school better served bureaucratic than rehabilitative goals.

A friend of world-renowned penologist Enoch C. Wines,[9] Hendrickson conspicuously portrayed himself as a "scientific" philanthropist.[10] Identifying the congregate design of the burned facility with other correctional anachronisms, he predicted the family plan would change the very nature of correctional work. While showing high regard for Barrett's noble intentions, Hendrickson still considered the former institution "a juvenile prison . . . with its crowd of boys in a single herd."[11] Barrett's evangelical enthusiasm harkened to an older style of reformist thought which, it appeared, embarrassed the new superintendent.

One indication of Hendrickson's "scientific" approach was his belief in the inheritability of criminal traits. Though hereditarian ideas did not become popular until the last quarter of the century, some practicing correctional administrators had broached the subject.[12] Moses Barrett, for example, had spoken occasionally about hereditary factors accounting for growing numbers of juvenile criminals. But it was plain from his usage that he was not referring to personality traits transmitted through the genes, but rather to the totality of a youngster's past. To Barrett "heredity" actually meant the family, home, and community environment of a child.

When Hendrickson emphasized the "permanence of hereditary traits and tendencies," his meaning was different from Barrett's. Although the superintendent's thinking on the subject was anything but doctrinaire, he generally described two types of delinquents: the born and the created. "The one inherited proclivities to wrong; the other has acquired such tendencies—the former are naturally vicious, the latter were made so by bad associations—in the former it is hereditary, in the latter it is the result of unfavorable surroundings."[13] Whereas Barrett had blurred distinctions between relatively innocent and criminal youngsters, hoping thereby to foster hope and trust within all, Hendrickson sharpened those distinctions. His viewpoint inevitably predisposed him to consider persistently disobedient inmates as hereditary criminals impervious to all treatment. Those who did not bend to his wishes could easily be dismissed by Hendrickson as born criminals.[14]

Hendrickson also conceived the role of the superintendent differently from his predecessor. The new superintendent's stress was on strict regimen and on maintaining social distance between himself and inmates. He considered it more important to devise elaborate schemes to keep inmates busy than to uplift them through personal contacts; more important to enforce precise time schedules than to participate actively in treatment. Like Barrett, Hendrickson emphasized the need to instill "habits of subordination." But unlike his predecessor, he did not temper this conventional aim with the kindness and sensitivity so characteristic of the Victorian Barrett. "In truth, the discipline is the one thing useful in rearing the young," wrote Hendrickson. "Good discipline implies obedience. Obedience is not consistent with self will. . . . When a horse is trained—disciplined—he delights in yielding obedience to the rein. The same law governs animals and boys."[15] Plainly, Hendrickson was influenced little by notions of affectional discipline, or at least did not consider such notions appropriate to the rehabilitation of juvenile offenders.

Hendrickson also introduced material incentives to good behavior. Boys would be paid nominal sums for conforming to all institutional rules. Conversely, he wanted to charge inmates for basic necessities (although where many of them would get the money remained unclear). "We have little opportunity to cultivate economy," he observed. "The boy is now clothed and fed, whether he works well or not."[16] This "scientific" approach to rehabilitation, the superintendent promised, would not only teach inmates the material rewards of social conformity—a valuable lesson to learn before release—but would also deter escapes. Boys who fled would lose their savings in the school's bank, and an inmate who assisted another to escape would be assessed proportionally for the cost of the escapee's return.

As superintendent of Waukesha's public schools, Hendrickson

had been part of an educational vanguard demanding practical updating of school curricula. Moses Barrett's inexperience as a schoolteacher, Hendrickson felt, explained his exaggerated confidence in the relevance of academic instruction to juvenile offenders. While Hendrickson conceded that academic training might provide a stimulus to character development in America's brightest youth, he saw little benefit in such training for the inmates of a reformatory. Many graduates of the common schools actually became welfare recipients as adults, Hendrickson charged, because they wasted precious time on irrelevant school subjects as children.

Curricular revamping, though, could hardly begin to mitigate the dangers Hendrickson foresaw as arising out of the school system. The superintendent intended the reform school to serve as a model of social control for Wisconsin's parents and teachers. "The idleness during the long vacations of the year, during Saturday and Sunday of each week, during the morning and before school and particularly the long, late evenings after school of each day, is alone sufficient to corrupt any child."[17] Only the omniscient supervision of children possible in a reform school, Hendrickson contended, fulfilled the goals of socially responsible and efficient educational institutions. He prophesied that reformatories would provide the nation "with a larger proportion of self-supporting, productive citizens, than the average public schools of the land."[18]

In retrospect, these distinctions between the two superintendents seem fairly obvious. More subtle differences between the two further undermined the practice of affectional discipline in Wisconsin's "progressive" reform school.[19]

Like his predecessor, Hendrickson stressed the primacy of moral education. But whereas Barrett believed intellectual growth was a necessary prelude to ethical awareness, his successor considered the development of "habits of industry" not only a prelude but the only visible sign of moral understanding. For Hendrickson "love of labor" was the only sure manifestation of piety. "Honest, productive labor," he intoned, "is ordained of God to restore the fallen. Here faith and works unite."[20] By compelling inmates to work as long and as hard as they could, Hendrickson could thus claim to be teaching morality.

It was one thing to eulogize work in the abstract, quite

another to decide which types of work best built character. Hendrickson did not believe strongly in the moral influence of agricultural employment. Contact with nature was pleasant and should form part of every child's experiences, he felt, but it did not compare with disciplined hard labor as a rehabilitative tool. Whereas Barrett had sent his most promising and best behaved boys to work the institution's farm, Hendrickson sent only the youngest and least skilled.

The moral attributes of the skilled tradesman were far more attractive to the superintendent than values gained from agricultural employment. Each year he requested and received funds to enlarge the number and size of institutional workshops and to hire local artisans to supervise instruction in the trades. Sensitive, perhaps, to Barrett's earlier remonstrances against shop labor, Hendrickson denied that he was training mere factory hands. Instead he argued, "Intellectual labor develops manhood."[21] Renouncing what he saw as the timidity of his predecessor, Hendrickson affirmed that the reform school, just like the public schools, had an obligation to supply inmates with vocational skills before discharge. "Without a trade or its equivalent, not only will the labor and means expended in the youth's so-called, reformation, be lost, but he himself for want of remunerative employment, will be liable to fall into dissolute habits and share the common fate of the idler."[22] In Hendrickson's family reform school, work replaced personal interaction between staff and inmates as the primary means of moral uplift.

Hendrickson's emphasis on shop work posed a pedagogical dilemma he never resolved, indeed, never recognized. Delighted by the acclaim the reformatory was receiving under his direction, he never seriously considered what had made the idea of the family reform school unique. His dilemma was nonetheless real: how was he to incorporate into the family design, without destroying its singular advantages for rehabilitation, the types of work and degree of regimentation which had characterized the older houses of refuge?

The superintendent sincerely felt shop work was rehabilitative; he did not advocate it merely as a means of producing revenue.[23] Yet legislators demanded material returns in payment for large legislative-sponsored investments in machinery. Since Hendrickson never objected (as had Moses Barrett) to legislative intrusions, he was in a weak position to counter their demands and stem the emerging factory orientation of the reformatory. With his consent the shops began to produce for the open market, in addition to supplying uniforms and chairs for Waupun Prison. Supervisors of the reformatory's cane and tailor shops contracted with retail merchants in Waukesha to manufacture whatever goods the retailers desired. The institution's shoe shop in particular experienced rapid growth and soon became a statewide wholesaler—much to the chagrin of skilled shoemakers. The shop was renamed the Wisconsin Boot and Shoe Factory, thus symbolizing the shift from affectional discipline to the gospel of remunerative work.

In short, Hendrickson wanted to change the methods more than the ultimate aims of treatment. Whereas Barrett had emphasized intellectual growth and evangelical religion, Hendrickson stressed conversion to the secular god of work as a prelude to ethical awareness. Within a decade Hendrickson's successors would build on his innovative methods but discard his goals—all within the structural facade of the family reform school.

Furthermore, Hendrickson's lack of sympathy for the affectional mainsprings of Victorian juvenile justice pointed up how the family design could be manipulated to serve the ends of administration more than treatment.[24] A family reform school offered Hendrickson two advantages his predecessor never enjoyed but which Barrett's correctional method required. First, every child could receive individual care from overseers acting as surrogate parents. Second, separate cottages made it possible to classify inmates, however rudimentarily, according to their distinctive temperaments and patterns of behavior.

Both Barrett and Hendrickson believed that small groups of similarly dispositioned boys were more amenable to moral uplift than large heterogeneous groups. In the intellectual climate of the 1870s and after, however, a concern for precise classification of inmates tended to dovetail with newer conceptions of hereditary criminality.[25] Rather than a means to an end, which it had been for Barrett, classification of inmates began to enjoy scientific standing as an end in itself. Hendrickson's ideas led him to erect a separate but highly visible House of Correction, symbolizing that disobedience would be viewed as hereditary depravity, to be controlled if not eliminated by brute force in a building designed especially for that purpose.[26] The appeal here was to outright fear, not to the subtle orchestration of affection, trust, work, and religion which had inspired Victorian correctional ideals.

Whatever the superintendent's initial reason for isolating inmates in the house of correction, it inevitably became tempting for overseers to excuse those boys who remained recalcitrant as natural-born criminals. This type of rationalization probably had a snowballing effect. A boy sent from his cottage to the house of correction would be stigmatized as irredeemable in the eyes of his overseers—one less boy to worry about. "House boys" would then be returned to special cottages for their "kind," further isolating them as a class apart and justifying explicit custodial care and additional punitive controls. Thus, when divorced from the premises of affectional discipline—the view that every child possessed an inborn potential for good which needed to be drawn out by love—the family design helped bring into existence a veritable caste system for inmates who refused to conform. It provided, in effect, both the setting and justification for a self-fulfilling prophecy.[27]

Until the late 1870s the shell of the family design remained intact. Inmate population expanded to over three hundred, but the number of cottages grew apace. Neither legislative stinginess, epidemic, fire, nor public criticism overtly influenced internal affairs. To all appearances, Wisconsin had a thriving Victorian reform school.[28]

But form and substance were entirely different matters. Indeed the state's "progressive" reform school began to gain nationwide praise only after its initial reason for being had subtly been co-opted to facilitate the maintenance of order.[29] In practice, classification of inmates was less an aid to rehabilitation than a tool of bureaucratic management, a highly appealing tool because it offered both a means and a "scientifically" approved rationale for isolating malcontents who threatened the institution's public image. Earlier educational goals were transformed into mere strategies of control.[30] These were unintended, but nonetheless real consequences of Victorian correctional theory which the family reform school, ironically, both made possible and helped to obscure.

Unmasking the Facade: The Exposure Ritual

With financial backing from a legislature sympathetic to his interest in shop labor and remunerative employment, A. D. Hendrickson had shaped the renamed Wisconsin Industrial School for Boys in his own image. Outside events had impinged very little on the institution's internal programs. Had the superintendent actually tried to apply affectional discipline, developments might have been different. The legislature, after all, had agreed to fund a family reform school only in the wake of frustration over the burning of the original facility. Legislators could easily have sabotaged a sincere attempt to apply Victorian correctional stratagems by refusing to appropriate funds for building new cottages to keep pace with rising inmate population. But these drastic steps proved unnecessary, since Hendrickson established a good nationwide reputation for the institution at a relatively cheap price. Public officials could bask in the state's philanthropic glory.[31]

This idyll began to come to an end, however, in the mid-1870s, although Hendrickson was not there to witness the demise. His burgeoning reputation at the national and international levels (he was one of several Americans to participate in the prestigious London penological conferences in 1872) could not prevent credibility gaps on the local level. An investigation of the financial situation and accounting procedures at the reform school turned up a sizable imbalance in the budget and a number of irregularities in the books. Seeking to avoid scandal and possible prosecution, Hendrickson resigned in 1876 and hired a bookkeeper to help trace the missing monies. When the bookkeeper was unable to do so, the superintendent left town.[32]

Hendrickson departed at an opportune moment, for the impact of the severe depression of 1873 had yet to be felt at the reformatory. The legislature responded to a shortage of hard cash just as it had during the recession of 1857; it reduced allocations for both operating budgets and new construction costs in correctional and charitable institutions. The reformatory was unable to replace outworn machinery and eventually had to fire several shop foremen, thereby threatening established work routines and, inevitably, overall discipline. Equally important was the fact that the depression diminished the market for the institution's manufactured and agricultural products. The reform school became ever more dependent on the diminishing legislative allotments.

Finally, deteriorating social conditions throughout the state encouraged many local judges, especially those from towns with inadequate welfare or workhouse resources, to commit large numbers of noncriminal, dependent youth to the reformatory.[33] Taking advantage of a revised law eliminating county payments for children committed on criminal charges, these judges knowingly branded innocent youngsters as lawbreakers in order to shift welfare responsibility for them to the state. An upstate judge described the procedure: "The town where the child was born would get one of the neighbors to swear that the boy was incorrigible, and he would then be sent to the State Industrial School. The townships thus get rid of the burden of supporting such children, and they have come to regard [it] in large measure as designed to meet such cases."[34]

Internal problems at the reformatory were intensified by a decision of the managers not to parole inmates whose parents were jobless, or for whom apprentice or indenture positions were unavailable. Throughout the 1870s the managers, like most Americans of means, underestimated the severity of the nation's economic ills and anticipated momentary recovery.[35] By 1879 the number of inmates had soared to well over four hundred. Flushed with a sense of achievement and renown gained under Hendrickson, the managers never doubted that the reformatory could weather the current financial storm. Indeed during the height of the depression they recommended a bill for legislative approval (which was denied) to permit neighboring states to confine delinquents in Waukesha at a relatively nominal fee![36]

The depression was not the only event threatening to unmask the institution's "progressive" facade. Of several controversies which rocked the reform school in the late 1870s, the issue of religious freedom for inmates probably affected established routines least. Since its inception under the evangelistic Moses Barrett, the reformatory had taught Protestant theology. Sporadic protests by Catholic laymen and religious leaders had

impeded proselytizing efforts, but not until Milwaukee's Archbishop Henni became actively involved did Catholic groups
organize to assure delinquents freedom of worship.

Henni's most vitriolic opponent was Andrew Elmore,
secretary to the board of managers and also now head of the
Wisconsin State Board of Charities and Reform.[37] Like many
nineteenth-century reformers who combined social conscience
with nativism, Elmore considered Catholicism as much a political as religious threat. He held that whereas Protestantism
taught devotion to democracy and self-reliant individualism,
Catholicism preached idolatry and subservience to a foreign
potentate.[38] Wisconsin Catholics understandably responded
with skepticism to Elmore's claim that only "nonsectarian Christianity . . . a sort of State religion" was taught in the institution.
In reality, they countered, "the bible, the hymns, the Sabbath
school books and the religious teachers are all Protestant. . . .
This may not be sectarian between Protestant sects, but to the
Catholic inmates it is Protestantism."[39]

After the governor had placed pressure on them to find an
equitable solution, the managers, with Elmore dissenting, voted
to excuse Catholic inmates from Protestant services and to force
the superintendent to receive priests approved by Archbishop
Henni.[40] This decision was unsatisfactory to many Catholics in
Milwaukee, however, especially novitiates at St. Francis Seminary for whom Catholic education had become a lively issue.[41]
Not only did reformatory officials exclude Catholic priests with
force, the seminary students charged, but the dearth of Catholic
priests in Waukesha imposed a de facto ban on Catholic worship. The suggestion of Manager Edward O'Neill to hire a full-
time Catholic clergyman to correct this injustice, though, met
with little support, and further deliberations proved incon-
clusive.[42] Indeed for the remainder of the century the religious
issue went unresolved, in large measure because religion itself
was increasingly devalued as a rehabilitative tool.

Another thorny problem which placed the institution's previously untarnished reputation in jeopardy involved A. J. M.
Putnam, Hendrickson's replacement as superintendent. A former provost marshall in the Civil War and three-time sheriff of
Rock County, Putnam was probably a political appointee. Not-

withstanding his background, Putnam's approach to rehabilitation was actually less punitive than Hendrickson's.[43] This less
punitive approach, in fact, proved to be his undoing.

Despite, or perhaps because he could draw upon a long experience in law enforcement, Putnam found corporal punishment
less essential than Hendrickson had in commanding the respect
of inmates and in maintaining order. The superintendent established new restrictions on the freedom of cottage parents—
particularly those in charge of the most troublesome boys—who
prided themselves on strongarm methods. Hendrickson had entrusted cottage parents with prime responsibility for punishing
disobedience. This arrangement actually conformed to the practice of the foreign family reform schools, but when joined to
Hendrickson's hereditary rationale it fostered heavy reliance on
physical coercion. Putnam therefore centralized punitive authority in the superintendency: overseers were forbidden to inflict beatings without his prior knowledge, and physical punishments were confined to the house of correction. To the chagrin
of disgruntled employees who predicted the opposite, the escape
rate apparently declined in the months after this policy took
effect.[44]

Their independence and pride now challenged, several cottage
parents, led by Assistant Superintendent William Sleep, charged
publicly that discipline in the institution had declined due to
Putnam's unnecessary regulations. According to this group, inmates neither respected nor feared their overseers; this made the
youths more difficult to rehabilitate and control. The group also
charged that Putnam had further impaired the overseers' effectiveness by scolding them within earshot of inmates. Several
employees quit the already understaffed facility and told newspaper reporters to expect anarchy to erupt momentarily. The
managers were forced to intervene.

Late in 1878 the managers asked Putnam to resign. The superintendent asked for reasons behind their request but received
none. Finally Putnam resigned under protest in January and
demanded, in a public letter which created quite a sensation in
Waukesha and Milwaukee, a full investigation. The managers
denied his request and then took the offensive by hurling false
accusations. First they alleged Putnam was incompetent, a
charge they quickly retracted in light of his lengthy police expe-

rience. Then they maligned his reputation by claiming he had entered the room of a female employee while she was sleeping, a charge they also retracted after considerable controversy. Outraged but powerless, Putnam returned to his home in Janesville and peppered Waukesha and Milwaukee newspapers with letters asking for public exoneration.[45]

Journalistic interest in the affair dampened after the first round of accusations and counteraccusations, but the issue again became newsworthy the following year. Putnam bided his time until another reformatory issue resurfaced and then redoubled his efforts to obtain an investigation of the events surrounding his forced resignation. His pleas merged with another unresolved grievance, the poor health of inmates, and added to the administrative headaches that plagued the institution during the depression.

Despite the reformatory's new location, typhoid fever struck the inmate population again during the summer of 1879. Because their policy of retaining as many inmates as possible during the depression made them vulnerable to criticism on medical grounds, the managers tried to keep the presence of typhoid a secret in the hope that the disease could be contained. Amazingly enough, they succeeded for two months. But with the deaths of three inmates and some alert snooping from a *Sentinel* reporter, the story finally broke. The managers assured residents of Waukesha that the reformatory's water supply was uncontaminated, but the town called in its own doctor to investigate. The doctor found the water highly suspect and recommended the immediate erection of tents for inmates along several of the town's pristine springs. But the managers chose to ignore the doctor's advice, hoping to ride out the public frenzy.[46]

After the deaths of six more inmates, local politicians convinced the governor to order the board to find a new water supply and to call in Milwaukee's health commissioner to determine the causes of disease. The commissioner concluded that first, the primary cause of typhoid was the institution's covered privy vaults which extended far enough into the ground to infect water conduits; and second, that overcrowding had facilitated contagion. Cottages designed for three dozen boys now housed more than fifty, he noted. The bunks were "on the plan of steamboat berths," jammed so closely together that there was "barely room for a person to pass between tiers." The overall conditions were nothing short of "barbarous."[47] The *Sentinel* picked up the assault, labeling the institution a "State Charnel House" and implying that the governor had not ordered a more extensive inquiry because he had wanted to protect friends on the board of managers.[48] To abbreviate a story which captivated the press for months and thrust the reformatory managers uncomfortably into the public limelight, there were several additional investigations but their effect on the design or routines of the institution was minimal.

Religious freedom for inmates, the forced resignation of Superintendent Putnam, and the latest typhoid calamity were all lively issues in 1879 when the managers fought bitterly over the choice of a permanent successor to Putnam. William Sleep, leader of the protest against Putnam, had been appointed interim superintendent, but when Sleep was incapacitated by typhoid the managers were forced to step up their search for a successor. Meanwhile, for reasons that can only be guessed at, Andrew Elmore attempted to take advantage of Sleep's illness by substituting Madison's S. S. Rockwood, one of the state's best-known educationists, in Sleep's position.[49] The board remained stalemated for several months before overriding Elmore's veto and appointing Sleep as superintendent.

Sleep was undeniably different from his predecessors, all of whom had been men of renown in their local communities. Sleep's work experience, on the other hand, was almost entirely in the institution. His appointment represented the first instance of inbreeding.[50]

Beginning in 1870 as "a very good teamster," Sleep had worked his way up under Hendrickson. Sleep's friends contended that his career as a poor boy who made good would encourage inmates to copy his example, but there were detractors who felt his narrow experience and limited intelligence were grave liabilities. The *Sentinel* argued the point with tact: Sleep's deficiencies were rather those "of head than of heart. He is not big enough for the place and has not had the proper training for so important a position."[51] Another commentator, recalling the stature of prior superintendents, put the issue sharply: "It takes a little more brains to conduct properly the *most important penal institution* of the state of Wisconsin than is likely to be stored in the cranium of a man of absolutely no education."[52]

Sleep's methods for maintaining order in the overcrowded institution became frighteningly apparent soon after his appointment. In the spring of 1881 escapees from the reform school began to inundate Milwaukee. City officials had concluded, based on past experience, that the escape rate was a fairly reliable index to overall conditions in the institution[53] and therefore questioned Sleep about the influx of escapees. The superintendent evaded their questions and responded that he had just taken care of the problem by discharging a female employee who had assisted inmates to escape.

Still the number of runaways continued to escalate. An inquisitive reporter offered one explanation, although Milwaukeeans were at first reluctant to believe it. Boys who had been recaptured, he wrote, complained of "inhuman treatment on the part of the superintendent." One inmate's "bare back [was] perfectly raw from the effects of brutal whipping."[54] Not for another three months, however, would most observers take these charges seriously.

An irate ex-employee of the institution helped to expose Sleep. The former director of the boot and shoe factory who was then residing in Appleton, Mr. Conklin wrote a letter to the *Sentinel* charging the reformatory's factory with hampering his own city's efforts to industrialize. His attempt to establish a shoe factory had floundered, he said, because the reform school, with neither overhead nor wages to pay, could undercut his prices. With promises of more scandalous news, Conklin enticed reporters to Appleton to corroborate his charges. Four local youths, he stated, would testify graphically to the inhumane methods of punishment now in use at the reform school. The reporters scurried upstate.[55]

The ex-inmates' descriptions of reformatory life were published in early November, along with supporting evidence from other children and staff. Widespread use of corporal punishments was undeniable. The *Sentinel* delighted in providing gruesome details. After his father had unsuccessfully filed a habeas corpus petition, one inmate tried to escape but was caught. Sleep placed the boy in the house of correction, where he was put in ball and chain, fed bread and water, and whipped regularly. The

twenty-inch sole leather whipping strap was soaked in oil, with
its ends burnt to harden them. Former inmates sketched dozens
of similar brutalities, but the one dominating their portraits was
the thrashing of an emaciated, sickly boy who was "beaten until
he went into a fit, and in that condition was taken down to the
pump-room and had cold water pumped on him to bring out the
fit."[56]

Other revelations were equally shocking. Unlike Superintendent Putnam, Sleep permitted cottage parents to inflict beatings without giving prior notice. The most feared flagellants,
though, were the officer in charge of the house of correction and
Sleep himself. According to one boy, Sleep gained sadistic
pleasure from beating children, often doing so until he fell from
exhaustion. A staple and less severe punishment was putting
boys "on the line," where they stood silently at the position of
attention all day, fed only bread and water. The daily food was
also miserable. Breakfast consisted of rye coffee, bread, and
paste "made out of salt pork with flour which used to stink very
badly if several of the boys were spreading their bread together."[57] Several youngsters also recalled finding bugs and
worms in the bean soup.

A former employee charged that Sleep had suppressed stories
of the many attempts to burn down the institution and had also
squelched reporting of several abortive suicides. Some reports,
furthermore, challenged the superintendent's sanity. One held
him responsible for the earlier typhoid epidemic and numerous
dysentery cases because he insisted on slaughtering cattle and
hogs in the hot sun. Indeed Sleep was so temperamentally explosive, one report said, that he had thrown away the pure
spring water procured by Waukesha residents to stem the epidemic. One boy tried to sum up the frustrations of inmates: "To
what extent and how the boys are punished is known to few
outside the school. No wonder the boys misbehave and run
away."[58]

In addition to these reports, the current foreman of the boot
and shoe factory verified most of the inmates' charges. The
reformatory was able to market its goods cheaply, he explained,
because the superintendent avidly enforced production quotas.
If a boy was lazy or evinced tiredness, Sleep beat him on the
spot; if the boy failed to meet his quota, Sleep beat him later.

The foremen of other shops in the institution were equally demanding, and for good reason: they received a share of the profits. Under Sleep's administration, the older and stronger a boy, the more time he spent producing marketable goods.[59]

Sleep denied every allegation, although, interestingly, he never denied that the main purpose of having inmates work in factories was for profit, not treatment. He charged that Mr. Conklin was a "sorehead" manufacturer who fabricated the exposé for selfish reasons. The charges of brutality, Sleep said, were also either outright lies or distortions. The superintendent, in self-defense, invited reporters to visit unannounced and observe daily routines.[60]

This they did—on the one day of the week when Sleep customarily left the institution to shop in Milwaukee. Infiltrating the reform school, the reporters questioned inmates at length before the astonished overseers learned who they were. "When the boys discovered that their cause was to be pleaded before the public in the columns of the *Sentinel*, it was almost impossible to get away from them so anxious were they to tell their stories." Sleep got word of the invasion in Milwaukee and hurried back in time to admonish reporters that inmates tended to exaggerate the extent of their misfortunes.[61]

Rather than becoming involved in public controversy, Sleep entrusted his friends with defending him to the press. One close acquaintance serenely observed that none of the overseers he interviewed could recall ever having seen excessive punishment used at the reformatory.[62] E. B. Shaw, a former employee, called Sleep the finest superintendent in the institution's history, although he at least granted that physical punishments were commonplace. Shaw's defense illustrated just how far the institution had drifted from the precepts of affectional discipline, in theory as well as in practice. "It is right to have humane societies for the prevention of cruelty to animals," he noted, "but when you compare a wild, ungovernable boy to a vicious horse, the comparison is nowhere. The horse can be managed by kindness, the boy, in nine cases out of ten can not." The potential for good in all youngsters, not their predispositions for evil, had underlain initial enthusiasm for the family reform school; but it was a point of view entirely absent from Shaw's remarkable defense of the status quo. "Boys have got to know that they are obliged to obey, they will not do it of their own free will nor out of respect to any officer. I am aware that many people will differ with me, but experience is my teacher."[63]

In a curious way Shaw was wrong: there were very few people, especially in government, who were willing to differ with him. This became apparent during the investigation of the reformatory by the newly appointed State Board of Supervision. The board decided to conduct its hearings in secret. This antagonized reporters who labeled the investigation a "whitewash" even before it began, and concluded that the public could not "look, as it was reasonable to expect it might, to the State Board to carry out the necessary reform."[64]

The report fulfilled the journalists' expectations. Only forty of the three hundred forty inmates questioned had legitimate gripes, according to the board. Most complaints were "utterly frivolous," nothing "different from what is of daily occurrence in public schools."[65] The report said that inmates who had recently entered the institution admitted that their parents had whipped them more severely than had Sleep or his underlings. Finally, according to the report, the food at the reformatory was superb, better than one could find in the average hotel.

The board's report revealed incredible naiveté, as the newspapers noted in their continuing sensationalistic coverage of events. Inmates on parole had been threatened with having their leaves terminated if they dared to volunteer criticism of the institution.[66] The present inmates had been coerced to remain quiet by promises of later retribution. The verbal assaults occasionally displayed political malice: "It is to be hoped that our next legislature can get free enough from machine control . . . to drive out from our public institutions that class of brutes and hypocrites, who have so long been disgracing the good name of the state."[67] Reports of atrocities at the Wisconsin Industrial School for Boys soon spread to the East Coast, and the whole episode descended into caustic name-calling.

For all the hullabaloo and righteous indignation, no substantive alteration of policy emerged. Public interest in the internal affairs of the reformatory soon receded. To be sure, the smug assertion of the board that what went on within the institution was the superintendent's concern alone aroused considerable, if short-lived, protest. Several citizens argued it was

their civic responsibility to penetrate the facade of all philanthropic institutions to verify that these institutions were fulfilling
the public's trust. "The sleeping rooms in the institution are
grated like jails," observed the *Sentinel*. "High walls surround
the buildings. . . . If brutality is used there, the boys have no
remedy except from public opinion."[68]

Public opinion—the point was exactly on the mark. But what
the *Sentinel* failed to note in its spirited defense of the public's
right to know was just how long ago that anonymous public had
lost interest in the plight of delinquents once they were taken off
the streets; how the patina of penological "progressivism" had
shielded the reformatory from outside purview; how administrators had exploited the family design to serve mainly bureaucratic aims of efficiency and order; and how easily the institution
had drifted toward the traditional house of refuge in its policies
and practice. Even as the family reform school became more
widely celebrated throughout the country, the Wisconsin Industrial School for Boys increasingly became an isolated and
forgotten fortress, a dumping ground for the state to pour its
human refuse.

Conclusion

In the aftermath of "crisis," the board ordered the release of
inmates en masse. Three hundred children were paroled or freed
unconditionally within a year. Not long after, the board reported facilities were adequate, employments plentiful, and discipline not unduly harsh. The *Sentinel*'s recent fury had ebbed to
complacency. Its inspection of the reformatory revealed that,
"as usual, everything under Superintendent Sleep's management
was found satisfactory."[69]

Public opinion, then, was fickle indeed. When it came to the
lives of delinquent youth, it was easy for purported guardians of
the public conscience to forget past atrocities and assume that
until the next crisis emerged, everything was satisfactory. After
all, the state did have a "progressive" reform school. What better
evidence could there be of its benevolent intent?

7

**The Juvenile
Court Movement
in Microcosm:
Milwaukee**

Remarkably little is known about how
juvenile courts worked in practice in the
early years of the twentieth century.[1] In
part this is a result of poor—intentionally
poor—record keeping. In their quest for
informality, many courts never employed
stenographers and kept only skimpy,
unsystematic data on their clients.[2] In
part, too, restrictions on public access to
court records have contributed to the
dearth of accurate information.[3]

Still, these explanations are inadequate.
Historical blind spots generally result
from more than insufficient or restricted
evidence; they derive equally from the
conscious or unconscious choice of scholars not to raise certain questions or delve
too deeply into commonly held assumptions. In the case of the juvenile court,
two tendencies appear to have thwarted
empirical analysis. First, diverse legends
about the court at its inception, its heyday, have been enshrined in the social-
work profession as lore, the accepted wisdom the initiates of a profession dare not
challenge.[4] Second, most histories of philanthropic institutions have concentrated
on legal frameworks, theoretical formulations, and reformers' backgrounds, to the
exclusion of operating realities. Together

these tendencies have focused attention on what the juvenile court movement was supposed to achieve, not on how it actually operated.[5]

The traditional story of the juvenile court in its heyday might be rendered as follows. In the beginning, the guilt or innocence of offenders was of marginal concern to the court. Rather, the fundamental issue was the determination of what social factors had compelled children to commit illegal acts, and what elements in their home situations and communities were unconducive to proper child care. Criminal procedures were anathema: their focus on guilt and innocence, and the adversary procedure used to weigh the merits of conflicting evidence, impeded the intervention of government as *parens patriae*. The court viewed customary responses to delinquency as ineffective because such responses encouraged isolation of children in nonrehabilitative institutions and, moreover, ignored the latest findings of developmental psychology. Children and adults held fundamentally different conceptions of reality; consequently, the court asserted, children could not be judged by impersonal moral and legal codes.

Rather than deciding a youngster's guilt or innocence, the juvenile court relied upon its diagnostic component—the detention center—to determine the causes of delinquent behavior and/or the likelihood that a child would commit criminal acts in the near future. The court also brought together offenders and potential offenders, their families, judges, probation officers, and interested community representatives in the hope of finding nonpunitive remedies which would spare children the stigma of criminality and let them remain in accustomed social settings (probation was seen neither as stigma-producing nor as a serious deprivation of liberty).

In his humanitarian concern for children and his utter disregard of criminal law procedures, Ben Lindsey—the "kid's judge," as Lincoln Steffens dubbed him—exemplified the new approach to juvenile justice. Lindsey insisted that the juvenile court was an educational institution; its main goal, like that of the public schools, was to turn out well-adjusted future citizens. Its methods were ameliorative and persuasive. The underlying assumption was that all children, however misguided their early upbringing, retained an inborn potential for good which only needed to be drawn out by sympathetic adults. The court's immediate objectives were to convince children that the state wanted to help and not to punish them, to convince parents to exercise careful guardianship and become exemplars of upright behavior, and to keep the vast majority of offenders and would-be offenders at home under probationary watch.

A new physical setting facilitated attainment of these goals. By discarding his judicial robe, hearing many cases in chambers, and eliminating juries and counsel, the judge was to provide an atmosphere conducive to honest communication in order to convince offenders of his sincere interest in solving their problems, not in punishing them. The court was to be friend and moral guardian; confessions by clients were to be a sacred trust, promises made a sacred duty. Personalizing the dispensation of justice to children, the court would teach them that law was not an arbitrary or rigid code of conduct. Instead clients would learn that law took account of individual problems and rendered judgments in accordance with individual needs. When children and parents understood this elemental truth, they would become more obedient citizens.[6]

So the traditional rendition goes. Those sympathetic to the juvenile court applauded it and called for additional funds to finance its operation;[7] those critical denounced it as false humanitarianism and regretted substitution of unbridled judicial discretion for the conventions of criminal law.[8] Both viewpoints, however, speak more to the ideology of the court movement than to the actual operation of juvenile courts. They leave unaddressed a variety of intriguing questions.

For instance, were the persuasive techniques Lindsey relied upon, the trust he instilled, and the successes he achieved typical of most juvenile courts? Did cities with larger and more heterogeneous populations than Denver present judicial problems Lindsey never faced and for which his methods were perhaps inappropriate? Did most judges trained in the procedures and rules of criminal law adjust as easily as Lindsey to their quasi-parental, educational roles, or live up to new responsibilities which the abrogation of due-process safeguards thrust upon them? Did probation officers generally empathize with their clientele as fully as Lindsey empathized with his? Was the spirit of rapprochement which seems to have characterized the decision-making process in Denver—of parents, children, and court officials working amiably toward mutually agreed-upon solutions—duplicated elsewhere? These are issues neither traditional nor revisionist interpretations of the court have attempted to answer, and for which existing legal and literary evidence is inadequate.

To begin to answer these questions, I obtained access to records of the Milwaukee Juvenile Court for the period from 1901 to 1920. Though imperfect in many respects, the records provide an intimate glimpse into the daily life of the court and a new empirical base for evaluating the practice of Progressive juvenile justice. In the following chapter I shall have more to say about the nature of these records, but first it is essential to describe the social and intellectual setting in which the Milwaukee Juvenile Court originated.

From Facade to Farce:
Politics and the Reformatory

As suggested in chapter four, there was an obvious economic reason for the popularity of the juvenile court movement: in an era of rapid social and demographic change, courts were a much cheaper response than reformatories to the anticipated growth of juvenile crime.[9] An additional though less direct reason probably lay in the peaking of eugenic thought, especially in Wisconsin, as documented by Rudolph Vecoli. With the aim of preventing propagation of society's "unfit," reformers seriously contemplated (in addition to sterilization) a massive building program designed to provide facilities where a wide range of hereditary deviants could be institutionalized for life. The economic argument in favor of probation was surely enhanced when reformers considered the large sums of money which would be needed to finance such alternative projects.[10]

Though important, these explanations are less readily demonstrable than two previously examined developments on the national level: increasing public awareness of institutional failures and newly heightened sensitivity to the value of preserving natural family units whenever feasible.

William Sleep managed to sustain the facade of the family reform school for most of the 1880s, aided, no doubt, by the managers' policy of paroling inmates en masse whenever the institution was threatened by overcrowding. Although Sleep, unlike Hendrickson, did not command nationwide admiration as a correctional innovator, the institution under his direction remained one of the half dozen or so most highly regarded simply because of its "progressive" family design. There were no further epidemics and only random reports of blatant brutality; when Sleep retired, few could recall the earlier "crisis."[11]

This low profile vanished in the 1890s as a result of overt political jockeying. After nearly two decades of Republican hegemony in Wisconsin, the Democrats, led by Governor George Peck, capitalized on widespread displeasure among immigrants at a discriminatory school act—the famous Bennett Law—to win the election of 1890. Quickly abolishing two supervisory bodies which had competed acrimoniously in the 1880s for power and influence, the legislature appointed a new Board of Control. Though ostensibly created to eliminate political bickering and assure neutral management, the board had the opposite effect and amplified the impact of politics on public philanthropy. Frustrated Democratic office-seekers now sought positions in the Peck administration, and the governor acquiesced by distributing places on the board as patronage.[12]

Barely a month after assuming office, members of the Board of Control became enmeshed in a political squabble involving the reformatory. In 1891, against the advice not only of Republicans but also of Waukesha County Democrats, they appointed M. J. Regan to succeed Sleep as superintendent. Regan's background was hardly distinguished. Until 1885 he had resided in the town of Eagle (within Waukesha County), employed at "superintending a stock horse on routes through the adjoining districts." A perennial Democratic candidate for whatever minor office was vacant, he had always been defeated. Disgruntled over his political bad luck in Eagle, Regan had moved to the village of Waukesha, where he sought but failed to win nomination for postmaster. In financial distress, he finally managed to be elected town marshal, a position he held for two years before losing it in 1890. After an unsuccessful bid for county sheriff, Regan persuaded several local and statewide business interests to employ him as a lobbyist. During this time he apparently secured political connections which later prompted the Board of

Control to offer him the superintendency of the reform school. If ever there was a party hack, it was M. J. Regan.[13]

Waukesha Democrats joined Republicans in attacking the Board of Control, fearing Regan would discredit the Peck administration. Philip Carney, editor of the *Waukesha Democrat*, minced no words in denouncing the board as "a sort of kindergarten for teat fondlers in the party and discarded political blood-suckers who had caught onto the skirts of the new dispensation."[14] Local citizens who knew the extent of Regan's incompetency were "involuntarily forced to the conclusion that he is by nature, associations, education, and in diverse other regards absolutely unfitted for one of the most delicate and correspondingly responsible superintendencies of any of the state institutions."[15]

Waukesha Democrats missed no opportunity—and Regan gave them many—to impugn the new management. Late in 1891 an inmate died of diphtheria and the superintendent, perhaps fearing a scandal, failed to notify the boy's father. Eventually the father learned of his son's death and sued the state for criminal negligence. Of this unfortunate incident editor Carney observed that never in the institution's history had there been such an uproar over sanitary conditions and overall management.[16]

Another incident enabled Carney to voice a more pointed complaint. One day a tramp wandered into the institution and stole several pigs. Until the man was arrested two days later for carrying the pigs into town, Regan remained unaware of the theft. Incidents like these, Carney raged, were undoubtedly more common than anyone dared imagine, for Regan, never confident about future income, continued to serve as a lobbyist in Madison. It was time for the Board of Control, Carney wrote, to insist that Regan "pay more attention to the discipline and sanitary conditions . . . and devote less time to gratifying his personal motives."[17] Though it is impossible to prove, Regan's frequent absences may have accounted for an escape rate four times higher than it had been during most of the 1880s.

Public censure of the institution now became frequent, for the first time in a decade. Another reason for a rising escape rate, charged Carney, was that Regan relied heavily on physical coercion to maintain order. To punish "certain bestial practices," notably masturbation, he stripped inmates and flogged them

vigorously with a rawhide lash. He often assaulted boys "with
implements of torture after the manner of the cowboys on the
plains with refractory animals until wounds are inflicted and
blood runs over the victims."[18] Regan, in short, was giving the
state and the Democratic party a bad name. Only half-
facetiously did Carney suggest that the board blink a mass
escape while it searched for a more humane superintendent.[19]

Rising concern over the high escape rate and excessive punishments peaked in 1892, after a group of citizens from the town of
Calhoun wrote to Carney about a scene they witnessed in their
railroad station. Accosting a boy who had recently fled the
institution, two officials from the reform school "struck and
pounded him black and blue, and tore the clothes from his body
and otherwise brutally assaulted the poor boy until he was
covered with blood and scarcely able to stand. And then while
the boy was bleeding and sore and naked," the letter continued,
"the two brutes got into their dog cart and each one took hold of
the boy and drove off at a lively rate, dragging him after them in
a most cruel and inhumane manner."[20] Although they had been
skeptical about Carney's trenchant editorials, the citizens of
Calhoun now agreed that the superintendent and perhaps even
the Board of Control encouraged such violent treatment.

Regan's defense of the arresting officers was similar to the
defenses employed in the early 1880s to excuse Superintendent
Sleep. Threatening to sue the *Democrat* for defamation, Regan
contended, with remarkable ingenuousness, that the boys had
not been stripped naked. Rather, their clothes had simply torn
off when the officers lifted them by the shirt collars to beat them
with clubs and fists! This reply infuriated Carney all the more.
To a "bar room politician" like Regan "a person must be hacked
to pieces, or blown to atoms before severity is exercised. And
therein lies the whole difficulty."[21] The *Democrat* ignored the
libel suit and called for an investigation of the incident. Perhaps
when confronted with the results of such an investigation, noted
Carney, the Board of Control would be awakened from its
customary slumber.

As in earlier years, it is impossible to be certain whether all the
charges hurled against the superintendent were true, whether the
markedly increased journalistic attention represented an actual
deterioration in internal reformatory affairs, or whether the

community at large was now more concerned about the care of juvenile delinquents. Certainly partisanship had influenced the selection of reformatory officials in the past. Still, the impact of partisanship had never been as blatant or as disruptive as it was in the 1890s. The facade of the family design could no longer mask the custodial and punitive nature of treatment. Despite its "progressive" exterior, the Wisconsin Industrial School for Boys was receiving the same type of criticism that reformers like Homer Folks were leveling at institutional care in general. Thus the overt decline in management—the fact that the lid was no longer being kept on—contributed to an atmosphere in which alternative methods of dealing with delinquents would at least be seriously considered.

The Familial Persuasion: Reeducating the Urban Poor

A subtle shift in social thought in Progressive Wisconsin also helped legitimate the goal of noninstitutional treatment for the great majority of juvenile delinquents. Like most nineteenth-century Americans, Wisconsinites had believed that the sooner a child was removed from a poor home or inadequate parents and placed in a quasi-familial institutional setting, the better. This view, to be sure, remained influential among charity workers (and probably more so among the larger middle-class public) in the early twentieth century.[22] Nevertheless, what made charitable opinion in the Progressive period distinctive was a growing interest in the need to keep impoverished families together and a measured optimism that with proper training parents of the poor could become effective crime prevention resources.

As a consequence of this emerging belief in the utility of keeping families together, citizens throughout the state and especially in Milwaukee became increasingly concerned with such issues as the viability of the family as a socializing agent in an industrial age; the rising divorce rates and their dangerous implications for social order; the necessity of mothers' pensions to shore up impoverished and/or single parent families; the need for day nurseries (generally subsumed in Wisconsin under the kindergarten crusade) to provide for the well-being of children whose mothers worked; the potential uses of domestic science to enhance family life, of special significance in Milwaukee due to Catharine Beecher's role in founding Milwaukee-Downer College; the widespread popularity of Hallian child psychology, which became a lively topic in Milwaukee women's clubs and University of Wisconsin extension courses; and, finally, the role of mothers' clubs, generally a part of local women's organizations, religious groups, and social settlements, in disseminating the latest scientific information on good parenting.[23]

New attitudes toward the family of a poor youth as a potential ally in the campaign against juvenile crime began to surface in meetings of the Wisconsin Conference of Charities and Correction in the late 1890s.[24] Professor A. L. Graebner of Concordia College, St. Louis, who grew up in Milwaukee and whose brother was very active in Wisconsin philanthropies, succinctly captured both the old and the new viewpoints.

No sentimentalist on the quality of home or community life among the poor, Graebner called attention to the damage incompetent parents and miserable slum environments inflicted upon innocent children. He presented the traditional argument in favor of quick removal of youngsters from egregiously inadequate households. "A home which becomes a hot-house of lewdness and debauchery and crime in any form is no longer a place where a child's life and health, liberty and honor are secure, or where it may remain without detriment to the community, and it is in the interest of the child and of other members of society to whom the state owes protection of their civil rights, that no child unable to look to its best interests should remain in such surroundings."[25]

Yet what made Graebner's talk an example of Progressive rather than Victorian sensibilities was that removal of children from impoverished homes was neither his first nor his foremost concern. His main interest was in developing new means for government and private welfare agents to work together in assisting poor parents to raise their children. Like Homer Folks, Graebner was not a doctrinaire opponent of institutional treatment per se. But, also like Folks, he held few illusions about the rehabilitative potential of reformatories, even those with a family design. "The state," he granted, "must forever grapple [with] the impossibility of finding a real equivalent for a home with a natural father and mother."[26]

Most significant was Graebner's argument against the nine-teenth-century tendency to consider institutionalization a first resort. Instead, he affirmed the obligation of both government and citizens to assist lower-class parents in improving their own lots and in maintaining their homes at least at minimal standards of decency and proficiency. "The last thing . . . to which the state should allow itself to be driven," he insisted, "is to take a child away from its natural home. The home may need reform. Then let it be reformed if possible. The home may need subsidy from the state; then let it be subsidized; and only when it is beyond reform or remedy, then let it be abandoned and sup-planted."[27]

Graebner's priorities, then, were clear: "Resort to every avail-able measure for saving the child by saving the parent." In an apt analogy, he blended diverse elements of familial thought in the Progressive era: "As the presumption should always be for, not against matrimony, and undue readiness to grant divorces tends to undermine the very foundations of society, so the presump-tion should likewise be in favor of the relation of the parent and child with its rights and duties, and even under adverse circum-stances every measure to better those circumstances should be exhausted."[28] Hardly the sentiments of a social radical, Graeb-ner's ideas were nonetheless inconceivable against the back-ground of charitable and correctional thought in Jacksonian or Victorian America.

Two privately sponsored organizations emerged in late nineteenth-century Milwaukee which, like Graebner, stressed the upbuilding of poor families instead of institutional treatment as the most effective response to juvenile crime. Naturally enough, the two organizations provided the nucleus of support for the city's juvenile court movement.

Of the two, the Associated Charities had less influence in providing support for the court. Founded in 1882, the organiza-tion's initial goals were starkly economical and punitive: to eliminate "excessive" charity expenditures by individual donors and to punish lower-class Milwaukeeans who fraudulently col-lected more in alms than they "needed" to survive. Like most charity organization societies in America, Milwaukee's Asso-ciated Charities never fully outgrew its fetish for "efficiency" in the distribution of alms.[29] As members repeated ad nauseam, theirs was a sympathy of the head not of the heart. Still, the Milwaukee group did change in two ways in the late 1890s. First, as David Thelen has noted, the depression of 1893 taught them the absolute necessity, ideological reservations notwithstanding, of public relief to families in need.[30] Second, partly as a result of their own experience and partly in response to new ideas on child rearing, household management, and religious duty, they learned to downplay vindictive investigations of the poor for more constructive efforts in parent education.[31]

These shifts in the attitude and strategy of the group should not be exaggerated, but neither were they unique to the Associated Charities. Such policy shifts reflected a subtle change of tone evident in the works of prominent charity spokespersons, as evidenced by the contrast between Mary Richmond's *Friendly Visiting* (1899), for example, and Josephine Shaw Lowell's *Public Relief and Private Charity* (1884) or Robert Hartley's earlier reports to the Association for Improving the Condition of the Poor in New York City.[32] Rather than ladies bountiful or ladies vindictive,[33] Milwaukee's friendly visitors in the Progressive era strove to become patient moral guardians, economic counselors, amateur child psychologists, and domestic science instructors. Their aims increasingly reflected those of the National Congress of Mothers.[34] Preserve rather than disrupt lower-class families by teaching housewives to manage their homes, rear their children, and entertain their husbands: this was increasingly the ideal, if not necessarily the practice, of charity workers in Progressive Milwaukee. It therefore was natural for agents of the Associated Charities to serve as volunteer probation officers of the juvenile court, since both types of work emphasized rehabilitation of children at home and treatment of families as cohesive units.

The group that provided the most important support for the juvenile court in Milwaukee was the Boys' Busy Life Club.[35] The boys' club—Milwaukee's was the first west of the Alleghenies—embodied three key elements in late nineteenth-century charitable thought. First, and least significant for the juvenile court, was the impact of G. Stanley Hall's theories on play and childhood development. As pointed out earlier, Hall's ideas were instrumental in a variety of reform proposals in the Progressive era, but they contributed little to the growing popularity of the juvenile court and probation.[36]

Second, the boys' club embodied the growing interest in municipal mothering, which enjoined well-to-do women to teach poor parents the techniques of efficient household management and child care. The boys' club program was deceptive; sponsors were interested in much more than supplying deprived children with suitable outlets for their play instincts. The sponsors' larger goal—which updated the aims of the Sunday school movement in the early nineteenth century—was to gain access to homes that were potential "breeders of crime" and had perhaps escaped the watchful eye of the Associated Charities. Claiming that it was futile to expect the boys' club to exert a lasting impact on children who returned to homes of degradation and squalor, the sponsors incorporated personal visitation into a larger strategy of social amelioration and control. To help with the visitation program, they recruited young volunteers and later paid workers from Milwaukee-Downer College, which from Catharine Beecher's founding had placed great emphasis on domestic science as a lever of social reform.[37] From the club's inception its paid staff devoted more time to home visitation than to amusing children in the clubrooms.[38] In short, the Boys' Busy Life Club, like the Associated Charities, joined science and sentiment in the pursuit of a more moral and "efficient" family life among the poor.

Third of the elements embodied by the boys' club was the influence of the Social Gospel. The role of the Gospel in Milwaukee juvenile justice was profound and easily demonstrable. "Applied Christianity" and the "institutional church" were the clarion calls to social reform through religious activism. Gospel advocates in Wisconsin interpreted Christianity as a living creed embodied in the sufferings and sacrifices of Jesus. According to these advocates, true communicants revealed their faith not by profession alone but by missionary activities to less fortunate neighbors. This activist theology broadened the role of the church to include social services and encouraged use of the meeting house as a community center where believers and non-believers of various social statuses could meet on terms of relative equality. Children of the poor, it was thought, especially benefited: they found soothing, low-keyed religion, witnessed uplifting models (young and old) for emulation, and played in healthy recreational environments.[39]

The ties between the Gospel and the Boys' Busy Life Club could not have been more direct. The boys' club had actually begun under religious auspices. In 1887 a group of young men calling themselves the Plymouth Atheneum had started the club in the basement of Congregationalist Plymouth Church, one of the two centers of Gospel thought in Milwaukee (the other center was instrumental in establishing social settlements).[40] Led by the articulate, moderate social activist Reverend Judson Titsworth, Plymouth Church, for nearly a decade, supplied most of the volunteers needed to supervise play activities and visit poor families.[41] Even after the club became more autonomous in 1900, leaving the church basement for larger quarters and expanding its directorship to include members of other congregations, it remained an appendage of Plymouth Church, which continued to supply more than half of its leadership.[42]

Members of the club considered the juvenile court movement a logical extension of their missionary activity. The court, like the boys' club, emphasized personal intervention into the family life of the poor. Understandably, then, several representatives of the club—and hence the Plymouth Church congregation—served as members of the volunteer probation staff when the court opened in 1901. Indeed for at least two years before the court's official opening, the club superintendent served unofficially as a "friend in court" to young offenders. Other members of the club visited the local jail to comfort alleged juvenile criminals before and after trial and ministered informally to these youths at home after their ordeals.[43] Thus to these individuals the idea of noninstitutional treatment flowed easily from more than a decade of church welfare and club experience. The Social Gospel, municipal mothering, and probation went hand in hand.

The Juvenile Court Movement in Milwaukee

If blatant mismanagement of the reform school and select developments in social thought and welfare practice enhanced the appeal of new correctional programs, the immediate spark for the establishment of Milwaukee's juvenile court was the recent Chicago example. After only two years, the achievements of Chicago's juvenile court had begun to assume legendary proportions, especially in the Midwest. Court enthusiasts in Milwaukee highlighted the Chicago successes as a spur to Wisconsin achievement.[44] In Milwaukee as in Chicago, prominent, well-to-do women with prior experience in charitable affairs led the court movement: Mrs. Annabelle Cook Whitcomb, head of the boys' club; Miss Marion Ogden, daughter of a wealthy real estate agent and a frequent visitor of children in the jails; and Mrs. Kathryn Van Wyck, head of the Associated Charities.[45] Personal acquaintances of Jane Addams and Louise DeKoven Bowen, the three Milwaukeeans traveled to Chicago on a number of occasions to see its juvenile court in operation and to discuss legal strategies with Richard Tuthill, who had drawn up the Illinois juvenile court law. In fact, the three virtually copied the Chicago law and persuaded Chief Probation Officer Timothy Hurley and several other Chicagoans to testify in Madison on the law's constitutionality and workability.[46]

In short, the court movement in Milwaukee was led by knowledgeable, energetic, and socially elite women who orchestrated a sophisticated political campaign. After gaining formal endorsement from a half-dozen newspapers (including ethnic papers) and a variety of civic groups, they steered their bill easily through the legislature in 1901.[47] The initial stage of the juvenile court movement was over, having experienced none of the frustrations which impeded the creation of a family reform school several decades before.

This seeming consensus persisted through the first decade, resulting in incorporation of many features considered essential to the proper operation of a juvenile court. But in one area, probation, the court's structure did not keep pace with reformers' evolving goals.[48] Local government representatives refused to finance a probation staff anywhere near the size sanctioned by the nationwide movement. Sponsors of the juvenile court in Milwaukee by and large had their way, but not in this critical area.[49]

One factor with which the Milwaukee court did not have to contend was serious opposition on constitutional grounds. Not until the 1918 case of *State* v. *Scholl* did any parent or guardian challenge the court's mandate. The issue in *State* v. *Scholl* was somewhat anomalous: it centered not on the more common argument against committal without due process, but on the right of the court to place children not formally convicted of crime on probation.[50] Since this challenge cut to the core of noninstitutional remedies, it evoked a vigorous response from the state supreme court.

On the right to trial by jury, the supreme court offered a standard reply: proceedings in juvenile court were civil, not criminal, and children were not convicted or punished. The juvenile court was a "legitimate exercise" of the state's "police powers, or, in other words, its right to preserve its own integrity and future existence." Moreover, contended the judges, the benevolent purpose behind the law overrode petty concerns about denial of due process: "We know of no rule which prevents the use of investigation and unsworn testimony in ascertaining the essential facts. The desideratum is to obtain, by the use of kindness and sympathy, the confidence of the child and of its parents if possible, to convince them that the judge and probation officer are friends and not the avengers of offended law." A more Lindseyesque view of affectional discipline could hardly be found than in the contention that the juvenile court brought parents and children "before an experienced and humane judge who shall inquire into the situation, not with the awe-inspiring and frigid methods of a criminal court, but informally and intimately, like a wise and gentle brother, or like the good Samaritan of holy writ, and who shall, when fully advised, do that which is best for the child's future, either by way of sending it to an institution or by providing for kind and tactful but in no sense degrading surveillance for a limited time at home."

Other legal pitfalls impeding the development of juvenile courts in New York City and elsewhere did not arise in Milwaukee. The enabling legislation in Wisconsin reiterated and expanded loose nineteenth-century definitions of delinquency, dependency, and neglect.[51] The law did, though, simplify procedures for bringing cases into court; almost any citizen could file a valid complaint with ease. To avoid constitutional challenge, and with the expectation (which was correct) that it would rarely be used, the legislature initially provided that a parent or guardian of a child on trial could demand a jury of six.[52]

Another section of the law prohibited confinement of children under fourteen in a jail or police station, or confinement of youngsters between fourteen and sixteen in the same jail cells as adults. An overly optimistic assumption underlay this provision. Sponsors of the court expected the county to fund a separate house of detention where children could be held before and after trial. From 1901 to 1904, however, the county refused to finance the facility. Contrary to law, the judge of the juvenile court kept many youngsters in jail (although as isolated as possible from adult offenders). Miss Ogden continued her ministrations to the youngsters.[53] Late in 1904 the Milwaukee Home for the Friendless offered use of its top floors as a detention center. For diagnostic and educational purposes this left much to be desired, but it was clearly an improvement over the local jail. Finally, in 1909, the county funded an entirely new court complex, considered to be the best in the country, complete with detention quarters.[54] Thus Milwaukee was slow in fulfilling a critical prerequisite of the court movement, although after it did, the court's physical facilities were inferior to none.

The passage of an adult or contributory delinquency law in 1905 indicated how readily the state legislature supplied the court's nonfinancial needs. In many states this was the most difficult piece of legislation to pass, but in Wisconsin there were no problems whatever. A triumphant visit to Madison and Milwaukee by Ben Lindsey laid the groundwork for the law's approval, which came shortly after his departure.[55]

The legislature also approved the principle of payment for probation officers in 1905, a measure not considered vital at first (either in Milwaukee or the rest of the country).[56] Under this legislation William Zuerner was appointed chief probation officer. Until 1907 Zuerner's main job was to coordinate activities of the volunteer probation staff. Thereafter the number of paid probation officers grew, so that by 1913, 90 percent of the children on probation were supervised by paid, full-time officers.[57] Obviously, payment was one matter, an adequate supply of probation officers another. But the principle of payment was accepted in Milwaukee with less resistance than in several other cities.

The Milwaukee facility also did not experience serious religious and political rivalries disruptive elsewhere. The prosectarian sympathies of judges in Milwaukee (as contrasted, for example, with those in Chicago) defused a likely source of conflict. They acknowledged the right of parents to determine the religious affiliation of foster parents and of institutions where their children were to be committed.[58] True, there were fewer dispositional options—aside from probation—for delinquent than for dependent or neglected youth. Most male delinquents, regardless of religion, were sent to Waukesha. But the reform school by this time had been obliged to provide Protestant and Catholic clergy and to respect the religious preferences of inmates.[59] Furthermore, whenever possible the court sent Catholic delinquents whose "crimes" were not serious—for instance, truancy—to the St. Amelianus Orphanage which, though nominally for parentless youth, clearly functioned also as a reformatory. The options were simpler for female delinquents: Protestants were sent to the Wisconsin Industrial School for Girls in Oregon (south of Madison), and Catholics went to the privately funded House of Good Shepherd in Milwaukee. And, finally, the court attempted to place youngsters on probation with members of their own ethnic group and faith (particularly if there was a language problem).[60]

As control of probation moved into the hands of paid officers, complaints about political interference were voiced in Milwaukee as throughout the nation. It may well be that several paid officers received their appointments as political favors (although I have no evidence of this, pro or con).[61] Still, another question is more important, especially in light of the elitist, Protestant backgrounds of the founders of the court and the ethnic origins of many paid staff members.[62] Were political appointees necessarily less qualified to deal affectionately with children in their home and community surroundings than volunteers or civil servants? In the next two chapters I shall address this question indirectly in the context of actual cases; for now it can simply be suggested that the opposite may be closer to the truth. If politicization of probation actually occurred, it appears to have equalized the distribution of positions among the city's ethnic groups. This made it possible for judges to assign probation officers to children of similar cultural backgrounds. Without these officers as intermediaries, encounters in and out of court might have been more tension-ridden and alienating than they actually became. Thus, when considered against the backdrop of a multi-ethnic community and the extremely personal nature of the services to be rendered, there is no ipso facto reason to judge political influence destructive of the court's mission.

Finally, the publicly recorded response of the community to the court did not appear to go to the extremes it did elsewhere, notably in Chicago and Denver.[63] Despite occasional complaints by neighborhood groups about the prominence of youth gangs, criticism remained relatively low-keyed and infrequent.[64] There were no scandals or exposés involving the court to compare with those involving the reformatory. The only issue that sustained journalistic interest was whether juvenile courts should remain branches of district courts or become separate legal entities. Although tempers flared for a while, founders of the court argued both sides of the issue.[65] Until the 1940s the juvenile court in Milwaukee remained a branch of the local district court. But this was nothing worse than the administrative arrangement Ben Lindsey accepted, indeed desired, in order to avoid constitutional objections. Thus, the most notable controversy involving the juvenile court was peripheral to its method of treatment.

In short, except for not being able to provide for an adequate supply of probation officers—admittedly a critical issue—partisans of the court achieved most of their initial objectives.[66] By 1905 and certainly by 1909 the court's legal and structural framework seemed solidly grounded—almost as solidly as the family reform school had appeared after its inauguration a half-century earlier.[67]

8

The Operational Meaning of Noninstitutional Treatment

What was the operational meaning of treatment in the Milwaukee Juvenile Court? Three bodies of information survive which help in varying degrees to answer this question.

One is the statistical record. Beginning in 1905 the court's chief probation officer, William Zuerner, began to keep rudimentary records on what transpired in court each year. These records were not published and never became widely available, which may help to account for their poor quality. Particularly for the Progressive period, the statistical information is incomplete and inconsistently recorded.[1] Nonetheless, the data are essential for understanding the dimensions of the court's task and for assessing the consequences, intended and unintended, of its creation for the administration of juvenile justice.

A second body of information concerns the most elusive sphere of the court's work, the out-of-court settlement.[2] Such a settlement involved a probation officer's attempt to resolve problems of children and their families before a formal appearance in court became necessary. A single surviving log book kept by several probation officers between 1914 and 1916 indicates what types of problems came within

142

the officers' purview, the kinds of intervention they usually employed, the role of the out-of-court settlement in the court's overall rehabilitative effort, and the relation of the probation staff to their "potential" clientele.

The final body of information derives from a sample of twelve hundred randomly selected cases which came before the court between 1901 and 1920 (almost exactly 10 percent of the total number of cases during this period). In approximately one-fifth of the cases included in the sample, trial transcripts or reasonably accurate accounts of what various participants said in court are still on file. Some of the transcripts are brief, no longer than a page or two. Others are considerably longer, running anywhere from ten to fifty pages. In many cases, moreover, there are multiple transcripts, one for each of a youth's many separate appearances in court. In sum, these transcripts (which I shall examine separately in chapter nine) reveal graphically the day-to-day operation of a juvenile court.[3]

The Dramatis Personae

Before examining the official data, it is useful to consider briefly the backgrounds of the participants—those connected with the court and those brought before it.[4] It must be emphasized that my information, culled from city directories and diverse secondary sources, is inadequate to produce a convincing collective biography of these participants.[5] What follows necessarily caricatures actual persons. Still, it is possible to suggest the extent to which the findings confirm or challenge existing portraits of "child savers" and their clientele in the Progressive era.

Most historians have emphasized the social and psychological distance separating Progressive reformers from those they hoped to uplift. They have portrayed reformers as a distinctive "social type": upper and upper-middle class, highly educated, prudish, probably anti-Catholic, with a small-town or rural conception of social order. Contrastingly, their clientele are portrayed as being lower-class, poorly educated, immigrant, Catholic, formerly peasant, and ghetto-dwelling.[6] One can generalize from this overall portrait to the particular situation of the juvenile court, to wit: however well-meaning those who founded and ran juvenile courts might have been, honest communication with their clientele was impossible because of the profound cultural and experiential gaps between reformer and client.[7] How well does this characterization apply to the social scene in the Milwaukee Juvenile Court?

Turning first to the parents of children in court, it is clear that the great majority were in fact lower-class, ghetto-dwelling, Catholic immigrants with minimal educations (although it is impossible to say with certainty how many had previously been peasants). Over 90 percent of the children brought into court between 1907 and 1911 were the offspring of European immigrants. Of these, three out of four were either German or Polish. The predominance of ethnics in court was consistent with the backgrounds of reform school inmates in the nineteenth and early twentieth centuries, when approximately 75 percent of the inmates prior to 1900 (it is impossible to single out the Milwaukee youth) were the sons of European immigrants. (See appendix two, table 6; and appendix one, table 2.)

That most parents were relatively poor was evident in several ways: first, from the salaries earned by the fathers, generally reported to be below ten dollars per week;[8] second, from records showing that the residences of families in court were concentrated in the poorer immigrant neighborhoods surrounding the city's scattered railroad network; and third, from occupations revealed in city directories.[9] Relying on addresses supplied in court to distinguish individuals with the same names, I have traced the backgrounds of 235 parents who appeared before the court in the years 1911 and 1916.[10] The bulk of these parents were clearly lower and lower-middle class—based on their reported occupations. The single largest job category, accounting for about 25 percent of the total, was that of laborer. An additional 8 percent of the group traced were listed as widows. Other job categories with representations of around 5 percent were clerks, machinists, and teamsters, with the remainder spread among sundry occupations of low to middling status including peddlers, saloon keepers, tailors, mechanics, window washers, plumbers, bricklayers, and so forth. In short, of those parents who can be traced, the great majority were of relatively low social status.

What of those who ran the juvenile court? A distinction must first be drawn between those who sponsored the court in the legislature and promoted its virtues in the press and those who actually performed most of the daily work. As observed in chapter seven, well-to-do women provided the driving force behind the juvenile court movement. Mrs. Whitcomb, Mrs. Van Wyck, and Miss Ogden were undeniably upper-crust, and all were native-born Protestants. But, except for Miss Ogden, few female sponsors participated in the court's daily work. Even before 1905, when all probation officers were volunteers, and women from Plymouth Church and the Boys' Busy Life Club showed greatest interest in the court, men rather than women predominated. Of the sixty volunteers who can be positively identified between 1901 and 1920, two-thirds were men.[11]

Furthermore, the majority of volunteers were not from the city's social elite. Of the sixty, 80 percent of their or their husbands' occupations can be identified. Fully half of this identifiable group were paid directors of charity organizations or truant officers in the public schools.[12] Four were policemen, three were newspaper reporters, five were ministers, and the remainder were in business for themselves as grocers, dressmakers, carpenters, shoe salesmen, tailors, photographers, real estate agents, saloon keepers, teaming contractors, stenographers, foresters, and physicians. Active participation in the voluntary phases of juvenile court work thus passed quickly out of the hands of a small elite into a diverse group of middle-class citizens and private charities (most of which, though, did receive financial support from the city's well-to-do).[13]

The backgrounds of the court's paid probation officers, who after 1905 handled the bulk of the cases, did not conform to a conventional "social type" either. Of the ten officers whose backgrounds can be identified, five were raised in rural areas and five grew up in Milwaukee during the period of the city's most explosive growth. At least three were Polish immigrants, and at least four were Catholics. Of the four women, none graduated from college and only Miss Ogden ever attended (one year at Wells College in New York).[14] The women were far from uneducated, however: two came from established Milwaukee families, one was fluent in three languages, and another had been a teacher. Of the six men, two had previously worked in law enforcement, one as a deputy sheriff and the other as justice of the peace. A third was the brother of Milwaukee's most famous Polish prelate, and a fourth was a well-regarded educator, musician, and occasional politician. A fifth had operated a collection agency, and the sixth had been an engineer.

In short, these individuals did not conform to a stereotype. Though of a higher social status than their clientele, there was great diversity among them in terms of religion, ethnicity, prior occupations, and so forth. No striking commonalities in their backgrounds, at least of the kind used by several historians to understand the mind-set of Progressive reformers, can convincingly be said to have predisposed them to behave toward their clientele in a single or distinct way.

While their careers inevitably displayed certain commonalities, the four judges who manned the court during most of the Progressive era were not cut from the same mold either.[15] In fact, three of the four, like most of the court's clientele, were Catholics and the sons of immigrants.

Neele B. Neelen, who had the longest tenure, was a Baptist. Born to immigrant farming parents and educated in district schools near Rockford, Illinois, he completed a two-year degree at the University of Rochester before taking a law degree at the University of Buffalo in 1891. Franz D. Eschweiler was born in Houghton, Michigan, studied for two and a half years at the universities of Iowa and Michigan, and was admitted to the bar in 1889. The son of a Bohemian father, John C. Karel was born in Schuyler, Nebraska, although the family moved to Kewanee, Wisconsin, when Karel was very young. He was educated in Kewanee public schools before studying at Prague and then at the University of Wisconsin for both baccalaureate and law degrees. Michael S. Sheridan, the son of Irish immigrant parents, was reared in South Coventry, Connecticut, where he was trained as a machinist. After moving to the Midwest, he studied law at night school for two years, gaining admission to the bar in 1892. In short, although all four judges were "professionals," native-born, and reared in rural areas, their ethnic, religious, social, educational, and legal backgrounds were too diverse to warrant predicting that they would behave toward children and parents in a single or set pattern.[16]

Although neither judges nor probation officers constituted an obvious "social type," they did in fact behave in similar ways both in and out of court. To be sure, personality quirks could spell the difference between freedom and imprisonment in individual cases. Clara Smith, for example, was noticeably more offended by female unchastity than other probation officers. Michael Sheridan resorted more quickly to threats than other judges. Overall, though, these differences were minor, making it possible to portray the court, unlike the reform school, less in terms of chronological developments than in terms of modal procedures. The important point is that, based on the limited information available, these similarities in behavior cannot reasonably be attributed to the distinctive social origins of judges and probation officers. Indeed, if all behaved similarly, that appears to have resulted from common allegiance to values and beliefs acquired more in spite of than because of their unique social origins.[17]

The Out-of-Court Settlement

As is often true in historical research, the types of human behavior that seem potentially the most intriguing also prove to be the most inscrutable. No facet of the court's rehabilitative task was considered more important than the elimination of "delinquency-producing" home conditions before a formal court appearance was necessary.[18] A log book kept between 1914 and 1916 provides some indication of the problems encountered, the assistance offered, and the resolutions apparently achieved in pursuit of this goal.

The log book contains information on 356 cases (about 20 to 25 percent of the total number handled by the court in this time period). Immediately striking is how rarely the court's intervention was precipitated by specific problematic behavior of children. In ten percent of the cases the allegations (if any) could not even be identified. Nineteen percent of the total, and the cases considered most serious, involved instances of parental neglect; these almost never included specific allegations (criminal or otherwise) against children.

Twenty-eight percent of the cases alleged nothing more concrete than that family members could not get along with one another. These conflicts usually involved disagreements between parents and children on such issues as refusal to work or to turn wages earned over to parents, staying out late, general disobedience, and so forth. They also included disagreements between parents themselves, especially on monetary and sexual matters. Parents most often initiated these interventions, using the probation staff to resolve intrafamilial problems.

The largest portion of cases, 43 percent, could nominally be termed delinquency according to broad legal definitions which continued to prevail in the Progressive era. But the category of delinquency, as has already been apparent, covered an enormous range of conduct which the probation staff tended to lump together and treat with equal seriousness: larceny, "bad associations," intercourse, assault and battery, truancy, cursing, masturbation, and so on. Analysis of actual conduct in these cases indicates that no more than a third—or 14 percent of all out-of-court settlements—involved clear-cut criminal offenses, and most of these were petty thievery.

A further indication that most problems settled out of court involved little overtly illegal or disruptive behavior derives from the origins of the complaints. Unlike delinquency referral patterns today, policemen initiated complaints in only 6 percent of the traceable cases. Public school officials, private charity organizations, and public relief authorities together accounted for an additional 14 percent. In sum, only one out of five cases resolved out of court was brought to the attention of the probation staff via public and quasi-public sources.[19]

By contrast, in nearly a third of the traceable cases parents initiated proceedings against their own children, hoping thereby to shore up their waning parental authority in the domicile. Still more illuminating, fully a third of the complaints originated with neighbors who for one reason or another had become disgusted with children who lived nearby, or who intended to avenge a grievance against an adult by swearing false charges against his children. In short, the probation staff was frequently used by lower-class immigrant adults to relieve private familial frustrations and to satisfy personal grudges.[20] Probation officers, to be sure, recognized this and resented the many frivolous complaints they received. But their aim of "preventing" delinquency and searching for vague "underlying causes" required them to take each complaint seriously, to intervene on the basis of uncertain allegations, and to assume the worst about a parent or child unless proven otherwise.

Brief summaries of actual cases will suggest the superficial nature of many complaints and the haphazard kinds of settlements generally effected.[21]

In July, 1914, a probation officer received word that sixteen-year-old Gerald Muldower refused to work, stayed out late at night, and smoked cigarettes. Upon investigation it was learned that Gerald's parents were dead and that he was living with his grandparents, who had filed the complaint. Further inquiry revealed that Gerald had been unemployed for nearly two years, refusing to work ever since he lost a finger on his last factory job. Confronted with these "charges," Gerald promised the probation officer that he would seek employment and pay board to his grandparents. Whether Gerald was threatened with a court appearance is impossible to determine. But he quickly corrected his errant ways and obtained a job in a hardware store, after which the officer closed the case as a successful settlement. Was Gerald "on the road to delinquency"? No one knew, of course, but at least for the moment the intervention of the officer seemed to improve intrafamily relations.

Three weeks earlier a similar case had required more affirmative action. Mr. Pildowski complained about his two teen-age boys who refused to work or attend school and who spent their days "bumming around" railroad tracks or frolicking in outlying woods. The probation officer advised the boys to find work, but to no avail. After two unsuccessful visits to their home, he called them into his office and employed scare tactics, threatening to bring formal charges (probably for truancy or incorrigibility) against them. The ultimate fate of these boys remains unclear; presumably they found the officer's threat frightening enough to find employment. At any rate, this case was also listed as a successful settlement.

As will be revealed in the trial transcripts, the complaints parents brought against their own children were often extreme, leaving the court with few dispositional options. It was a pleasurable, if rare achievement to resolve one of these cases out of court.

An example was the case of Mrs. Sherman, who accused her son Israel of staying out late at night and stealing. At first Mrs. Sherman insisted that Israel be locked up for at least a year, but a probation officer convinced her to see whether the three of them might be able to talk out their problems. Israel, perhaps realizing that unless he agreed to the talk he would be taken into court and possibly committed, volunteered to place himself on probation. The officer approved and also forced Israel to plead for forgiveness while on his knees. Were it not for the probation officer's early intervention, Israel would surely have been brought into court on a charge of incorrigibility and would have been subject to the vagaries and uncertainties of the judicial decision-making process.

Other cases similarly highlighted ambiguity in probation officers' attempts to "prevent" delinquency. Overt criminal acts rarely entered into complaints. Consider the accusation of Mrs. Elvehrer, who alleged that her children were being molested by a neighbor's child. Upon investigation, the probation officer realized the complaint had no basis in fact; the children were being used as pawns in a quarrel between two adults. The officer sternly warned both parents to stop their fighting; once they agreed he closed the case as a successful resolution. Similar to the Elvehrer case was a neighbor's complaint charging a young girl with truancy. Investigation revealed the girl had a valid work permit and that the neighbor was simply trying to upset the girl's mother.

This type of complaint frequently backfired. For instance, Mrs. Wolenski charged in April, 1915, that Peter Czerzak, who lived in a nearby rear basement apartment, was neglecting his four-year-old daughter. Unable to locate Czerzak, the probation officer decided to investigate Mrs. Wolenski's house. Finding it in a "very filthy condition," she warned Mrs. Wolenski to clean up or she would bring her family into court and charge her with neglect. Similarly, Mr. Padrewski complained that three neighborhood youths had attacked his son Lewis. The investigating officer learned, however, that Lewis had actually instigated the quarrel and, moreover, that the boy surreptitiously smoked cigarettes. The officer concluded that Lewis was "to all appearances a bad boy and will need watching." From accusers, Mr. Padrewski and his son had become the accused.

However ambiguous the relation of out-of-court settlements to delinquency "prevention," such settlements were often accompanied with extrajudicial punishments. Two cases in August, 1916, demonstrated this practice. In the first case, Mr. and Mrs. Esk complained that their thirteen-year-old daughter, Denise, was incorrigible. When they brought her to the probation office, she was "very saucy" to her mother, accusing her of immorality, among other things. Thereupon the probation officer, on her own initiative and against the parents' remonstrations, placed Denise in detention for four days. Realizing that they had no control over the proceedings, the Esks dropped the charges against Denise after her release. In the second case Mrs. Debrink complained about her daughter Ellen's "sauciness" and brought her to the probation office to discuss their problems. Ellen, however, refused to pay any attention to the probation officer, whereupon he placed her in detention for several days and then put her on probation.[22]

The cases examined so far are representative in that they all originated with parents or neighbors. While charitable agencies and school authorities initiated fewer complaints, theirs generally required more immediate and affirmative action. For example, in November, 1916, a public school teacher alleged that every day all the Mordinski children arrived at school hungry. Upon investigation the probation officer uncovered a rather bizarre situation. Mr. and Mrs. Mordinski had been having a bitter dispute over the latter's refusal to transfer half of her property rights to her husband. In the interim Mr. Mordinski had refused to provide money for food and had not eaten at home in six months. When the probation officer arrived at the house the cupboards were indeed empty. Somehow the probation officer was able to effect a quick reconciliation between husband and wife; Mrs. Mordinski agreed to her husband's demands and Mr. Mordinski promised to give her money for food. The officer's early intervention may not have prevented delinquency, but it certainly prevented malnutrition.

Compared to their representation in cases brought to court, girls appeared disproportionately in out-of-court settlements.[23] About half of the cases in the log book involved girls of varying ages. Moreover, in stark contrast to their response in cases brought to court, the probation officers generally responded pragmatically to female moral improprieties. Seemingly comparable offenses could be found before the court as well as in

out-of-court settlements, thus highlighting the centrality of discretion in the court's modus operandi. One never knew quite
what to expect from the probation officers.[24]

Consider the investigation of a complaint (origin uncertain)
that sixteen-year-old Eloise was pregnant and was bragging
about her condition to young girls in her neighborhood. Eloise's
mother had died seven years earlier, her father worked half
days, and three of her five siblings still lived at home. Eloise
cooked and kept house for them and her father, thus helping to
keep the family intact. Although she admitted to being pregnant,
Eloise denied having told anyone but relatives. Furthermore, she
was to be married to the child's father in less than a month. The
reaction of the probation officer—nearly always a woman in
cases like this—was temperate. After due consideration of alternatives, the officer decided to wait out the month and let the
marriage take place. Thus the probation officer, who was clearly
shocked at Eloise's condition, held her moralism in check. One
may conjecture, based on other cases involving young unwed
mothers, that had Eloise not been engaged she would have been
allowed to have the baby and then would have been sent to the
House of Good Shepherd. But in this instance, quite reasonably,
the officer left well enough alone.

Another sex-related case further demonstrated the use of noninstitutional remedies for female sexual promiscuity. This time a
group of boys and girls, schoolmates, were involved equally,
but the boys, as usual, escaped with little more than a stern
warning. The boys had formed a club devoted to group masturbation and the enticement of young girls into intercourse. The
probation officer was content to break up the club and did not
insist that its members be tried in court. For the boys' indiscre-
tions she urged an educational solution. "I advised the parents
that as each of these boys had now arrived at the age of understanding that it would be well if instead of administering corporal punishment they would take their boy and advise and
educate him along the lines of sex hygiene and point out the
danger they were putting themselves in by their acts."

Though the girls received harsher treatment, none was institutionalized. Jamie, age ten, whose immorality was confined to
necking in nickel shows with the most amorous of the boys, was
confined indefinitely to home under parental supervision.

Nancy, age eleven, who had played kissing games regularly with boys and masturbated with female partners, was similarly confined. Even Irma, age fourteen, who admitted to frequent casual intercourse with numerous paramours, was merely forced to transfer schools.

This brief review of out-of-court settlements suggests a number of conclusions. First, intervention of the probation officer probably helped resolve a number of individual and family problems among the poor, but in most instances there was no way to link this accomplishment to delinquency "prevention." In only one way was the out-of-court settlement demonstrably related to delinquency prevention, and this connection had nothing to do with criminal behavior among children. Rather it derived entirely from the probation officer's arbitrary power: if a child agreed to do exactly as an officer wished—or at least pretended to do so—then the officer would "prevent" a charge of delinquency from being lodged against the child.

Furthermore, interventions by probation officers probably exerted little lasting impact on their clients. The officers rarely followed up initial inquiries and resolutions. Instead they closed cases immediately after the first positive sign of family reconciliation, promise of reform, acquisition of a job, and so forth, hoping against hope that nothing more would go wrong.

Finally, what seems most remarkable in retrospect is not that these children were spared appearances in court, but that they came to public attention in the first place. The out-of-court settlement encouraged probation officers to drum up their own "business," and at the same time increased their leverage over the poor; they did not need a judge to make the poor conform to their wishes. Whatever its rehabilitative impact on parents and children, the out-of-court settlement provided a new mechanism of moral surveillance and social control—although one that, in retrospect, appears to have been more threatening in its potential than in its actual use.[25]

The Appearance and Reality of Noninstitutional Treatment

Though the statistical record of the Milwaukee Juvenile Court is far from complete, the range of activities it covers goes beyond

my immediate concern. The following discussion is highly selective. It seeks mainly to enhance understanding of the human
element in the court's modus operandi, not to give a comprehensive summary of the court's evolution or to indicate the extraordinary variety of services and functions it performed.

Until 1905 the court was an amateurish operation. Staffed by
volunteers (except for the judge), the court met only one afternoon per week. Case intake remained small. Fewer than one
hundred fifty cases were decided during the first year. Though
successive years saw relatively small increases, by the end of four
years the court had decided fewer than one thousand cases.

This pattern changed with the appointment of a full-time chief
probation officer, the establishment of a separate detention center, and the passage of an adult delinquency law—all in 1905.
Immediately thereafter intake increased considerably (see appendix two, table 1). The reasons for the increase probably had
little to do with the growth of misconduct, dependency, or
neglect among Milwaukee's youth, or with a sudden marked
increase in the age-specific population.[26] Rather, I would suggest, the caseload tended to grow with the court: enlargement
and improvement of machinery for enforcing the court's original
mandate generated "business."[27] On the one hand, police, agents
of charitable organizations, and citizens proved more willing to
bring children into court after separate, "safe" detention quarters
were secured and after parental deficiencies became punishable
offenses. On the other hand, a full-time probation officer had
more time and interest in ferreting out juvenile misconduct and
in following up local gossip on neglectful parents and abettors of
crime than did volunteers.[28]

Despite increases in the probation staff from one in 1905, to
seven by 1909, to fourteen by 1920, individual caseloads remained remarkably high. Although Chief Probation Officer
Zuerner regularly complained about this, neither he nor anyone
else involved in the court's intake process attempted to decrease
new intake in order to make treatment (or at least surveillance)
more efficient.[29] Beginning in 1910, perhaps earlier, no fewer
than one thousand children were on probation in any one year
(about 30 percent were holdovers from previous years). This
supervisory burden—for reasons not entirely clear—was generally not distributed equally among the staff.[30] In 1913, for exam-

ple, one officer supervised fewer than 100 children, two supervised between 150 and 200 children, and four supervised between 200 and 300 children. These caseloads—at a time when Zuerner considered 60 the absolute maximum for effective treatment—required and received extraordinary expenditures of energy. In 1919, eleven probation officers paid over 8,000 visits to individual homes and received more than 21,000 visits by probationers at their offices. Still, this left precious little time for the individual attention and omniscient supervision believed necessary for treatment.

Probation accounted for the great majority of dispositions (see appendix two, table 2), with the modal period of supervision running about one and a half years.[31] The heavy reliance on probation, especially for male delinquents, is confirmed by records showing a rather small number of commitments to the state reform school at Waukesha during this period (see appendix two, table 3). Between 1905 and 1916, the average number of youths committed each year was only thirty. Moreover, although the number of reformatory committals varied from year to year, it clearly did not increase at a rate proportional to rising case intake in the court. Indeed, if anything, it decreased. For example, in 1906, 55 boys were committed to the reformatory, out of 536 new delinquency cases; in 1911, 15 boys were committed out of 705. To sum up, the odds of being committed to a reformatory for boys charged with delinquency in the Progressive era were rather small. Despite increases in intake, the court's reliance on long-term committals actually diminished after 1905.[32]

To grant this, however, is not to generalize glibly—as advocates of the court frequently did—that the number of children incarcerated declined in the Progressive era. While the juvenile court sent relatively few children to reformatories, it held large numbers on short-term sentences in the detention center before, during, and sometimes after trial. Especially after the city completed its modern detention facility in 1909, short-term imprisonment was fully integrated into the court's intake and dispositional process. The majority of youth placed on probation also spent several days in detention for observation and safekeeping. Furthermore, the proportion of those placed in detention increased over time. Whereas in 1905 approximately one-third of the children who appeared in court were held in detention, by 1916 the proportion was about three-quarters (see appendix two, table 4).

These data suggest an important facet of Progressive juvenile justice that can easily be obscured by the statistical salience of probation or by the traditional scholarly focus on what took place in court.[33] By establishing secure, segregated detention facilities for children, Milwaukee resolved a dilemma that had been troublesome since the 1850s (indeed, as argued in chapter two, a dilemma apparent as early as the 1820s on the East Coast). The dilemma centered on a paucity of dispositional options: with a choice between long-term committal to a reformatory and short-term sentencing to a county jail, some judges and juries appear to have informally exempted many children from the sanctions of criminal law. Detention provided a way out of this dilemma. Though sponsors of the court touted the detention "home" primarily as a diagnostic center, a place to deal with children individually and to determine their distinctive needs prior to court appearance, in practice the center served as a comparatively safe children's jail. Police, charity agents, truant officers, parents, and probation officers presumably had fewer reservations about bringing children "to justice" after having been assured that these children would not be "contaminated" by adult criminals in the process.

It would seem, then, that detention reintroduced the likelihood of short-term and frankly punitive sanctions into the administration of juvenile justice. In the Progressive era, especially after the modernization of detention facilities, increasing numbers of youth were being sent to jail both to "cool off" and to be impressed with the majesty of the law. Short-term detention served as a mechanism of deterrence in a way that long-term reformatory committals could not, and it also served as an alternative—symbolically, perhaps, even as a rebuke—to the institutional apparatus that had been so ineffective in curtailing delinquency during the previous century.

The Heyday of the Juvenile Court?

The operational meaning of treatment in the Milwaukee Juvenile Court was most graphically revealed and recorded in trial transcripts. For reasons of practicality and readability, I have chosen a small but representative group of sixteen cases for close analysis. Three were dependency cases resulting in removal of a child from his or her home; six were delinquency cases resulting in a child's commitment to an institution; and seven were somewhat vague in nature, although all appear to have resulted in probation.

No brief synopsis can possibly do justice to the variety and complexity of all the transcripts or fully evoke the frustration, anxiety, confusion, and anguish so often in evidence in the court's proceedings. Although selected with an eye toward the exemplary and archetypal, each case was necessarily idiosyncratic because, obviously, no two children or their parents were exactly alike. The sixteen cases that follow should be appreciated much like opera highlights, as suggestive of a larger drama and of characteristic patterns of interaction among protagonists—except that in the juvenile court, the play was real.[1]

The Panacea of Probation

As has already been made clear, the men and women who ran
the court took its preventive mission seriously. Their aim was to
nip criminality in the bud, even if that required placing children
innocent of criminal acts on probation. With this goal in mind,
children were frequently brought into court for "bad associations." While most parents did not object to remedial measures
the court deemed necessary, some occasionally did and even
persuaded judges, against the judges' own inclinations, to apply
more stringent rules of evidence than were considered ideal for
treatment. A case in the summer of 1912 demonstrates this type
of situation and its outcome.[2]

Four teen-age boys were brought into court for breaking
school windows, on a complaint filed by the school's principal.
As was customary, the judge failed to inquire at length into the
truth of the principal's allegation, preferring instead to place all
the boys—none of whom had ever been in juvenile court before—on probation and to assess their parents proportionally
for the cost of replacing the windows.[3] To the judge's obvious
surprise and chagrin, one of the boys' fathers, Mr. Hackenbruck, objected because his son had not actually broken any
windows. The judge was aghast, but the father persisted in his
assertion that both probation and the fine were unfair, perhaps
even illegal. "You are taking the wrong attitude," snapped the
judge. "Your boy was in the crowd; he had the stones in his
hands, and was about to throw them. I don't know why we
should pick him out as being better than the others." Unwilling
to accept this construction of the law, however, Mr. Hackenbruck retorted: "The guilty goes with the innocent, is that it?"
The judge hesitated then, admitting that young Hackenbruck
had not thrown any stones and that none of the boys "were
exactly guilty," but insisting that the determination of guilt or
innocence was not the court's objective.

Finally, the judge compromised: he absolved the father of the
need to pay a fine but placed his son on probation. The judge
remained angry, though, about what he saw as the father's
ill-advised challenge to the court's authority. "But I want to tell
you your boy is just as much to blame as the other boys, and I
think you are taking the wrong attitude in standing here and

talking the way you are, you are simply encouraging your boy to get into mischief of this kind." Though absolved of guilt, young Hackenbruck was now subject to possible committal to a reformatory should he break the rules of his probation.

In the spring of 1916 another case also captured the court's determination to root out future evil by resorting to "coercive predictions."[4] While the disposition in this case was somewhat extreme, the decision-making process used in achieving it demonstrated how the court generally disregarded facts in favor of "underlying causes."

The official complaint against Alex Milentz was the theft of a bicycle. Investigation by a probation officer turned up Alex's poor education and work record. After leaving school in the fifth grade, Alex apprenticed himself to a barber, quit, then became an errand boy, quit again, and then remained at home for two weeks before being arrested for the alleged theft and placed in detention.

The probation officer, though, was sure the cause of the bicycle theft was a combination of Alex's poor home environment and the boy's immoral habits. Demonstrating the casual way evidence was customarily introduced into the proceedings, the probation officer observed: "I questioned Alex as to his habits, and he informed me that he was smoking butts, picking them up along the streets, smoking cigarettes; it shows that the boy is nervous; he also masturbates quite a bit; in fact, he is—I am satisfied that he has been doing that while here; the bed-clothes show evidence of that. The parents—I have spoken to them, and they don't seem to have any idea that the boy might be practicing something of that kind." After presenting this "incriminating" evidence, the officer concluded: "The boy needs very close attention; he is in bad shape."

To the probation officer the links between a bad home, ciga-rette-smoking, masturbation, and bicycle theft were clear. A circular causal sequence was posited: everything led to every-thing else. The judge agreed with the probation officer's assess-ment of the case. After consulting with Alex's mother, the judge announced that Alex would be allowed to go home on probation to await placement with a farm family. Reflecting the pastoral ideals which remained powerful in the Progressive period and the degree to which the court was willing to intervene into intimate family affairs, the judge ordered Alex to the farm "until he is straightened out" and ordered the mother to have him circumcised.

Whether Alex actually went to the farm or, if he did, when he returned home is impossible to determine from the court records. But whatever the final disposition, Alex certainly would not have been the only boy brought into court on a criminal charge and then removed from home mainly because of poverty and "immoral" habits. The particulars varied from case to case (smoking and masturbation were probably the most common), but a child not proven guilty of a definable crime could easily be placed under supervision for an "underlying cause." The broad definition of delinquency under which the juvenile court continued to operate and the creation of a probation force to implement its preventive ethos combined to produce and legitimate this result.

Most dependency cases generated heated controversies between judges, probation officers, and parents. The parents in these cases were almost always impoverished. They were generally called to the court's attention by private and public charity officials who, in the course of processing the parents' claims for financial assistance, decided that in the interests of juvenile welfare, the children should be removed from the home. When brought into court and threatened with loss of their children, most parents responded hostilely, refusing to believe that the court genuinely had the children's best interests at heart.

A case in the spring of 1916 typified this parental attitude toward the court. Mrs. Wilowski, a mother of three children, whose husband was suffering from tuberculosis, was brought into court on a charge of neglect. She had been having difficulties with the city's health officials, who wanted her to bring the children to the health department for a physical examination, whereas she had insisted on using her own doctor. The judge decided to take command of the case himself by ordering the children into court that very afternoon.

Mrs. Wilowski objected: "No, I ain't coming here this afternoon; you think that I got money for streetcar fare, coming all the time; you must know that I ain't so rich." Obviously angered, the judge promised to have the children forcibly brought into court, and then he threatened: "I am going to have that thing done, or I am going to take the children away." Undaunted, the mother responded: "You will never take the children away from me." Their deepest emotions now stirred, the judge and Mrs. Wilowski continued to shout at each other, neither giving ground. Mrs. Wilowski had suffered one bad experience too many with public officials and would not sanction their intervention into family affairs again, even if her children were sick.

> My husband was in the Sanitorium four months, and the
> nurse she don't come and see that my children get some-
> thing to eat; only she come and told me that I should have the
> children examined by the doctor. I says, I wouldn't stand for
> that, that they wouldn't look after my children. . . . They are
> making such trouble for me; he was in the Sanitorium; I was
> talking to the doctor, and the doctor told me, if you want him
> you can take him along, that is the way the doctor told me;
> and the doctor make so much trouble; I ain't no sinner, no
> drinker; I support my children so long, and I want to stay
> with them to the end.

In the end, though, Mrs. Wilowski submitted to the judge's order and had her children inspected by the health department. Her defense that she was poor, virtuous, and loved her children obviously did not impress the judge, who placed her on probation for six months. Now a probation officer rather than a charity official would determine whether Mrs. Wilowski and her husband could retain possession of their children.

Although the absence of a probationary report makes it impossible to determine the final outcome of the case, the dialogue in court suggests the skepticism with which many parents viewed the court's concern for their children's well-being. A spirit of hostility and fervid emotion was evident on all sides and distinguished proceedings in the Milwaukee Juvenile Court from those reported by the amiable Ben Lindsey in Denver.

Despite differences in practice between Milwaukee and Denver, the several judges of the Milwaukee Juvenile Court considered themselves disciples of Lindsey (this was especially true of the first judge, Neele B. Neelen). In court they oftentimes imitated Lindsey's most characteristic mode of treatment, his attempt to convince accused delinquents that he was their friend, their "pal." Generally, though, the imitation was imperfect, as exemplified in a case before the court in the summer of 1912.

Caught in the act of stealing money, Walter Mikva experienced a fate common in juvenile hearings, that of being tried primarily for prior offenses, in his case a persistent record of truancy. In court Walter's school principal testified vigorously against him until, as if on cue, he reversed the gist of his argument and began pleading with the judge to show mercy for Walter. How does one interpret this strange behavior on the part of the principal? From numerous similar "performances" by other school and charitable officials, it is clear that this was a stylized dramatization staged by the court. Its aim was to impress upon youngsters both the court's peremptory authority and, equally important, its willingness to forgive. The judge certainly played his part with flair, addressing Walter: "I am not inclined to be as easy with you as your principal is. I can't make you believe that this is a serious matter, I can tell that from looking at you. You just got a notion in your head that we are going to preach to you awhile and talk and then we are going to let you go home. Now, I will tell you, I am going to try to do you some good. I am going to try to get under your skin, if I can."

Get under Walter's skin he did, by placing the boy in the detention center for a night. The next day the judge again approached the chastened lad, and asked in Lindseyesque fashion for voluntary, "contractual" compliance between friends. "I want to make a bargain with you," the judge told Walter, "that you will agree, if you run away from school again, you will come up and report it to the probation department. . . . And if you run away from school again that you will come up here and report to me and tell me to send you to Waukesha." Walter, not surprisingly, responded favorably to the idea, and the judge placed him on probation—but only after having threatened the boy with certain institutional commitment and having placed him in detention, two significant Milwaukee modifications on the Lindsey method.

Dramatizations like these often approached the comically absurd, although most children, knowingly or not, played their parts as officials of the court hoped they would. The keynote was on penitence: if a child seemed genuinely contrite, he or she would almost always be placed on probation and might even have the case dismissed. It is difficult to believe that young Marsha Bowman's testimony in the spring of 1920 could have fooled anyone, but her case did demonstrate that a smart child could manipulate a confession scene to serve his or her own ends.

Marsha had run away from home. After her arrest for loitering with a group of boys, she was found to be carrying douche medicine, which led the probation staff to suspect her of immorality. A doctor's examination confirmed her virginity, however, and she was placed on probation. One month later Marsha was back in court on a charge of attending German dance houses and remaining away from home an entire evening. This time the judge resorted immediately to threats: after a few days in the detention center, he threatened, she would be sent to the reformatory for girls in Oregon. Marsha spent a few days in detention; upon her release, as the judge doubtless anticipated, she was not only chastened but apologetic with a vengeance. "I am going to be so good. I want everybody to say: No, I can't go out. I won't go out anymore. Won't you shake hands with me?" The court could only respond affirmatively, to which Marsha replied: "Thank you. Oh, I am so glad. I will promise everyone that is in this court room, I promise I won't—I will be a good girl from now on."

Marsha had learned to play the game well, to meet the court on its own affectional grounds. Indeed judges generally found it difficult to be hostile to anyone, parent or child, who was so profusely contrite. Had more youngsters and parents adopted a similar strategy and become servile, they might have spared themselves later difficulties.

But parents in court, whatever their social status, were generally not servile. The consequences of asserting one's parental prerogatives, however, did vary according to one's social standing. Whereas a lower-class parent who challenged the court was likely to place himself or his child in deeper trouble, a middle-class parent could often exploit legal loopholes. A parent could, for example, bail out a child placed in detention before trial. This privilege, however, was rarely invoked, for reasons illustrated by a case in the spring of 1920.

Arrested for stealing a bicycle, Paul Gmiczyk was sent to the detention center for "observation" prior to his appearance in court. Paul spent only one night in detention, however, as his mother put up bail and had him released. When the superintendent of the detention center so informed the court, the presiding judge immediately called the case and raged at the mother's interference. For a time the mother insisted on her legal prerogatives. It soon became clear to her, however, that the law was on the court's side and that she had better retreat before the judge carried out his threats.

> Court: Why didn't you leave this boy stay here a little while to think over the stealing of this bicycle, why did you bail him out right away?
>
> Mrs. Gmiczyk: Because I thought it was lesson enough for him . . . .
>
> Court: Are you willing now to take down your money and let this boy stay here a week to think this thing over, or, do you want to send him to Waukesha until he is eighteen years old?
>
> Mrs. Gmiczyk: He didn't commit such a serious crime. Where would he reform now? . . .
>
> Court: I want you to take your money and I want this boy to stay here a week so he can get a little time to think this over, and see our probation officers, so that they will get a little chance to talk this over with him. If you don't do that we will have to send him away somewhere.
>
> Mrs. Gmiczyk: I am satisfied, whatever the court does.
>
> Court: Well, that is what the court wants you to do. I don't like the idea if a boy steals, of you people running up and bailing him out of here. We want a little time to let him think it over upstairs. Let him stay here a week, it will do him good. This case is continued for an hour, until she makes up her mind, and if she doesn't do it, I will seriously consider sending this boy to Waukesha.

Mrs. Gmiczyk wisely relented, and Paul went "upstairs" for a full week before being placed on probation. Clearly the court would not brook this type of challenge to its legal authority and rehabilitative method. The liberal use of detention to chasten young offenders, before and after trial and as a corollary to probation, and the use of threats to compel parental cooperation were better integrated into the court's modus operandi than the pursuit of affectional discipline.

If raising bail was counterproductive, hiring a defense attorney was not. Attorneys appeared in only 3 percent of the sampled cases; in most instances the children involved in these cases were middle and upper-middle class.[5] When confronted by a vigorous defense lawyer, the judges of the juvenile court were less apt to insist upon their judicial right to do whatever they pleased, as evidenced by a case in the spring of 1919 involving two runaway girls, Betsy Parker and Carol Mahler.

During her runaway period, Betsy had stolen some money. Her ultimate fate in court remains unclear; she may well have been sent to the girls' reformatory in Oregon. The Mahlers, however, were taking no chances with Carol, for they already considered themselves victims of the law's "benevolence." Though they had asked the police to help find their daughter, they had never intended to punish her and were consequently appalled when a probation officer dragged the entire family into court. They therefore hired an attorney who confronted the judge on these grounds when he proposed to place Carol on probation: "I move to dismiss the case at this time. There is absolutely no ground for bringing a charge of delinquency against this girl—not according to the testimony produced in this court." Typically the judge responded in the language of *parens patriae:* "What do you consider delinquency? We are here to help this girl." But the attorney stood his ground, insisting that the court's proposal represented an infringement of parental rights and of the child's liberty.

When he could make no headway against the lawyer, the judge pleaded with Mrs. Mahler—pleaded, did not threaten, largely because, one may guess, Mrs. Mahler had an attorney to back her up. "We ask you to cooperate. She has gotten away from you and she is only a small child and in the formulative period. What I want to do is help you. We are not here to punish the child . . . [or] to reflect on you folks, but the fact that this girl got away and slept out nights and did what she did do, indicates that this child should be on probation." When it became clear that Mrs. Mahler would not budge, the judge continued the case for a week, with the explicit purpose of unearthing more damaging evidence. Carol spent the entire time in the detention center.

The case resumed with Carol's school principal on the stand to testify against her. The judge, if no one else, found his testimony incriminating for both Carol and her parents.

Principal: Well, she at times has had a little trouble with not
being able to get along with other children very well and she
is a child that of course will have to be watched by the
teacher.
Court: Why?
Principal: Well, she is not very truthful. . . .
Attorney: May it please the court, it wasn't this girl who took
the money; it was the Parker girl.
Court: The principal has no knowledge of that. I want to
know whether [Carol's] . . . conduct is such to warrant her
being placed on probation.

In this case as in most, there was no limit to the types of
evidence considered relevant. Since Carol's "condition" was at
issue, the court was willing to accept even the most circumstantial information to shed light on that condition. Even an attorney was unable to stop the following "evidence" from being
introduced.

Court: Who did she say those things to?
Principal: She told those things to her father.
Court: And he in turn told it to you.
Principal: He in turn told it to people who again told me those
things.

Still the attorney refused to accept probation for Carol. For
the moment the judge decided to abandon his attempt to obtain
voluntary compliance but made it clear he would try to find
unimpeachable grounds for placing her on probation in the near
future. Addressing the principal, he announced he would continue the case and "allow Carol to go home without putting her
on probation but I want you to promise this court to watch her
and if you catch her at any time not only lying or doing anything
that is irregular, I want you to report to me."

Next time, not surprisingly, came soon enough, as the principal construed the judge's instructions liberally. Carol's bad
character and potential for ruin in the future were, in the court's
estimation, at last confirmed. In good conscience the judge now
placed her on probation, over the attorney's objections and the
frustrated interjections of her father, who demanded, "Your
honor, what is the charge against her? Why did she come up
here; who had the authority to put her up here?" To which the

court glibly, and truthfully, responded: "Anybody that believes she is delinquent—anybody can."

A defense attorney, then, was useful, but only up to a point. In the end the judge could play all of his legal trump cards and do whatever he pleased. In most instances an attorney could prevent the committal of a child who had not perpetrated a serious crime, but rarely could he restrict the liberal use of probation or detention. When the court wanted to intervene in intrafamilial affairs in order to "prevent" future delinquency, there was virtually nothing anyone, even a lawyer, could do about it except to delay the inevitable.

Of the sixteen cases to be examined, the seven just described were most illustrative of the court's modus operandi, since none resulted in immediate long-term removal of a child from his or her family. Though the circumstances and participants varied enormously from case to case, probation and short-term detention were the types of treatment administered to all. If an empirical base existed for the frequent claim that the court revolutionized the treatment of juvenile offenders, cases like these constituted it. What, then, did such cases reveal about the operational meaning of treatment in the Progressive era?

First, the cases reveal that by no stretch of the imagination did the interactions between court and clientele embody the theory of affectional discipline. Rather than assuming that an innate potential for good was common to all children and trying to develop that potential in friendly, compassionate communications, à la Ben Lindsey, judges and probation officers in Milwaukee relied mainly on fear, threats, and short-term imprisonment to render children malleable and "cooperative." The relations between court and clientele were generally hostile and always superficial. Instead of providing treatment, the court engaged its clientele in role-playing. True, the majority of children were placed on probation, a relatively noncoercive sanction. But this certainly did not imply, as the faithful application of affectional discipline would have necessitated, that the court retained confidence in the family as a locus of treatment, as a setting for moral education and uplift. In practice, neither judges nor probation officers showed more than passing interest in developing strong personal relationships with clientele. As later cases will reveal more graphically, the court employed harsh criteria to judge parental intentions and abilities and almost invariably found parents wanting in these categories. Moreover, the heavy reliance on probation did not preclude punitive sanctions. Indeed, detention and probation tended to go hand in hand; any parent who objected to the former was likely to prejudice the judge into begrudging or revoking the latter.

Second, the cases demonstrate the readiness of the court to explore the outer limits of its legal mandate. Unrestricted by customary rules of evidence and procedure, judges, probation officers, and district attorneys asked every conceivable form of improper question, probing at length into hearsay and circumstantial evidence. They placed children in double jeopardy, "convicted" them of prior offenses, and used confessions to further implicate them and their parents. Ostensibly the objective in such proceedings was to bring to light all relevant information pertaining to a child's condition in order to develop a sophisticated diagnosis of his or her needs. In practice, however, remarkably superficial inquiries into "underlying causes" of a child's behavior pattern sufficed and, furthermore, appeared to satisfy the court.

However valuable for diagnostic purposes, the immediate effect of these inquiries was to incriminate defendants and their parents in innumerable misdeeds—moral, criminal, or otherwise—for which they could be held liable. After establishing the depravity of defendants, the court could then portray acts of "leniency"—like probation—as evidence of judicial kindness, mercy, and love. Thus in the Milwaukee Juvenile Court, adversary procedures remained de facto, if not de jure, integral to the modus operandi of the court. Instead of eliminating all trappings of criminal procedure, especially the concern for guilt or innocence, the juvenile court eliminated mainly those due process safeguards with which children and parents could defend themselves.

A third element evident in the cases was the persistence of Victorian moral attitudes toward children's noncriminal transgressions. The men and women who ran the Milwaukee Juvenile Court, unlike Ben Lindsey, had not genuinely assimilated the latest theories of human development and sexuality into their moral philosophies. They might and often did acknowledge verbally a stage in natural development termed "adolescence," but they had not internalized its implications for rendering moral judgments. In practice if not in theory, the natural instincts of youth still remained strange, forbidding, threatening, and fundamentally perverse to them. The more they discovered how adolescents, particularly children of lower-class immigrants, behaved when left to themselves, the less tolerant they became of parents whose economic or physical circumstances made constant surveillance of children impossible.

The Decision to Commit: Delinquency

In practice the legitimacy of the juvenile court, as of all courts, hinged on power. The right of the court to commit any child who came before it, whatever the alleged crime or "condition," provided the main source of leverage for obtaining compliance from children and parents. But parents and children were not equally powerless before the court. Nothing so jeopardized a child's freedom from incarceration as his or her parents' insistence that the child was beyond parental control. Thus the decision to commit, like the decision to place on probation, did not conform to a simple pattern. The choice between committal and probation sometimes depended on nothing more than whether the judge had awakened in a good or bad mood that morning; at other times such a choice reflected constraints imposed on the court by parents who refused to keep their children at home any longer.[6]

Consider the situation of fifteen-year-old Bronislaus Labarski in the summer of 1901. His father had initiated proceedings, charging that Bronislaus "loafs around the streets of the city of Milwaukee, and steals everything he can lay his hands on and does not [obey] him and is a bad boy in general." Mrs. Labarski had died or deserted her husband, leaving him to contend with their eleven children. Bronislaus, the father alleged, had been away from home for two months—or so he thought until Bronislaus took the stand and surprised everyone.

Court: Where were you during all that time?
Bronislaus: Walking.
Court: Walking around—where did you sleep, in box cars and sheds and so on?
Bronislaus: No.

Court: Where did you sleep?
Bronislaus: Slept in the cellar.
Court: Whose cellar?
Bronislaus: Ours.
Court: Home?
Bronislaus: Yes.
Court: You came back in the evening and would sleep in the cellar?
Bronislaus: Yes.
Court: And sneak away early in the morning, is that it?
Bronislaus: Yes.

This testimony both verified the boy's artistry at concealment and convinced the court that his father was incapable of providing the most basic supervision. The court went on, though, to validate the father's petition in three additional ways customary in cases of this sort.

First, it asked someone, in this instance a policeman, to corroborate the boy's vagrant habits. As often happened, the judge found himself having to temper a policeman's desire to remove potential troublemakers from his beat. At best, though, the judge supplied the policeman's testimony with a patina of evidential regularity.

Policeman: Your Honor all I know the father has been complaining that he has been running away from home and I would see him on the street and just as soon as he would see me he would run. I saw him running around with the other boys and it took me two weeks to catch him.
Court: That is nothing against him. It is natural he would run away. Did you find out anything about this boy that indicated he is incorrigible? Can his father control him?
Policeman: No, he can't do anything with him. I have had complaints from other people saying that he has been doing mischief.

Second, the court established the boy's backwardness in school. In the following dialogue the judge's reasoning may appear obtuse, a result, most likely, of his having decided upon a final resolution before the questioning even began.

Court: Did you go to school in your life time?
Bronislaus: Yes.
Court: Can you spell any words with three letters in it?

Bronislaus: Sure.
Court: What grade were you in?
Bronislaus: I was in the fifth grade.
Court: Now why didn't you stay at school?
Bronislaus: It was just vacation.
Court: Were you at school last winter?
Bronislaus: Yes, sir.
Court: Well, I think I better send you to the Industrial School.

Third, the judge spent little time inquiring into the father's motivations for seeking committal because he found communication with Mr. Labarski extraordinarily difficult. The two generally spoke right past each other. Transcripts of numerous other cases clearly reveal that the judge was often obliged to conclude that neither he nor the parent under examination had the faintest notion of what the other was saying. At this juncture the judge would simply stop the inquiry and ask the parent to confirm his desire to get rid of the child. There was no easy explanation for this persistent and frequently pitiful phenomenon. But whatever its cause, judges quickly became frustrated in trying to converse with their clientele. Even when a translator could surely have alleviated difficulties, judges rarely bothered to sustain even the pretense of meaningful communication. Consider the following "dialogue":

Court: How many children have you?
Mr. Labarski: Eleven.
Court: Eleven?
Mr. Labarski: Yes.
Court: Is this one of the oldest or youngest?
Mr. Labarski: No, third older than he.
Court: Older?
Mr. Labarski: Younger.
Court: Have you had any trouble with any of your other children?
Mr. Labarski: No. I can't speak so good English.
Court: Oh, you do well enough. . . .
Court: How many times has he been arrested before, do you know?
Mr. Labarski: No, not to this time.
Court: This is his first time?
Mr. Labarski: First time.
Court: How many times has he run away?

Mr. Labarski: Eight weeks, pretty near.

Court: He has been away for eight weeks. Where has he been do you know?

Mr. Labarski: What?

Court: Where has he been during that time? Where was he?

Mr. Labarski: I don't know; I can't tell. I told him to the police. I can't talk so good English.

Court: How long has he been away? You said about eight weeks? Now didn't you see him at all during those seven, eight weeks.

Mr. Labarski: Yes, he was home so long time.

Court: He has been away from home?

Mr. Labarski: Yes.

Rather than continue this farcical conversation, the judge's next remarks indicated that he had had enough. He abruptly changed the direction of his questions and asked:

Court: You mean to say you can't do anything with him at all?

Mr. Labarski: I can't—

Court: Now if you pay attention to me you can understand me. Now I say you cannot do anything with this boy. That is you can't bring him up as he should be?

Mr. Labarski: I can't.

And that was that for Bronislaus. Having opened the dispositional option of reformatory committal to unwilling parents, the court generally acceded to a parental desire to commit, with or without proof that the alleged delinquent had committed a specific offense. The point at issue was the social situation in which the child found himself, not the particular behavior of which he was accused. In this instance Bronislaus could do little more than expect the worst: his father did not want him, he had clearly shown himself to be beyond parental control, and his father was already under an incredible family burden. Probation, in the court's view, was useless without cooperation, or at least feigned cooperation, from the parent. Too old for adoption, Bronislaus was also too young to be declared independent. What alternative was there, the court reasoned, to a reformatory committal which would spare him the harshness of life in a home where he was not wanted? In short, while the court granted that no institution was an effective parent surrogate, in practice it regarded committal as a far lesser evil than returning children to overburdened or uncaring parents.

A somewhat similar case in the spring of 1904 demonstrates that the court at times tried to reconcile parent and child in the hope of avoiding institutionalization for the child, but that this attempt at reconciliation was generally to no avail. The testimony of the first witness illustrates an anomaly in the Milwaukee juvenile court movement. Even though there were no criminal charges against Wadislaus Debilowski, Clarence Hadden, superintendent of the Boys' Busy Life Club, recommended immediate committal for the boy. Given that the superintendent and his organization had spearheaded the drive for noninstitutional care, especially for first "offenders," Hadden's recommendation seemed out of place. Wadislaus, after all, had done well at the club's summer camp and had trekked several miles weekly just to attend manual training sessions. Still Hadden concluded that the boy's problems at home and school, plus his precocious physical development, made institutionalization the only suitable disposition.

The judge was surprised by Hadden's recommendation. He wondered out loud whether a reformatory committal was appropriate. Hadden replied: "I think if he had a term at the Industrial School he would be he would do [sic] very good work and turn out a good man. I see no reason why he cannot be. He should be trained." But the judge remained unconvinced; perhaps if removal was necessary, he suggested, the county Home for Dependent Children would be a more suitable location. Hadden remained firm: "I think, in my judgment, the school at Waukesha would be the place for him. Of course we don't claim to know anything about these necessities." Admitting not to "know anything about these necessities," the head of the boys' club nonetheless recommended institutionalization. With this example set by the group most actively campaigning for noninstitutional treatment, it was little wonder that unwilling parents viewed the court as a vehicle for discharging their burdens.

Ostensibly truer to the goals of the juvenile court movement than the superintendent, the judge attempted to determine for himself whether Wadislaus should remain at home. His hope was for reconciliation between father and son. Addressing himself first to Wadislaus, he attempted to portray the father's attitudes in a kindly light. "Your father is a pretty good man isn't he? Come on—tell us Wadislaus. He has always been pretty good to you when you was a good boy, wasn't he?... Now he might have whipped you a little more than what he ought to but you see your father doesn't want a bum out of you. He wants a good man out of you. He is better off to have no boy at all than a bad boy, isn't that right?"

Slowly the judge penetrated to the heart of the matter: whether Wadislaus wanted to return home or not was irrelevant because his father no longer wanted him. The judge was at first incredulous: "Why do you say he won't take you? How do you know he won't take you? You love your father, don't you?" But after calling the father to the stand, there was no longer any question; reconciliation was impossible. The judge criticized, scolded, cajoled, but the father stubbornly insisted that enough was enough. "It is all well and good but if I go to work and try to make two ends meet and my wife goes to work and he can't help us a little bit and if he would only behave himself and not go into stores and get foods on my name and steal things and don't want to behave himself it is too hard."

As this case indicated (and without reflecting adversely on the motives of those who brought their children into court on the grounds that they could no longer care properly for them), the clientele of the court could easily manipulate the judicial process if what they wanted was commitment. In numerous instances parents of the poor served as the principal aggressors against their own children, portraying them as potentially dangerous future criminals. Cases like these hamstrung the court, leaving few dispositional options to impose in good conscience. Though the court rarely attempted to apply in practice an affectional mode of treatment, it often lectured parents on their own empathetic failings. Witness the judge's final peroration:

> You tell him that if he has any feeling for his child or has any love for his own offspring it is always the parent's duty to do what he can for his children as long as there is hope. Now this boy is only thirteen years old and he hasn't done anything very serious up to now but of course he stole some money from him but he hasn't from anybody else and it seems to me that a father ought to step in and help him and see that this boy is brought up to take the right course and become a good

citizen. Why he ought to go to work and be willing where
there is even a ray of light left he ought to be willing to extend
a lifting hand to his son it seems to me.

Curiously, then, judges in juvenile court were most articulate
in affirming the virtues of affectional treatment precisely when
the theory was least appropriate to the situation at hand. Complaints of parents against their own children unquestionably lay
behind a sizable proportion of cases resulting in reformatory
committals.[7]

A parent's consent, however, was hardly a prerequisite for
committal. The court often ignored parents entirely during the
course of a proceeding as it attempted to determine the "underlying causes" of delinquent behavior and the consequences of leaving a child with his family. A case in the fall of 1906 demonstrates this process.

Fifteen-year-old Peter Forsza was arrested by the police on a
neighbor's complaint that he had exposed himself to her. At least
this was the formal charge, although it received no attention
whatsoever in court. Testimony focused instead on "underlying
causes," particularly the parents' inabilities and Peter's lower than
average intelligence. Though the quality of Peter's home life was
a central issue in the case, his parents were never asked to testify
and explain why they considered themselves capable of rearing
Peter properly. The evidence used to justify committal was
typical in its vagueness and loose moralizing:

Court: Now, officer, what do you know about this boy?
Policeman: Oh, he has been a bad boy the last two years.
Court: Well, in what particular.
Policeman: Going around stealing, skipping school, hitting
    other children, running away from home and hid himself,
    run away from home staying in barns, I think, at night.
Court: What kind of home has he?
Policeman: His folks are not proper persons to take care of
    that boy.
Court: In other words it is just as much the fault of the home
    as it is of the boy?

Peter's lack of achievement in school also served to incriminate him, reinforcing the policeman's contention that the
boy could not be helped if allowed to remain at home. In this

case and in numerous others, the judge was not above playing demeaning intellectual tricks on simpleminded children:

> Court: What grade were you in when you quit school?
> Peter: First. . . .
> Court: Can you spell "cat"?
> Peter: No.
> Court: Can you spell "dog"? How do you spell it?
> Peter: D—o—g
> Court: Where do you live?
> Peter: Milwaukee.
> Court: What county is it in you know?
> Peter: Yes, sir.
> Court: What county is it in?
> Peter: Wisconsin.
> Court: Wisconsin. Do you know what state we live in?
> Peter: Yes sir.
> Court: Isn't it Illinois? Don't you know we are living in Illinois? You don't think we are living in Illinois, do you?
> Peter: No.
> Court: What do you know what the capital is of this state?
> Peter: Yes sir, Washington.

And so on, endlessly and pathetically, with Peter flunking the judge's tests just as he had undoubtedly flunked tests a hundred times before in school. What finally clinched the court's decision to commit, though, was the policeman's reiteration that the home was unfit and that Peter's presence there endangered the moral welfare of his brothers and sisters. Functioning informally as the court's probation officer in this case, the policeman advised: "I think if this boy gets a lesson out to the school it would be good for him. You've got two more brothers after you, and a small sister yet." Thereupon Peter was committed, the official charge on his record: exposing himself to a neighbor.

Luck—or the lack of it—often figured prominently in the work of the juvenile court. Twelve-year-old James English surely must have spent many sleepless nights at the reformatory bemoaning the bad luck that had brought him into court in the first place and the unfortunate coincidences which lay behind the court's decision (in winter, 1907) to commit him to the reformatory.

James was spotted smoking cigarettes in a local park by a factory inspector looking for someone else. Suspecting James of wrongdoing, the inspector played on the boy's vanity and extracted a boastful admission that he had just received fifteen dollars for lying in a civil court suit against his former employer. Without further ado the inspector took James into custody and dragged him home where his mother, apparently waiting for such an opportunity, declared she was fed up with her son and wanted him sent to a reformatory. The inspector was only too accommodating.

James now found himself charged with loitering and incorrigibility because he happened to be in the wrong place at the wrong time and was unduly talkative. Worse still, when he appeared in juvenile court it was before the very judge to whom he had lied in the previous civil suit! The judge at first could find no obvious "underlying causes" behind James's behavior. He had not lied chronically in the past and did not stay out late at night—two staple accusations usually made with or without evidence. But the judge was determined to punish James, whose fate was sealed regardless of the quality of the evidence against him.

> Court: Now you smoked occasionally?
> James: I only smoked once.
> Court: Only once. Did it make you sick? . . .
> James: No sir.
> Court: Then you have been in the habit of smoking before?
> James: No sir. . . .
> Court: Did you ever tell your mother to go to hell?
> James: No sir.
> Court: Didn't you tell her the other day? You swore at your
>   mother, didn't you?
> James: No sir.
> Court: [addressing the factory inspector] What did he say?
> Inspector: He says, "You don't know what you are talking
>   about—Go on." In a very saucy manner—very saucy to
>   her—and when I talked to her she says he is always that
>   way—could not do anything with the boy.

The judge finally confronted James with his earlier lying in the civil suit. Without hesitation James responded that his employer had threatened to have him committed to reform school on a trumped-up charge if he refused to cooperate. Without inquiring into the validity of James's account, the judge became outraged and committed him on the spot to Waukesha. "You wouldn't want me to believe all that. I am afraid my boy that you are a kind of pleasant prevaricator. You are a dangerous boy and need training.... You must be taught the difference between right and wrong—you don't seem to comprehend it.... you started out on a bad road. You would land, after you grow up, with the training you have now, you would kill somebody—that is, if you thought you could get away, and I am going to send you to the Industrial School."

Brought into court by accident, James was thus sent to the reformatory as a potential murderer, despite his plaintive plea, "I ain't so bad." The court's superficial mode of inquiring into "underlying causes" often led it to take such action.

Cases resulting in committal to the boy's reformatory, like the four cited above, existed in countless variations. If the "underlying causes" seemed serious enough, a "pleasant prevaricator" might be sent to an institution as readily as a juvenile with a criminal record. Unless the parents refused to take care of the child at home, it was impossible in most instances to predict from the specific charge, previous record, or testimony in court what the ultimate disposition would be. Given the heavy reliance on probation, it was impossible to determine which of several "potential candidates" for incarceration would be chosen. In the name of individualizing treatment, the court introduced an extraordinary degree of arbitrariness. The odds were against committal, but who would dare trust the outcome when the stakes were so high?

When girls appeared in juvenile court and were committed to reformatories, however, one factor was always present: sexual promiscuity, real or suspected. Two examples will suffice to demonstrate what usually went on in court.[8]

Of the many unusual life histories revealed in the transcripts, none was more heartrending than the story of Karen and Jean Lanowski, whose case came before the court in the summer of 1911. Sadly, if ironically, the court had placed them several years before with a rural foster family after declaring their natural parents unfit, only to have farm life prove a worse source of corruption. The girls' foster father had worked them to the point of exhaustion and fed them only potatoes and soup, saving all milk and meat for the pigs. Furthermore, the farmer's sons had regularly slept with the two girls, who at the time of the trial were ages fourteen and fifteen. The father had even prevented their acquiring any formal education, in defiance of the state's compulsory school law. Neither girl knew the days of the week, but of the two Jean was the more ignorant.

Court: Milwaukee is a big city, isn't it; do you know the name of the state?
Jean: What?
Court: Do you know the name of the state?
Jean: No.
Court: Did you ever hear of Wisconsin?
Jean: No. . . .
Court: Of course you don't know the name of the state; are we living in the United States or Russia?
Jean: I don't know.

Guided by court policy, the judge refused to consider sending girls who were not virgins to foster families or orphanages. Only the reformatory would accept them, he concluded, and he therefore attempted to convince the girls that the House of Good Shepherd was a wonderful place to live. "You wouldn't mind going to a place like that where there were a lot of girls going to school all the time, if you and your sister could go there; you would just as leave go there until you can get a nice home, where you got good wholesome food and clean clothes to wear, and have kind teachers?" In a trying case like this, the court could perhaps reasonably argue that life in a reformatory was bound to be an improvement.

Very different was the case in winter, 1907, of flamboyant Deborah Horwitz, who flaunted her precocious sexuality. Deborah freely admitted to staying out at night with boys on many occasions. The efficient snooping of a probation officer into Deborah's bureau at home turned up further incriminating evidence: an enchanting group of five Woolworth-type self-photos which the court considered racy and a remarkable series of intimate letters to a sailor friend which left nothing to the imagination. As was its wont, the court attempted to blame Deborah's parents for her brazen behavior, but Mrs. Horwitz would not stand for it: "I got lots of trouble with the other girl, she needs an operation, and I got lots of trouble with the other children." Neither would Deborah accept the court's harsh, sexually discriminatory evaluation of her behavior. "Well, Deborah, this is a very serious matter," the court intoned, "if you would live a good life you would be a good woman, and be useful to society, but you have started out very bad. There is only one way to reform you and that is to send you to an institution. I cannot let you go home to your parents. . . . How is it, can't you stop?" Deborah sharply retorted: "I can stop, of course I can." "Why don't you behave yourself, then?" the judge rejoined. "These boys tell me that you just coax them." "I never coaxed anybody," Deborah stubbornly maintained.

But her protestations had no effect. Though neither judges nor probation officers were inveterate prudes, they often sought committal for girls (never for boys) solely on the grounds of early sexual activity. Still, in these cases as in others, the ostensible "offense" gave no clear indication what the ultimate disposition would be. Had Deborah not affirmed her right to be sexually active, had her mother not alienated the court by refusing to be contrite, and had the probation staff not turned up the incriminating photos and letters, Deborah, like most girls who appeared in court, might well have been placed on probation.

The Decision to Disrupt Natural Family Relations: Dependency and Neglect

In both the theory and practice of Progressive juvenile justice, delinquency shaded imperceptibly into dependency and neglect, and vice versa. In dependency and neglect cases, the parents were explicitly on trial; not surprisingly, it was these cases that saw the most bitter controversies and gave rise to the most poignant human dramas. While probation officers often insinuated that the children of parents charged with neglect had long records of undetected criminal activity, the key issues remained the same as in delinquency cases: was the home fit and were the children and parents potentially upright citizens? The focus, again, was on nebulous "underlying causes."

More than the cases already examined, dependency and neglect trials conformed to a highly patterned set of procedures and interactions between court and clientele. Probation officers and prosecuting attorneys aggressively sought removal of children from their natural parents; the parents fought with equal vigor against intervention by the court; and the judges attempted to steer between the two, insisting that some evidential guidelines be followed. Dependency and neglect cases opened many opportunities for attorneys to defend basic parental rights. That few parents hired lawyers surely resulted less from a lack of desire to do so than from poverty and ignorance of the law. A case in the winter of 1903 suggested how useful an attorney could be and revealed again that in practice probation officers showed little faith in noninstitutional treatment and the theory of affectional discipline.

One of the volunteer probation officers had become acquainted with the children of Mr. and Mrs. Marshall in the course of charity work with a church missionary group. As often happened, particularly with volunteer probation officers, she capitalized upon her dual role to bring to the court's attention previously unsuspected instances of child neglect.

The probation officer began her testimony by accusing the Marshalls of keeping a boarder, a fact they readily admitted, as it was a common practice among lower-class immigrant families in Milwaukee. But the probation officer suspected the worst and insinuated that Mrs. Marshall was sleeping with the boarder.[9] In short order the Marshalls' attorney dispelled such unfounded notions and attacked the character of the probation officer for accepting gossip as impeccable truth. He thereby set the tone for the entire trial and by objecting to hearsay evidence may well have spared the Marshalls the loss of their child.

After the probation officer stepped down, a neighbor took the stand. To the horror of the district attorney, she retracted a number of accusations she had made out of court. Why? Perhaps the district attorney elicited the real reasons, but perhaps she did not want to undergo as careful interrogation from the defense attorney as had the probation officer.

DA: And you felt sorry for him?
Neighbor: Felt sorry for the children.
DA: Now isn't it a fact that you have changed your mind since you saw him cry about it and found out how sorry he felt to see his children taken away from him or that there was any chance of their being taken away?

Neighbor: No sir . . . .
DA: How many times in all since this matter was begun as a
    proceeding, has he spoken to you about it?
Neighbor: I could not tell.
DA: A number of times. Has he not asked you to be on his
    side in this matter, so the children would not be taken away?
Neighbor: No sir he has not.

When a policeman similarly failed to testify as the district
attorney had anticipated he would, the role of the defense lawyer in intimidating witnesses appeared even more likely. "Have
you ever arrested him?" asked the district attorney about Mr.
Marshall, to which the policeman replied negatively. "When a
man goes through the streets so drunk that he can't talk and
staggers you don't arrest him?" queried the prosecutor again,
attempting to elicit the desired answer about Mr. Marshall's
erratic behavior. But the policeman would not oblige: "Not as
long as he goes about his business and don't bother anybody."

A fourth witness not only provided another example of the
hearsay nature of evidence in the case, but also revealed that the
probation officer had worked actively to prejudice the witnesses
against the Marshalls. Speaking of an attempt to obtain employment for the Marshalls' eldest daughter, the witness, another
neighbor, testified: "I only know what I was told and if I can tell
that. I was in another room at the time the conversation took
place." Understandably, this testimony was objected to by the
defense lawyer and the objection was sustained by the judge.
Direct examination continued:

DA: What if anything do you know of your own knowledge
    as to why this girl was not employed at Mrs. Blakeley's?
Neighbor: Because Mrs. Blakeley asked the probation officer
    about the bringing up of the child and then she refused to take
    her.
DA: How do you know that Mrs. Blakeley asked the proba-
    tion officer?
Neighbor: The probation officer told me.
Defense Lawyer: Defendant's counsel moves to strike out that
    part of the testimony of the witness relating to a conversation
    between the probation officer and Mrs. Blakeley.
Judge: Motion to strike out granted.
DA: Do you know anything to your own knowledge about
    taking a house-keeper?

Neighbor: Just the same way; except what the probation officer told me.

At this juncture, testimony having gone on for some time without improvement in the quality of adverse evidence, the defense attorney moved for dismissal: "No proper evidence has been produced that the girls' morals are in danger and that they [the girls] have no proper place to live." The judge, whose role in this type of case was that of arbitrator between parent and probation officer, could do little more than agree. Although the law was fuzzy on this issue, had the judge accepted the probation officer's recommendations, the defense lawyer might have demanded a separate trial in criminal court and then demanded that a formal charge be lodged against the parents for contributing to the delinquency of a minor. A lack of evidence would unquestionably have made conviction impossible. The judge, recognizing this, probably decided to stop legal proceedings in order to avoid later embarrassment.[10]

The poor quality of evidence presented against the Marshalls was unusually transparent. Most dependency and neglect cases involved individuals and circumstances which did not admit of so clear a resolution, for example, that of Mr. and Mrs. Klaus in the summer of 1906.

A probation officer, who had previously arrested the Klauses for contributing to the delinquency of their children, brought them into court on a charge of neglect. The former charge was indisputable: Mrs. Klaus admitted in court that because of the family's dire poverty the previous winter, she had sent the children to steal food from a local grocer. After conviction the Klauses had been sent to jail for short terms, during which time their children were removed—"temporarily"—to the county's Home for Dependent Children. Without explicit orders from the court, the children had remained at the Home for Dependent Children for several months after the parents' release from jail.

Although she pleaded desperately for the return of her children, Mrs. Klaus, like many parents who appeared before the court on similar charges, had failed to visit them often at the county home. Several explanations for this persistent phenomenon (as suggested by the parents themselves) were likely: the parents' anguish at seeing their children in quasi-prison settings; the sneering disparagement the parents received from in-

stitutional staff; the need to work seven days a week or during
the hours designated for visiting; a lack of funds to travel to the
home, which was located beyond city limits (not far from the
reform school); or, in Mrs. Klaus's case, the sudden death of her
husband after their release from jail. But to the superintendent of
the home, who often served the court as a probation officer,
there could be only one interpretation: "There is absolutely no
motherly heart or affection for these children." Evidently the
superintendent had decided on his own to retain the children
after their parents' release, and he now recommended their permanent, official removal from their mother's care.

The judge, however, would not sever Mrs. Klaus's natural
custody right without corroborating evidence from the probation staff. Indeed at one point early in the proceeding, when the
evidence was particularly confused, he came close to stopping
the trial altogether. "Now, in order to try this case you have got
to have at least a half dozen witnesses if not more, who know all
about this woman," he admonished the chief probation officer.
"You have got to show that she is not a fit and proper person to
have the charge and control of these children. Now, you cannot
do that by insinuation or by what someone else told you.... I
cannot try any case of importance as this is, so we may as well
quit here." This rhetorical flourish, though, appears to have
been mainly for effect and future reference. The trial continued
as probation officers brought in witnesses who were supposedly
more reliable to bolster the claims of the superintendent of the
county home.

First, a policeman offered his opinion that Mrs. Klaus "ain't
right. She is a little demented, slightly demented.... you take it
last Monday when I came up there and talked about the circumstances, and finally she came up with all kinds of different
photographs, different dresses, white dresses and black dresses,
and finally she got a dress out of the closet, and she had one of
the dresses tacked down with paper flowers, something like a
masquerade suit. That is my opinion about her and her talk."

The probation officer's inquiry into Mrs. Klaus's mental
health was equally impressionistic, based entirely on hearsay.

PO: I inquired at the neighbors and they told me that they
    didn't think the woman is exactly right, that she is a little
    weak, but they urged upon me to suggest to the court that

these children should not be brought back to the woman, they don't think that she was a proper person to take care of them.

Court: Did they state any facts in regard to her conduct since that time?

PO: Why, I inquired and they told me that she answers marriage advertisements in the papers, etc.

Finally the grocer whose store the Klaus children had stolen from offered his opinion about Mrs. Klaus's "mental capacity": "I never had any conversation with them. Never been over there but I heard her talk to me once or twice and from that I should judge that she is not. She is somewhat demented."

However inadequate the evidence, the judge decided to continue the case for a week in order to give the probation staff more time to dig up damaging information (a decision prompted in part by the statement of the eldest daughter that she preferred living in the county home). Dig they did, scouring the neighborhood for anyone who knew anything about the family. The new group of witnesses, though, was even less convincing than the old. First came the local butcher, the best informed:

Butcher: Well, she goes around kind of funny, and she can't take care of the children, and dirty and everything.

Court: Now, when she would come in your butcher shop, what would she say? Would she stand and laugh?

Butcher: Sometimes and sometimes lots of people in there, and then just went out, and didn't want anything. . . .

Court: Now, what do you know about these children?

Butcher: Well, you see I know only that much, that they always in the house. They lock the doors, that they never get out, and if she gets out with the children, then she has one on the arm and the others all behind her.

Court: How about sending these children to school?

Butcher: They wouldn't—

Court: How do the children look, sickly?

Butcher: Very sickly.

Court: Under fed. Do you know of your own knowledge whether that woman ever got lost?

Butcher: Yes. . . . Well, that is one time about nine o'clock, she came in the butcher shop, and she came back about twelve o'clock, and she could not find home again.

Court: How long ago is that?

Butcher: That must be about twelve years ago.

Several other witnesses testified, all about as well-informed as a machinist who worked in the neighborhood and who obviously did not know why the probation officer had dragged him into court.

Court: [Are the children] Not very well taken care of?
Machinist: Well, I don't know. Hard for me to say.
Court: What is that?
Machinist: I say I can't say whether they were well taken care of or not. . . .
Court: Are they well fed?
Machinist: That is something I don't know.
Court: Did they look sickly to you?
Machinist: No, not to me. They didn't look sickly to me.
Court: Now, what is the mother's reputation in the community where she resides as to her mental condition. . . . Is she a woman of sound mind or weak-minded?
Machinist: Well, I could not say.
Court: Would you say that she is a proper person to take care of these children?
Machinist: Well, that is a hard thing to say, I could not say that.
Court: That is all.

The probation officers brought in numerous witnesses, apparently hoping to make up in quantity what the overall testimony lacked in quality. Whether the judge found the testimony any more convincing at the second hearing than at the first is impossible to determine. But he did order the children to be taken permanently from the mother and left at the county home to await adoption. With Mr. Klaus dead, the eldest daughter fighting against return to her natural home, and the mother's previous history of contributing to her children's delinquency—aside from the issue of her mental capacity—the case certainly admitted of no easy resolution.

In many dependency cases the burden of evidence in favor of removal was unambiguous and the court's dispositional options severely circumscribed. As in delinquency cases where parents refused to rear their children, the hard facts of extreme family situations often rendered the goal of noninstitutional treatment irrelevant to immediate needs.

Consider the trying circumstances of the case of Mrs. Amy

Mann, brought into court in the summer of 1906, eleven days
after her husband's death, for neglecting her two-year-old baby
boy. In the lengthy, bitter, and tumultuous trial numerous allegations were leveled at Amy about her conduct before and after
her husband's death. A former boarder described two scenes
which did much to convince the court to remove the baby from
Amy's guardianship.

First she recalled a quarrel between Amy and her husband
which took place in the boarder's room and had become the talk
of the neighborhood. "She came up there in the morning her
husband came up in the afternoon and told her to go home with
him and she was kind of intoxicated and she said, 'No, I won't go
home with him you dirty son of a bitch,' and he says, 'All right,'
and so they happen to quarrel and Mrs. Mann here took something and threw it at him—she was jealous of him—she thought I
had something to do with her husband and I was perfectly
innocent of it, and she took the baby and threw it in the hallway,
and she said, 'Keep your own God Damn Kid, it don't belong to
me anyway.'" Equally damaging were the boarder's accusations
about Amy's recent sexual promiscuity, which other witnesses
confirmed.

> Boarder: Me and the gentleman I am going with . . . we sat
> on the outside, and she had another gentleman friend up
> there with her, and when we went up together, and we had a
> little beer and so we had left and we come over there in the
> morning and I wanted to see this lady [Amy] and I see her on
> the floor with some different fellow.
> Court: When was this?
> Boarder: Little—short time after her husband died.
> Court: What was she doing?
> Boarder: Why she had connection with him.
> Court: You saw that?
> Boarder: Yes, sir, I did. . . .
> Court: Where were they—in the bedroom?
> Boarder: No, sir, in the kitchen on the floor.

Amy tried feebly to defend herself and to retain possession of
her child. She blamed many of her bad habits which the court
found incriminating, like smoking, on her husband. In the end,
though, she simply insisted that she was not as bad a person as
the witnesses made her appear, that she was not sexually pro-

miscuous, and that she was still in a state of shock over her husband's recent death. But in this case as in most others involving young fatherless children where the mother's temper and morals were called into question, the court felt compelled to take immediate action. It sent Amy's baby boy to the Home for Dependent Children to await adoption. The court, though clearly sympathetic to Amy's predicament, was not willing to take a chance on the baby's physical well-being.

Conclusion

Summaries and brief excerpts from sixteen cases between 1901 and 1920 barely begin to explore the wealth of evidence contained in the trial transcripts. Yet even this snapshot review of exemplary cases suggests how far the Milwaukee Juvenile Court was from applying the affectional mode of treatment its advocates espoused, and which at least one court in the Progressive era, Ben Lindsey's in Denver, appears to have employed. The persuasive techniques Lindsey relied upon and the trust he instilled in children and parents were largely foreign to the Milwaukee experience. No one in the Milwaukee Juvenile Court—especially not probation officers—empathized with the clientele as Lindsey empathized with his. Nor was the spirit of rapprochement—of parents, children, and court officials working amiably toward mutually-agreed upon solutions—duplicated in Milwaukee. This was, in part, a product of forces beyond the court's control, notably the willingness of many poor parents to use the court to unburden themselves of child-rearing responsibilities. But the essence of Progressive correctional theory lay in the quality of personal relationships, the emotional bridges which judges and probation officers built between themselves and their clientele. By failing to approach the parents of children in court with kindness, compassion, and sympathy, officers of the court undermined what made Progressive ideas unique in the first place, and left the promise of the juvenile court movement not only unrealized but untested.[11]

Ideally the court was a missionary agent for the educational and moral uplift of the poor. In practice it functioned more often than not as a source of arbitrary punitive authority, and an arena for the evocation of hostile emotions on all sides.

Epilogue

As observed in the introduction to part 1, this is a highly selective history of American juvenile justice, most notably in its use of the case study method, its emphasis on individuals and ideologies, and its concentration on the "progressive" motif. While my case studies offer much new information on the actual conduct of juvenile justice, they only begin to satisfy the need for sustained empirical research in the United States and throughout the world. Many significant questions remain unanswered and unaddressed.

Granted these limitations, several impressionistic reflections and judgments on the American experience seem in order. Most striking to me in retrospect is the superficiality of the "progressive" viewpoint. Advocates generally ignored or hedged basic questions: What is punishment? What is rehabilitation? When do children become adults in assessing culpability for crime? What is crime? What does it mean to be "on the road to delinquency"? Admittedly these are troublesome issues, whether viewed from the vantage point of the citizen, the philosopher, or the therapist. But the credo of affectional discipline, under the beguiling rationale that personal intervention and "love" were correctional panaceas and adequate responses to serious social ills, was inordinately evasive in regard to all of these issues.

Particularly in the nineteenth century, the "progressive" viewpoint was more befuddled than it need have been. American sponsors of the foreign family reform schools had, at best, a vague understanding of how their European models operated. They ignored fundamental differences among the foreign facilities, for example, the recruitment of unpaid seminarians as parent surrogates at the Rauhe Haus and the heavy reliance on military regimen at the Colonie Agricole. One can not help but agree with the contemporary, Bradford Peirce, who wryly noted that most enthusiasts of the "family idea" idealized the modus operandi of the foreign institutions to accord with their own preconceptions and sensibilities, and consequently did not know what they were talking about.[1]

Though attentive to details of method and organization, the juvenile court movement was ill-conceived in its main objectives. As argued in chapter one, a highly nostalgic vision of social organization had underlain correctional thinking throughout the nineteenth century. To this anachronistic view the sponsors of the juvenile court joined a glaringly inappropriate mode of enforcement. The process was two-fold. First they conceived of the modern city much as a seventeenth-century "little commonwealth," where moral boundaries were known by all and were easily enforceable. Then they cast the probation officer in the role of a Puritan tithingman, or moral inspector, who was to canvass individual households and assure uniformity in behavior and thought (along middle-class lines, of course). Together with truant officers, visiting teachers, visiting nurses, visiting home economists, public health inspectors, and a variety of other private voluntary organizations, probation officers were to be part of a new civic phalanx devoted to standardizing socialization practices in the modern urban community—the new tithingmen.

Size was one obvious problem in attempting surveillance of modern cities with techniques common in colonial villages. Imagine how many probation officers would have been necessary to oversee all families whom reformers considered morally suspect! Moreover, and an equal stumbling block, the sources of moral authority were no longer centralized and certain. Conflicts of power, not appeals to community moral sanction, provided the framework for determining hegemony and cultural supremacy in the early twentieth century.

Thus the juvenile court movement presented something of a paradox. At first glance it appeared to offer a creative educational alternative to incarceration or rural exile of troublesome youth. But what it offered as a substitute was remarkably inadequate to the scale and nature of modern cities. Not surprisingly, then, did the court become little more than a nuisance, a source of randomly exercised authority, rather than a humane agent of moral uplift and social control. The proper literary analogy to characterize the court is not, as some present-day critics have implied, Orwell's Big Brother. Instead it is Cervantes's pathetic creation, Don Quixote. Like the knight-errant, the court felled anyone who questioned its mission or happened into its way. True, the court, like Don Quixote, occasionally did good and assisted the needy. But the nature of both their missions inevitably undermined their efforts. How could it be otherwise? They were compelled to reach snap judgments about complex human affairs just to maintain their own dignity and the illusion of serving society well. Their failures were tragicomic and perhaps even welcome.

But one dare not be amused by the juvenile court, for it touched upon that segment of the population most vulnerable to governmental intrusions. If not the omniscient agent of control and repression some critics have painted it to be, the court nonetheless fostered a point of view which encouraged, for ill-defined ends, selective disruption of the family lives of the poor.[2] Proponents of the court, unlike their nineteenth-century predecessors, rarely viewed the poor as objects of derision, as beasts in human form. But neither did they accord the poor true dignity and equality, even by the standards of the Social Gospel, their moral frame of reference. Instead they viewed and treated the poor—the one-time "dangerous classes"—as immature, ignorant, almost childlike creatures who simply did not know enough to behave like their moral and social betters. Ideally they wanted to teach impoverished adults the same lesson that the children of the poor were learning in public schools: how to comport themselves as upright citizens despite their lack of material resources. In short, the sponsors of the juvenile court infantalized the adult poor while attempting to civilize them. The extent to which the poor were humanized in the process remains, at best, ambiguous.

It is one thing to point up deficiencies in "progressive" correctional theory—a task others have undertaken more rigorously than I—quite another to assess its influence on nationwide public policy.[3] To the extent that my case studies reflect national patterns, I have tried to show how wide a gap remained between the theory and practice of "progressive" ideas and how easily the differences between the form and substance of affectional discipline could be obscured. I hope that both of these developments will be remembered in upcoming years, especially by the growing body of spokespersons for the "rights of children," who form loose counterparts to the "child savers" of earlier years. For it is by now clear that genuine reform of the correctional system is, if nothing else, a tricky business indeed and that mere tinkering with existing legal and institutional apparatus is grossly inadequate to effect reform. What is needed, as Judge Justine Polier has suggested, is nothing less than a major reorientation in American attitudes toward children—all children—to bring public policy in line with our much-touted conceit of being a "child-centered" society.[4] Unfortunately, in an era where "law and order" serves as a byword for responsible citizenship, it remains doubtful whether Americans, however anxious they may be about "crime in the streets," possess the will to initiate such change. But substantive and lasting reform will come at no cheaper price than our becoming a "child-centered" society in deed as well as in aspiration.

To anyone not a specialist in the field who dares venture into the voluminous literature on the juvenile justice system today, it is obvious that the focus of correctional reform is increasingly on the related concepts of deinstitutionalization and diversion.[5] One cannot, of course, predict with certainty what their outcome will be in practice; history rightfully breeds skepticism, not cynicism or determinism. But continuities between these innovative concepts and the "progressive" ideas examined in this volume are readily apparent. For deinstitutionalization and diversion to become banners for meaningful change and not mere slogans—or, worse still, a cloak for hiding new punitive programs—will require a citizenry sensitive to children's developmental needs and willing to provide financial resources to satisfy them.[6] It will also require more exposure and elimination of systematic inequities in the delivery of justice to the poor and frank recognition that correctional innovations, however wise, are marginal and secondary to broader efforts at social reform.

I am well aware of the limited role historical analysis can play in laying the groundwork for change today. Study of our correctional past does not at all guarantee greater ability or insight into planning for the future. Still, it is imperative to study American correctional history if only for the illusions it can dispel, if only to see how important it is to penetrate the veneer of reform and distinguish clearly between theory and reality. History offers no panaceas for the present, but it does help to alert us to the temptation of self-deception in dealing with a problem no more soluble today than it was a century and a half ago.

Appendix 1

Table 1   Recorded Offenses of Inmates in the Wisconsin
State Reform School, 1860–99 (Percentages)

Years	Criminal Acts (Mainly Larceny and Assault)	Incorrigibility and Vagrancy
1860–69	57%	43%
1870–79	47	53
1880–89	50	50
1890–99	60	40

Note: As these data attest, a sizable portion of reform school inmates had
not been convicted of specific criminal acts. Most of the incorrigibles—who
far outnumbered the vagrants—were probably committed by parents, although we know so little about the processing of children in nineteenth-
century criminal courts that it is impossible to be certain. Similarly, we
cannot be sure that all children accused of specific crimes had actually
committed them. As argued in the text, local judges falsely accused an
indeterminate number of inmates of specific crimes in order to shift the cost
of their support at the reformatory entirely onto the state.

But if interpretive problems remain, one important point about these data
is unambiguous. Throughout the nineteenth century vague delinquency
statutes resulted in incarceration of criminal and non-criminal youth on
indeterminate sentences. The Progressive period did not invent modern
conceptions of delinquency or so-called "status offenses."

Table 2   Birthplaces of Parents of Children Committed
                                to the Wisconsin State Reform School, 1860–
                                1919 (Percentages)

Year	Germany	Ireland	Poland	England	United States	Others
1860–69	16	24	—	10	29	21
1870–79	20	17	1	12	26	24
1880–89	32	₁7	6	7	28	10
1890–99	31	9	7	7	22	24
1900–09	31	9	15	6	12	27
1910–19	25	7	21	7	12	28

Note: The popular impression of delinquency as a phenomenon associated primarily with ethnic youth was largely correct. Over 90 percent of the inmates at the Wisconsin State Reform School were born in the United States, but approximately three-quarters had immigrant parents. As suggested by the data above, certain ethnic groups were statistically overrepresented at the reform school. For instance, between 1860 and 1879 there were about five times as many children with Irish parents in the reformatory as there were Irish immigrants in Wisconsin. Similarly, between 1900 and 1919 there were about ten times as many children with Polish parents in the reformatory as there were Polish immigrants in Wisconsin (data on immigration patterns drawn from the federal census). Many likely reasons for the predominance of ethnic youth among delinquents—e.g., difficulties in cultural adjustment, economic discrimination, school rigidities, selective enforcement of law against newcomers—lie beyond the scope of this book, but they are central to future research on the social history of criminal law. Unfortunately, the records of the Wisconsin State Reform School did little to illuminate the impact of a predominantly ethnic clientele on rehabilitative programs.

Appendix 2

Table 1   Children Appearing in the Milwaukee Juvenile
                               Court, 1905–11

Year	Number
1905	594
1906	663
1907	479ab
1908	1,968
1909	2,326
1910	2,455
1911	2,401

ahalf year
bexcludes old cases

Note: Fewer than one thousand cases were heard in the Milwaukee Juvenile Court during its first four years of operation. After 1905, following the appointment of a chief probation officer, the opening of a temporary detention center in the Milwaukee Home for the Friendless, and the passage of a contributory delinquency law, new intake increased measurably. More cases were heard in 1905 and 1906 than had been heard in the previous four years. Noticeable, too, is a sizable increase in total cases after 1907. This can probably be accounted for in large part by the appointment of four new probation officers in 1907. However, incomparable data in the years 1907 and 1908 make precise correlation uncertain.

Table 2   New Cases Placed on Probation by the Milwaukee Juvenile Court, 1908–14

Year	New Cases	Placed on Probation
1908	984	691
1909	847	555
1910	1,163	833
1911	1,290	787
1912	— —	— —
1913	1,321	827
1914	1,161	784

Note: Probation was the most common disposition in juvenile court, accounting for two-thirds of the children who appeared each year. This does not mean, as table 3 indicates, that the other one-third were sent to reformatories. Some had their cases dismissed entirely and a smaller percentage received suspended sentences (that is, they were officially judged guilty of an offense and then released outright, without supervision by the court). Furthermore, if it were possible in the years 1908 to 1914 to disaggregate the probation data and distinguish the delinquents from the dependents, the court's heavy reliance on probation for delinquent youth would become even more apparent. This is because a disproportionately larger share of neglect than delinquency cases resulted in temporary or permanent removal of children from their natural parents.

Table 3   Male Delinquents Committed by the Milwau-
                           kee Juvenile Court to the Wisconsin State Re-
                           form School, 1905–11

Year	New Male Delinquency Cases	Committals to Waukesha
1905	436	55
1906	536	54
1907	——	——
1908	658	24
1909	487	22
1910	731	22
1911	705	15

Note: As suggested in the text, long-term institutional committals were
relatively rare in the juvenile court; probation and heavy use of short-term
detention lay at the heart of treatment. The decreasing reliance on reformatories after 1905, despite increasing intake, suggests growing reliance on
preventive programs in public schools. From these data, however, one
cannot conclude that the likelihood of a court appearance terminating in
committal had declined relative to the nineteenth century, for we simply do
not know what percentage of children charged with crimes in the nineteenth
century were committed. Moreover, the juvenile court was not the only route
to the reformatory. Data from the 1920s indicate that fully one-third of the
inmates at Waukesha who had previously lived in Milwaukee were sentenced in municipal rather than juvenile court. See Francis Hiller, *Probation
in Wisconsin* (New York: National Probation Association, 1926), p. 79.
Obviously, full coverage of the judicial processing of juvenile offenders—
especially the more serious offenders—would have to include municipal
court records.
   I have not included female delinquents in these calculations because boys
outnumbered girls around ten to one up to 1910 (though only five to one
after 1916, when continuous data again became available). The numbers of
girls committed either to the Industrial School at Oregon, Wisconsin or the
Milwaukee House of Good Shepherd were generally too small to be useful
for statistical analysis, although a higher percentage of girls than boys
charged with delinquency were committed. Still, for both boys and girls the
odds were considerably against a reformatory committal.

Table 4   New Cases Held in Detention by the Milwaukee
                               Juvenile Court, 1905–17

Year	New Cases	Children in Detention (Indeterminate Periods)
1905	594[a]	195
1906	663[a]	282
1916	1,663	1,279
1917	1,724	1,405

[a]This actually includes old cases (holdovers) for
these two years; information on new cases alone
is not available. Thus the percentage of children
in detention in 1905 and 1906 may have been
somewhat higher than these data indicate.

Note: As these data suggest, large portions of the juvenile court's clientele,
and an increasing portion over time, were held in detention in addition to
whatever other disposition the court mandated. Much impressionistic evidence indicates that few children accused or convicted of crime actually
went to jail during most of the nineteenth century, as judges and juries
tended toward leniency rather than placing them in contact with criminal
adults. The extent to which this was true or not requires empirical investigation. In any case, it is clear that prior reservations disappeared with the
advent of segregated detention facilities for children. Short-term punishment became the norm for children accused of crime in Milwaukee; detention and probation went hand in hand. Unfortunately, except for the early
period, there is no information on the average number of days children
spent in detention. In 1905 and 1906 it was between five and six days. My
suspicion, drawn from reading trial transcripts where the length of time
spent in detention was occasionally divulged, is that once new detention
facilities opened in 1909 the average number of days tended to increase.

Table 5		Most Frequently Recorded Offenses against Children Appearing in the Milwaukee Juvenile Court, 1908–11 (Percentages)		
Charges	1908	1909	1910	1911
Disorderly conduct	9%	5%	6%	3%
Assault and battery	10	7	3	5
Incorrigibility	11	18	13	22
Disorderly person	18	11	21	6
Jumping on trains	—	6	2	—
Vagrancy	—	4	1	5
Truancy	4	4	4	3
Larceny	29	40	39	31
Burglary	17	7	3	—

Note: As had been true in the nineteenth century, there was great variety in the types of youthful activities that might be labeled delinquency (see appendix one, table 1). Though the above table does not include all the official charges against delinquents, it suggests the range and relative frequency. That some of the categories remain ambiguous—for instance, the difference between a disorderly person and disorderly conduct—is probably less important than that the court tended to ignore specific allegations in search of "underlying causes," and reached dispositions more on the basis of the latter than the former. Furthermore, it is somewhat questionable whether the specific charges listed above were lodged before or after trial, when prior conduct previously unknown to the court was divulged. Certainly my own sample of court cases indicated less specificity in initial charge than the chief probation officer recorded at the end of each year.

Table 6   Birthplaces of Parents of Children Appearing in
                               the Milwaukee Juvenile Court, 1907–11 (Per-
                               centages)

Country	1907	1908	1909	1910	1911
Germany	38%	36%	39%	30%	37%
Poland	36	42	35	43	34
Ireland	6	3	2	4	5
United States	9	5	10	6	7
Others[a]	11	14	14	17	17

[a]This group included small numbers of Jews, some of whom may well have
come from Germany and Poland as well as Russia.

Note: In the Progressive period, as earlier, the great majority of juvenile
delinquents—over 90 percent in the Milwaukee Juvenile Court—were
the offspring of European immigrants. Of these, three out of every
four were either German or Polish (the majority were born in the United
States, although the lack of data from the juvenile court, in contrast to that
available for the reformatory, makes it impossible to calculate the percentage). For comparison, see appendix one, table 2. Fortunately, the
probable implications of cultural estrangement on rehabilitative programs
can be more readily examined in the court than in the reform school. A
monumental attempt to explain the interaction of social and cultural factors
behind delinquency in the Progressive period which sheds considerable light
on the Milwaukee situation—although it occasionally comes close to
"blaming the victim"—is William Thomas and Florian Znaniecki, *The Polish
Peasant in Europe and America*, 2 vols. (New York: Alfred A. Knopf, 1927).

Notes

Introduction to Part 1

1. The spate of recent writings on educational and correctional innovations for children in the nineteenth and early twentieth centuries can easily mask how little we know about them as functioning realities, both internally and in relation to the communities which sustained them. Emphasis on the middle- and upper-class sponsorship of these institutions, and on the centrality of social control aspirations in correctional ideologies, has, it seems to me, done little more than highlight the obvious. In part two of this book I attempt to examine correctional institutions as functioning realities, but the social, political, and economic context of institutional change is largely untouched. Hopefully others better trained in sociological and anthropological method will attempt more systematically to link corrections to all threads in the social fabric. Two works which recognize the importance of drawing these linkages, although they fail to do so convincingly, are Alexander Liazos, "Class Oppression: The Functions of Juvenile Justice," *The Insurgent Sociologist* 1 (Fall 1974): 2–24, and Anthony Platt, "The Triumph of Benevolence: The Origins of the Juvenile Justice System in the United States," in *Criminal Justice in America*, ed. Richard Quinney (Boston: Little, Brown and Co., 1974), pp. 356–89.

Chapter 1

1. The standard works are Robert Pickett, *House of Refuge* (Syracuse: Syracuse Univer-

207

sity Press, 1969); Joseph Hawes, *Children in Urban Society* (New York: Oxford University Press, 1971); Jack Holl, *Juvenile Reform in the Progressive Era* (Ithaca: Cornell University Press, 1971); Anthony Platt, *The Child Savers* (Chicago: University of Chicago Press, 1969); Robert Mennel, *Thorns and Thistles* (Hanover, N.H.: University Press of New England, 1973); and Robert Bremner et al., eds., *Children and Youth in America*, 3 vols. (Cambridge: Harvard University Press, 1970–74).

2. For example: "Our country has inherited the English law and our courts of various name have inherited the powers of the ancient Court of Chancery which enable them to enforce the duties of parents and to protect the rights of infants. Our judges have recently discovered in these principles very large and unsuspected powers and have used them." Charles Henderson, "Theory and Practice of the Juvenile Court," National Conference of Charities and Correction, *Proceedings* (Fred J. Heer, 1904), p. 364. See also Bernard Flexner, "The Juvenile Court—Its Legal Aspects," *Annals of the American Academy of Political and Social Science* 36 (July 1910): 49–50; Herbert Lou, *Juvenile Courts in the United States* (Chapel Hill: University of North Carolina Press, 1927); Thomas Travis, *The Young Malefactor* (New York: Thomas Y. Crowell, 1908), pp. 184–85; Ben Lindsey, "The Reformation of Juvenile Delinquents through the Juvenile Court," National Conference of Charities and Correction, *Proceedings* (Fred J. Heer, 1903), p. 210; and Katharine Lenroot, "The Evolution of the Juvenile Court," *Annals of the American Academy of Political and Social Science* 105 (January 1923): 213. For useful overviews, see Margaret Rosenheim, ed., *Justice for the Child* (New York: Macmillan Co., 1962), pp. 1–21; Julian Mack, "The Juvenile Court," *Harvard Law Review* 23 (December 1909): 104–22; and Ellen Ryerson, "Between Justice and Compassion: The Rise and Fall of the Juvenile Court" (Ph.D. dissertation, Yale University, 1970), pp. 10–19.

3. See especially Sanford Fox, "Juvenile Justice Reform: An Historical Perspective," *Stanford Law Review* 22 (June 1970): 1187–1239.

4. Numerous recent books and articles speak to these general points, notably Francis Allen, *The Borderland of Criminal Justice* (Chicago: University of Chicago Press, 1964); Lois Forer, *"No One Will Lissen"* (New York: Grosset and Dunlap, 1970); David Matza, *Delinquency and Drift* (New York: John Wiley and Sons, 1964); Patrick Murphy, *Our Kindly Parent . . . The State* (New York: Viking Press, 1974); Edwin Schur, *Radical Non-Intervention* (Englewood Cliffs, N.J.: Prentice-Hall, 1973); Nicholas Kittrie, *The Right to be Different* (Baltimore: Johns Hopkins Press, 1971); William Stapleton and Lee Teitelbaum, *In Defense of Youth* (New York: Russell Sage, 1972); David Gottlieb, ed., *Children's Liberation* (Englewood Cliffs, N.J.: Prentice-Hall, 1973); Margaret Rosenheim, ed., *Pursuing Justice for the Child* (Chicago: University of Chicago Press, 1976); and Alexander Liazos, "Class Oppression: The Functions of Juvenile Justice," *The Insurgent Sociologist* 1 (Fall 1974): 2–24.

5. For general background, see Jeremy Felt, *Hostages of Fortune*

(Syracuse: Syracuse University Press, 1965), and Stephen Wood, *Constitutional Politics in the Progressive Era* (Chicago: University of Chicago Press, 1971).

6. Fox, "Juvenile Justice Reform," was the first to make this point crystal-clear. More detailed discussion of the origins of *parens patriae* can be found in Douglas Rendleman, "Parens Patriae: From Chancery to the Juvenile Court," *South Carolina Law Review* 23 (Spring 1971): 205–59; and Neil Cogan, "Juvenile Law, Before and After the Entrance of 'Parens Patriae,'" *South Carolina Law Review* 22 (Spring 1970): 147–81.

7. Eldon argued of the English Chancery Court: "It is not from any want of jurisdiction that it does not act but from want of means to exercise its jurisdiction, because the court cannot take upon itself the maintenance of all the children of the Kingdom. It can exercise the jurisdiction fully and practically only where it has the means of applying property for the maintenance of the infant." Quoted in Ryerson, "Between Justice and Compassion," p. 12. In the eyes of American legal expansionists, the advent of public schools and reformatories fully supplied "the means." The *Wellesley* decision was informally integrated into the legal rationale of American juvenile justice.

8. Ryerson, "Between Justice and Compassion," pp. 10–12.

9. *Ex parte* Crouse challenged an earlier Pennsylvania decision which had denied the reformatory jurisdiction over children who did not fall within traditional definitions of criminality or vagrancy. Whether this decision in fact limited the clientele to confirmed juvenile criminals and vagrants is a matter that, to the best of my knowledge, has never been investigated. No comparable decision in New York challenged the equally broad and vague jurisdiction of its House of Refuge. For a brief discussion, see Hawes, *Children in Urban Society*, pp. 57–59.

10. All committals were until age twenty-one, subject to early release upon recommendation by the institution's board of managers. I do not know when Mary Ann was actually released.

11. The tension between allegiance to the past and future in Jacksonian social policy is a theme imaginatively explored in Marvin Meyers, *The Jacksonian Persuasion* (Stanford: Stanford University Press, 1957). Most interesting was how a static conception of community went hand in hand, indeed, helped rationalize institutional innovations like the reformatories. On colonial views of community, see Edmund Morgan, *The Puritan Family*, rev. ed. (New York: Harper and Row, 1966); George Haskins, *Law and Authority in Early Massachusetts* (New York: Macmillan Co., 1960); Kenneth Lockridge, *A New England Town* (New York: W. W. Norton and Co., 1970); John Demos, *A Little Commonwealth* (New York: Oxford University Press, 1970); Michael Zuckerman, *Peaceable Kingdoms* (New York: Alfred A. Knopf, 1970); and David Flaherty, *Privacy in Colonial New England* (Charlottesville: University Press of Virginia, 1972).

12. *Ex parte* Crouse, 4 Wharton (Pa.), 9 (1838).

13. The centrality of the public school crusade to Jacksonian social

policy, before the famed reformer Horace Mann came onto the scene, has been underscored by several recent works, notably Carl Kaestle, *The Evolution of an Urban School System* (Cambridge: Harvard University Press, 1973), and Stanley Schultz, *The Culture Factory* (New York: Oxford University Press, 1973).

14. Joseph McCadden, *Education in Pennsylvania, 1801–1835* (Philadelphia: University of Pennsylvania Press, 1937), and Sam Warner, *The Private City* (Philadelphia: University of Pennsylvania Press, 1968).

15. On the managers, see Negley Teeters, "The Early Days of the Philadelphia House of Refuge," *Pennsylvania History* 27 (April 1960): 165–87. The single most important manager was Isaac Collins, a Quaker printer who had participated actively in educational and reformatory endeavors in New York City before moving to Philadelphia.

16. This recounting of "mental events" necessarily remains speculative, although I believe it complements what little we know about the public school movement in Philadelphia.

17. I shall examine this theme in the context of New York City's early public school system in the following chapter.

18. The People v. Turner, 55 Illinois 280 (1870).

19. Quoted in ibid.

20. See Edward Corwin, *The "Higher Law" Background of American Constitutional Law* (New York: Great Seal Books, 1955).

21. Numerous books and articles have appeared on these subjects, for instance, B. James George, *Gault and the Juvenile Court Revolution* (Ann Arbor: Institute of Continuing Legal Education, 1968), and Donna Renn, "The Right to Treatment and the Juvenile," *Crime and Delinquency* 19 (October 1973): 477–84.

22. Except for Illinois, where the decision—at least according to the traditional interpretations—had long-range effects on the state's juvenile justice system. See Platt, *Child Savers*, pp. 103–17. The anomalous legal developments in Illinois hindered the establishment of a state-financed reform school comparable to those elsewhere, and thus created an atypical setting for understanding the rise of the juvenile court movement.

23. *Ex parte* Becknell, 51 Pacific Reporter (Ca.), 692 (1897). See also State v. Ray, 63 New Hampshire 405 (1886).

24. Petition of Alexander Ferrier, 103 Illinois 367 (1882).

25. The judges who delivered the *Turner* opinion have not, to the best of my knowledge, been the objects of research. A fascinating study might be undertaken to assess the relation of their ideas on juvenile justice to their views on other social policies, to determine, for example, whether Turner was part of a consistent philosophy of civil liberties and/or laissez faire economics. It would also be intriguing to find out how other judges in the state responded to them, and what their individual fates were in the aftermath of *Turner*.

26. To be sure, as Ryerson and others have observed, the inclusion of criminal youth within the court's purview caused considerable discus-

sion in the Progressive period and led several reformers to argue that this represented a new application of *parens patriae*. In a sense they were right; children, at least in theory, had previously been subject in court to the procedures of criminal law. But whether this was in fact the way most children were tried remains unclear, as argued in Platt, *Child Savers*, pp. 183–202; Fox, "Juvenile Justice Reform," p. 1212; and J. Lawrence Schultz, "The Cycle of Juvenile Court History," *Crime and Delinquency* 19 (October 1973): 451–76. Furthermore, a misleading implication of this argument is that neglected and delinquent children were treated in entirely different ways in the nineteenth century. In fact, from the beginning of the century the lines between neglected and delinquent children were intentionally blurred in order to facilitate their committal to reformatories. Thus I consider it fundamentally mistaken to see the application of *parens patriae* to delinquent youth in the Progressive era as signaling a revolutionary shift in attitudes "from a doctrine of retribution to a doctrine of rehabilitation, from a tone of vindictiveness to one of sympathy, from rejection to assistance." Ryerson, "Between Justice and Compassion," p. 15. The blurring of legal lines between dependent, neglected, and delinquent youth was a product of Jacksonian rather than Progressive views of benevolence.

27. Commonwealth v. Fisher, 213 Pennsylvania 48 (1905).

28. A few academic commentators, though, did challenge the court's principal rationales, the first probably being Edward Lindsey, "The Juvenile Court from the Lawyer's Standpoint," *Annals of the American Academy of Political and Social Science* 52 (March 1914): 140–48. Aside from the inherent merits judges saw in the new courts, there may have been another, more pragmatic explanation for their diffidence. By the early twentieth century the child labor, compulsory education, and sterilization movements had reached maturity. Legislation designed to introduce or extend greatly the role of government in each of these areas was commonplace in every state. Inevitably, I would suggest, these reform movements intersected with the juvenile court: to deny the prerogatives of the court to inquire into the family situations of children who were "on the road to crime" was also to question the right of industrial commissioners, truant officers, and health officials to investigate possible instances of neglect, abuse, or inherited incapacity among noncriminal youth. What the consensus on the constitutionality of the juvenile court indirectly accomplished was to cement the legal groundwork for sundry other reform measures geared to aid, protect, and establish new means of surveillance over the lower-class immigrant family. On child labor, see Felt, *Hostages of Fortune*, and Wood, *Constitutional Politics in the Progressive Era*; on compulsory education, see Forest Ensign, *Compulsory School Attendance and Child Labor* (Iowa City: Athens Press, 1921); on sterilization and its relation to Progressive social reform, see Rudolph Vecoli, "Sterilization: A Progressive Measure?," *Wisconsin Magazine of History* 43 (Spring 1960): 190–203.

29. Mill v. Brown, 88 Pacific Reporter (Utah), 609 (1907).

30. Another decision which objected to portions of a juvenile court statute but sustained a very broad definition of *parens patriae* was Robison v. Wayne Circuit Judges, 151 Michigan 315 (1908). The legislation in question was somewhat anomalous; it authorized most of the paraphernalia of a juvenile court but retained both fines and jury trials (of six) for defendants. A jury of six was not in itself unconstitutional, but when attached to the possibility of fine it became so, argued the court in striking down the statute. But these objections did not affect the judges' overall enthusiasm for the juvenile court and their contempt for the *Turner* decision, which they caricatured as a classic "example of the vigor with which that which is not the law may be stated."

31. Not surprisingly, then, social reformers in the Progressive era found the juvenile court an excellent base on which to build their more general plea for increased governmental powers of intervention and surveillance over families of the poor. This derived from the unusual position of the juvenile justice system vis-à-vis other child welfare proposals. The juvenile justice system was, in a sense, the "granddaddy" of governmental programs in child welfare (together, of course, with the public schools). It was an institutional network in which the right of the State to disrupt natural family relations of the poor was well established. What better way, then, to make a case for *parens patriae* as the underlying rationale for other child welfare reforms than to emphasize its importance to the juvenile justice system, where the doctrine had long since been legitimated?

32. See J. Willard Hurst, *Law and the Conditions of Freedom in the Nineteenth-Century United States* (Madison: University of Wisconsin Press, 1956), and *The Growth of American Law* (Boston: Little, Brown and Co., 1950); Morton Horwitz, "The Emergence of an Instrumental Conception of American Law, 1780–1820," *Perspectives in American History* 5 (1971): 287–328; Stanley Kutler, *Privilege and Creative Destruction* (Boston: Little, Brown and Co., 1971); and Lawrence Friedman, *A History of American Law* (New York: Simon and Schuster, 1973).

33. Interestingly, the development of juvenile law in America and Britain appears to have been very different, especially on traditional distinctions between neglected, dependent, and delinquent children. Unlike the English, Americans devoted little time to discriminating among potential clienteles for government-sponsored rehabilitative institutions, and consequently, little attention to the legal rights of different types of poor children. The loose application of *parens patriae* to "predelinquents" in America from the early nineteenth century onward, and the legislative initiatives thereby facilitated, provided for a unique pattern of development whose significance will become clear only after further research on the comparative history of juvenile corrections. For the English story, see especially Harriet Schupf, "The Perishing and Dangerous Classes: Efforts to Deal with the Neglected, Vagrant and Delinquent Juvenile in England, 1840–1875" (Ph.D. dissertation, Columbia University, 1971), and John Stack, "Social Policy and

Juvenile Delinquency in England and Wales: 1815–1875" (Ph.D. dissertation, University of Iowa, 1974). For Canada, see Susan Houston, "The Impetus to Reform: Urban Crime, Poverty and Ignorance in Ontario, 1850–1875" (Ph.D. dissertation, University of Toronto, 1974).

34. On these themes see Kaestle, *Evolution of an Urban School System;* Schultz, *The Culture Factory;* Henry Perkinson, *The Imperfect Panacea* (New York: Random House, 1968); Michael Katz, *The Irony of Early School Reform* (Cambridge: Harvard University Press, 1968); Marvin Lazerson, *Origins of the Urban School* (Cambridge: Harvard University Press, 1971); and David Rothman, *The Discovery of the Asylum* (Boston: Little, Brown and Co., 1971).

35. The most explicit judicial opinion in the Progressive era tying the legal rationales of public education and juvenile justice was *In re* Sharp, 15 Idaho 120 (1908), 96 Pac. 563, where the judges admonished: "It would be fatal to the highest and greatest good, both of the individual and of the state, as well as a decided blow at popular education and enlightenment, if the state could not enforce compulsory school laws and direct parents and guardians to send their children to school during certain hours, or days, or months, as the case may be. The delinquent children's act carries this principle a step further."

36. See, for example, Michael Katz, *School Reform: Past and Present* (Boston: Little, Brown and Co., 1971); Frances Piven and Richard Cloward, *Regulating the Poor* (New York: Random House, 1971); Diane Ravitch, *The Great School Wars* (New York: Basic Books, 1974); Margaret Steinfels, *Who's Minding the Children?* (New York: Simon and Schuster, 1973); and Steven Schlossman, "The 'Culture of Poverty' in Ante-Bellum Social Thought," *Science and Society* 38 (Summer 1974): 150–66.

37. Ryerson, "Between Justice and Compassion," p. 10.

Chapter 2

1. Robert Pickett, *House of Refuge* (Syracuse: Syracuse University Press, 1969); Robert Mennel, *Thorns and Thistles* (Hanover, N.H.: University Press of New England, 1973); Joseph Hawes, *Children in Urban Society* (New York: Oxford University Press, 1971); David Rothman, *The Discovery of the Asylum* (Boston: Little, Brown and Co., 1971); and Sanford Fox, "Juvenile Justice Reform: An Historical Perspective," *Stanford Law Review* 22 (June 1970): 1187–1239.

2. See, generally, Leon Radzinowicz, *A History of English Criminal Law and Its Administration from 1750,* 4 vols. (London: Stevens and Sons, Ltd., 1948–68); Coleman Phillipson, *Three Criminal Law Reformers: Beccaria, Bentham, Romilly* (London: J. M. Dent and Sons, Ltd., 1923); Marcello Maestro, *Voltaire and Beccaria as Reformers of Criminal Law* (New York: Columbia University Press, 1942); W. David Lewis, *From Newgate to Dannemora* (Ithaca: Cornell University Press, 1965); Samuel Knapp, ed., *The Life of Thomas Eddy* (New York:

Conner and Cooke, 1834); Arthur Ekirch, Jr., "Thomas Eddy: His Ideas
and Interests" (M.A. thesis, Columbia University, 1938); Sidney
Pomerantz, *New York, an American City, 1783–1803* (New York:
Columbia University Studies in History, Economics, and Public Law,
1938); Raymond Mohl, *Poverty in New York, 1783–1825* (New York:
Oxford University Press, 1971); Carroll Rosenberg, *Religion and the
Rise of the American City* (Ithaca: Cornell University Press, 1971);
Sydney James, *A People Among Peoples* (Cambridge: Harvard Univer-
sity Press, 1963); Derek Howard, *John Howard* (London: Christopher
Johnson, 1958); Harry Barnes, *The Evolution of Penology in Pennsyl-
vania* (Indianapolis: Bobbs-Merrill Co., 1927); Carl Kaestle, *The Evolu-
tion of an Urban School System* (Cambridge: Harvard University Press,
1973); Pickett, *House of Refuge;* Fox, "Juvenile Justice Reform"; and
Lois Banner, "Religious Benevolence as Social Control: A Critique of an
Interpretation," *Journal of American History* 60 (June 1973): 23–41.

3. John Vanderbilt, Jr., *An Address Delivered in the New York Free
School . . . on the Introduction of Fifty Orphan and Helpless Children,
Belonging to the Masonic Fraternity* (New York: Southwick and Pelsue,
1810), pp. 9-10.

4. Kaestle, *Evolution of an Urban School System;* Mohl, *Poverty in
New York;* Rosenberg, *Religion and the Rise of the American City;* Julia
Duffy, "The Proper Objects of a Gratuitous Education" (Ph.D. disserta-
tion, Teachers College, Columbia University, 1968); and William
Cutler, "Philosophy, Philanthropy, and Public Education: A Social
History of the New York Public School Society, 1805–1853" (Ph.D.
dissertation, Cornell University, 1960).

5. The social impact of this wave of immigration has never received
the attention it deserves, even though charity and educational societies
considered it momentous. See Robert Albion, *The Rise of New York
Port* (New York: Charles Scribner's Sons, 1939), and Kenneth Miller,
Immigrant Life in New York City (New York: Macmillan Co., 1949).

6. In one form or another, as I shall demonstrate in succeeding
chapters, the goals of the early Sunday school movement continued to
influence a variety of educational, welfare, and correctional innovations. See Kaestle, *Evolution of an Urban School System,* pp. 120–26,
and Robert Lynn and Elliot Wright, *The Big Little School* (New York:
Harper and Row, 1970).

7. This was the renowned controversy between the Free School
Society and the Bethel Baptist Church, which resulted in the withdrawal
of public aid from the Baptists as well as several other denominations.

8. The relationship of this structural change to the later development
of school bureaucracies is explored in Kaestle, *Evolution of an Urban
School System,* and Michael Katz, *Class, Bureaucracy, and Schools*
(New York: Praeger Publishers, 1971).

9. New York Public School Society, *An Address of the Trustees of the
Public School Society . . . Respecting the Extension of their Public
Schools* (New York: J. Seymour, 1828), p. 9.

10. New York Sunday School Union, *First Annual Report* (New

York: Printed by the Union, 1817), p. 35.

11. Quoted in Lewis, *From Newgate to Dannemora*, pp. 29–30.

12. Quoted in ibid., p. 51.

13. On the differences between New York and Pennsylvania, see Barnes, *Evolution of Penology in Pennsylvania*; Negley Teeters, *The Cradle of the Penitentiary* (Philadelphia: Pennsylvania Prison Society, 1955); and Rothman, *Discovery of the Asylum*, chapter 4. In retrospect, the differences between the two systems seem less impressive than the similarities, especially the emphasis on silence at all times.

14. Lewis, *From Newgate to Dannemora*, chapter 3. Note Lewis's important reminder, p. 56, on chronology: "It should be remembered that the founding of Auburn prison and the birth of the Auburn system were not one and the same development. The latter did not occur until the mid-1820's."

15. See ibid., chapters 3 to 6, and John H. Griscom, *Memoir of John Griscom* (New York: R. Carter and Bros., 1859).

16. Rothman, *Discovery of the Asylum*, chapter 4, downplays the evolution of penal policies.

17. The best account of the managers and their diverse interests is in Pickett, *House of Refuge*, chapters 2 and 3. Though begun under private auspices, the Refuge soon gained public sponsorship and funding. Unlike the situation abroad, corrections in America was almost from the first a public enterprise.

18. Nathaniel Hart, comp., *Documents Relative to the House of Refuge* (New York: Mahlon Day, 1832), p. 140. On Lancasterian pedagogy, see Carl Kaestle, ed., *Joseph Lancaster and the Monitorial School Movement* (New York: Teachers College Press, 1973).

19. Hart, *Documents Relative to House of Refuge*, pp. 80–81.

20. In large measure, as noted in chapter one, because the vague definitions of delinquency, dependency, and neglect encouraged incarceration of children varying widely in age and condition.

21. A similar ambivalence surfaces almost every time a new correctional innovation for children is advanced, most recently in the so-called "community treatment" movement. See Paul Lerman, *Community Treatment and Social Control* (Chicago: University of Chicago Press, 1975).

22. This type of self-analysis was not, of course, limited to the sponsors of juvenile reformatories. Especially in the antebellum period, the managers of schools, prisons, and mental hospitals appeared to take special delight in communicating their rationales and problems. After the Civil War, as part of a more general concern for "efficiency" in the administration of benevolent facilities, the reports began to stress statistics and to downplay the managers' personalities and roles.

23. W. A. Coffey, *Inside Out, or An Interior View of the Newgate State Prison* (New York: Printed by the author, 1823); Charles Sommers, *Memoir of the Rev. John Stanford, D.D.* (New York: Swords, Stanford and Co., 1835); John Stanford, Petition of January 21, 1812, Stanford Papers, New-York Historical Society; and Society for the

Prevention of Pauperism in the City of New York, *Report on the Penitentiary System of the United States* (New York: Mahlon Day, 1822), p. 43. Though broached early in the development of juvenile corrections, this problem was not resolved—and then, only in large cities—until the early twentieth century with the advent of special detention centers. See chapters four and seven.

24. Hart, *Documents Relative to House of Refuge*, p. 16.

25. That the House of Refuge was, in Michael Katz's phrase, a "reform by imposition," and that it was intended to serve as an agent of social control, seem to me indisputable. To see the institution in this light, however, does not necessarily reflect badly on the founders' motives, nor does it assume that the controls were successfully implemented or effective. These are entirely separate matters requiring different types of research than undertaken here. To talk intelligently about motives requires careful biographical inquiry; to talk meaningfully about the impact of control requires exhaustive analysis of institutional networks before and after implementation. Most historical discussions of reform and social control in recent years have, I believe, shed more spark than light on the subject. See Michael Katz, *The Irony of Early School Reform* (Cambridge: Harvard University Press, 1968), part I.

26. Hart, *Documents Relative to House of Refuge*, pp. 125–26.

27. Ibid., p. 48.

28. Quoted in ibid.

29. Morton Horwitz, "The Emergence of an Instrumental Conception of American Law, 1780–1820," *Perspectives in American History* 5 (1971): 320, 326.

30. The traditional historical emphasis on educational and welfare reforms in the Progressive era has tended to obscure important changes in attitude and policy in the early nineteenth century, changes which Horwitz's article accounts for only in part. The role of government in spurring economic and technological innovation in this period has received sophisticated treatment in such works as Louis Hartz, *Economic Policy and Democratic Thought* (Cambridge: Harvard University Press, 1948); Oscar Handlin and Mary Handlin, *Commonwealth: A Study of the Role of Government in the American Economy* (New York: New York University Press, 1947); and J. Willard Hurst, *Law and the Conditions of Freedom in the Nineteenth-Century United States* (Madison: University of Wisconsin Press, 1956).

31. Hart, *Documents Relative to House of Refuge*, p. 190. A sympathetic treatment of this theme is Banner, "Religious Benevolence as Social Control"; less sympathetic is Charles Foster, "The Urban Missionary Movement, 1814–1837," *Pennsylvania Magazine of History and Biography* 75 (January 1951): 47–65.

32. Horwitz, "Emergence of an Instrumental Conception of American Law," pp. 320, 326.

33. Hart, *Documents Relative to House of Refuge*, p. 11. My strong debt to Peter Gay, *The Enlightenment*, 2 vols. (New York: Alfred A.

Knopf, 1966–69) is obvious here.

34. See Hermann Mannheim, ed., *Pioneers of Criminology* (Chicago: Quadrangle Books, 1960), passim, and Marcello Maestro, *Cesare Beccaria and the Origins of Penal Reform* (Philadelphia: Temple University Press, 1973).

35. The legal aspects of this change have been less well traced than the attitudinal. See, for example, E. Douglas Branch, *The Sentimental Years* (New York: D. Appleton-Century Co., 1934); Monica Kiefer, *American Children through Their Books* (Philadelphia: University of Pennsylvania Press, 1948); Anne Kuhn, *The Mother's Role in Childhood Education* (New Haven: Yale University Press, 1947); Bernard Wishy, *The Child and the Republic* (Philadelphia: University of Pennsylvania Press, 1968); Mary Ryan, "American Society and the Cult of Domesticity, 1830–1860" (Ph.D. dissertation, University of California at Santa Barbara, 1971); Kathryn Sklar, *Catharine Beecher* (New Haven: Yale University Press, 1973); and, for a somewhat different perspective, Barbara Finkelstein, "Governing the Young: Teacher Behavior in American Primary Schools, 1820–1880; A Documentary History" (Ed.D. dissertation, Teachers College, Columbia University, 1970).

36. Hart, *Documents Relative to House of Refuge*, pp. 78, 76, 13.

37. Ibid., p. 38.

38. Ibid., p. 22.

39. These comparisons can be extended. For one, English correctional reformers were concerned to draw careful statutory distinctions between neglected, dependent, and delinquent youth, and to establish separate facilities for each category of offender. Americans, by contrast, did not consider this a serious matter until the very end of the century. For another, the English actively discouraged indiscriminate commitments of children to reformatories by parents who no longer wanted to care for them. They demanded parental financial contributions to maintain inmates, and sought to apply to reformatories the more general penal philosophy of "less eligibility." None of these concerns, to say the least, gained much of a hearing in nineteenth-century American correctional circles. See Harriet Schupf, "The Perishing and Dangerous Classes: Efforts to Deal with the Neglected, Vagrant and Delinquent Juvenile in England, 1840–1875" (Ph.D. dissertation, Columbia University, 1971), and John Stack, "Social Policy and Juvenile Delinquency in England and Wales: 1815–1875" (Ph.D. dissertation, University of Iowa, 1974).

40. Hart, *Documents Relative to House of Refuge*, p. 187.

41. There were, in fact, glaring differences among the three institutions. The way the managers thought about them is apparent in John Griscom, *A Year in Europe*, 2 vols. (New York: Collins and Jannay, 1824). Griscom's work was completed several years before publication, and distributed in manuscript form to many of those who eventually became managers of the Refuge.

42. Hart, *Documents Relative to House of Refuge*, pp. 51–52.

43. Obviously, then, the Progressives were not the first to celebrate the virtues of discretion and highly subjective evaluations of children's moral and social status in juvenile corrections. When the managers said they intended to "prevent" delinquency by incarcerating children before evil propensities matured, they meant it.

44. Hart, *Documents Relative to House of Refuge*, pp. 44, 188.

45. In addition to the managers' own statements partially challenging this view (which I shall discuss shortly), their firing of the first superintendent, Joseph Curtis, for alleged leniency and inability to control inmates casts further suspicion. See Pickett, *House of Refuge*, pp. 82–83, and Catherine Sedgwick, *Memoir of Joseph Curtis, A Model Man* (New York: Harper and Bros., 1858).

46. Hart, *Documents Relative to House of Refuge*, p. 101.

47. Ibid., pp. 189–90, 180–81.

48. Pickett, *House of Refuge*, chapters 8 and 9; Rothman, *Discovery of the Asylum*, chapter 10; Mennel, *Thorns and Thistles*, chapter 1; Alexander Liazos, "Class Oppression: The Functions of Juvenile Justice," *The Insurgent Sociologist* 1 (Fall 1974): 2–24.

49. Although more detailed analysis of their thought is necessary to prove the point, I would suggest that the managers' ambivalence on the Refuge's mission paralleled their ambivalence on the nature of children. Traces of Calvinistic theology, even among the predominantly Quaker sponsors of the institution, lingered in their public statements long after they had ostensibly become Lockeans.

50. See especially Liazos, "Class Oppression," although his attempt to tie a demand for deference to the demands of an expanding capitalist economy is far from convincing.

51. As David Rothman has suggested, *Discovery of the Asylum*, the aim was to create within institutions a set of fixed social relationships unattainable in Jacksonian society.

52. For a somewhat similar analysis of the "curriculum" of public schools, see Robert Dreeben, *On What is Learned in School* (Reading, Mass.: Addison-Wesley Publishing Co., 1968). Of course in the Refuge, unlike the school, one does not have to distinguish too carefully between the "latent" and "manifest" curriculum.

53. One can follow architectural developments in the managers' yearly reports; see also Pickett, *House of Refuge*, pp. 53–54.

54. Hart, *Documents Relative to House of Refuge*, p. 132.

55. Ibid., p. 153.

56. Ibid., p. 102.

57. Ibid.

58. Ibid., p. 202.

59. I say rarely rather than never because the family metaphor occasionally appeared, although bereft of the ideological baggage it carried by mid-century. The more common usage was to refer to staff and inmates as one family under God, not to the institution itself as a domestic surrogate.

Chapter 3

1. A movie on the juvenile reformatory today, shown in spring of 1971 on NBC, "This Child is Rated X," is especially evocative. See also Howard James, *Children in Trouble* (New York: Pocket Books, 1971), and Larry Cole, *Our Children's Keepers* (Greenwich: Fawcett Publications, 1974).

2. See Paul Lerman, *Community Treatment and Social Control* (Chicago: University of Chicago Press, 1975), and Ronald Goldfarb, *Jails, the Ultimate Ghetto* (Garden City, N.Y.: Anchor Press, 1975).

3. The most reliable examination of the reform school after mid-century is Robert Mennel, *Thorns and Thistles* (Hanover, N.H.: University Press of New England, 1973), chapter 2.

4. In *The Discovery of the Asylum* (Boston: Little, Brown and Co., 1971), David Rothman attempts to integrate the house of refuge movement into his larger argument that Jacksonian correctional theory was institution-bound. But was the house of refuge as popular an institution as he implies before mid-century? I think not—indeed, in retrospect, what seems most notable is how little imitation there was of the first reformatories in New York, Boston, and Philadelphia in the 1830s and 1840s. Thus, two new questions about the evolution of juvenile reformatories emerge: why did the reformatory have so little appeal outside the nation's largest cities before mid-century, and what accounted for its enormous popularity thereafter? Obviously it will not do to explain the popularity of reformatories in terms of a distinctive Jacksonian Zeitgeist. More germane developments undoubtedly include: levels of urbanization and industrialization; the "new immigration" of the 1840s and 1850s; growing recognition that public schools were not serving as cure-alls for urban disorder; the development of diverse new mechanisms of law enforcement; a newly heightened sensitivity to the needs of children; and intensified fears about social change which these related phenomena occasioned. The reformatory movement, I would suggest, was part and parcel of an amorphous "search for order" which gained appeal first in the cities and then became, as Robert Wiebe has argued, a nationwide anxiety in the latter third of the century. See *The Search for Order* (New York: Hill and Wang, 1967).

5. Only a thorough investigation of institutional evolution in every state will show whether, and to what extent, other states and cities experimented with the family design before 1900. The willingness to experiment with the family design, however, especially toward the end of the century, may well have been dictated by considerations other than the ones emphasized here. Administrative concerns may have been foremost, a matter I shall discuss in chapter six.

6. Mary Carpenter appears to have been the most popular of the English reformers in America. See, as examples of her enormous literary output, *Reformatory Schools for Children of the Perishing and Dangerous Classes, and for Juvenile Offenders* (London: C. Gilpin, 1851),

and *Juvenile Delinquents: Their Condition and Treatment* (London:
W. F. G. Cash, 1853). Also very useful are Joseph Carpenter, *Life and
Work of Mary Carpenter* (London: Macmillan and Co., 1879), and
Margaret May, "Innocence and Experience: The Evolution of the
Concept of Juvenile Delinquency in the Mid-Nineteenth Century,"
Victorian Studies 17 (September 1973): 7–29.

7. Interestingly, an earlier group of appointees with the same mission
showed no awareness of the family design. See the *Report of the
Commissioners on the State Reform School to His Excellency the
Governor of the State of New Hampshire* (Manchester: State Printer,
1852). In 1855, though, the appointees wrote: the "family reform school
is not theory ... it is now universally approved by those who have
given attention to the subject, and had experience in institutions of this
kind, yet it has been practiced for many years in institutions on the
continent of Europe." Commissioners for Locating and Building House
of Reformation for Juvenile and Female Offenders Against the Laws,
First Annual Report (Manchester: State Printer, 1856), p. 19.

8. David Rothman has correctly pointed to the seeming duplicity, or
at least inconsistency, between the reformers' domestic metaphors and
actual institutional designs. See Rothman, *Discovery of the Asylum*,
pp. 234–36.

9. Robert Pickett, *House of Refuge* (Syracuse: Syracuse University
Press, 1969), chapter 8; Joseph Hawes, *Children in Urban Society* (New
York: Oxford University Press, 1971), chapter 3; Mennel, *Thorns and
Thistles*, chapters 1 and 2; Rothman, *Discovery of the Asylum*, pp.
257–59; and Robert Bremner et al., eds., *Children and Youth in
America*, 3 vols. (Cambridge: Harvard University Press, 1970–74), 2
(1971): part 4, chapter 1.

10. See Pickett, *House of Refuge*, chapters 8 and 9, and Mennel,
Thorns and Thistles, chapter 1.

11. Elijah DeVoe, *The Refuge System; or, Prison Discipline Applied
to Juvenile Delinquents* (New York: J. R. M'Gown, 1848), pp. 28–29.
DeVoe's critique must be read, of course, in light of his being a
disgruntled employee. But his book, in my estimation, rings true.

12. In short, there is hardly a criticism of American reformatories
today that was not voiced more than a hundred years ago.

13. Richard Hofstadter, *Anti-Intellectualism in American Life* (New
York: Alfred A. Knopf, 1963), part 5.

14. DeVoe, *Refuge System*, p. 11.

15. Boston Common Council, *Report of the Committee Appointed to
Investigate Alleged Abuses at the House of Reformation and House of
Correction* (Boston: City Printer, 1864), pp. 22–23.

16. See especially Samuel Knapp, ed., *The Life of Thomas Eddy*
(New York: Conner and Cooke, 1834), and Frank Thistlethwaite,
America and the Atlantic Community (New York: Harper and Row,
1963).

17. This subject has never been systematically investigated, even
though Horace Mann, Henry Barnard, Calvin Stowe, and Charles

Loring Brace, among others, acknowledged the importance of their Continental tours in formulating their own programs. On the other hand—and this is of particular importance in juvenile corrections—England often served as intermediary for Continental correctional ideas. The Anglo-American connection remained the most firmly grounded, as attested in John Resch, "Anglo-American Efforts in Penal Reform, 1850–1900: The Work of Thomas Barwicke Lloyd Baker" (Ph.D. dissertation, Ohio State University, 1969). Robert Mennel's ongoing comparative study of reformatories in the United States, England, France, and Germany promises to shed much new light on this neglected subject.

18. Quoted in Trustees of the State Industrial School for Girls at Lancaster, *First Annual Report* (Boston: State Printers, 1857), pp. 41–42 (hereafter cited as Trustees, *First AR*).

19. The only modern study to deal with either of these individuals is John Font, "Protestant Christian Socialism in Germany, 1848–1896; Wichern, Stoeker, Naumann: The Search for a New Social Ethic" (Ph.D. dissertation, University of Minnesota, 1969).

20. Horace Mann, *Account of the Hamburgh Redemption Institute* (n.p., 1843). I know of no earlier reference to the foreign reformatories.

21. Antedating the formation of the National Conference of Charities and Correction by more than a decade, these conventions appear to have been the first to draw together charity and correctional representatives from all parts of the country (although mainly from the East). A convention was scheduled for 1858, but I have been unable to determine why it did not take place.

22. Managers and Superintendents of Houses of Refuge and Schools of Reform in the United States, *Proceedings of the First Convention* (New York: Wynkoop, Hallenbeck and Thomas, 1857), p. 24.

23. See Bradford Peirce, *A Half-Century with Juvenile Delinquents* (New York: D. Appleton and Co., 1869), p. 248 and passim; Rothman, *Discovery of the Asylum*, pp. 259–60; Pickett, *House of Refuge*, p. 181; and Mennel, *Thorns and Thistles*, pp. 52–55.

24. The degree to which a generational gap paralleled differences in correctional orientation requires additional analysis. Many of the participants at the conventions had no personal acquaintance with the founders of the house of refuge. The lack of well-known spokesmen for the original refuge idea may have contributed to a willingness to look abroad for charismatic correctional leaders—which, all signs indicated, Wichern and DeMetz undeniably were.

25. Henry Barnard, *Reformatory Education* (Hartford: F. C. Brownell, 1857), pp. 351–52 and passim. Barnard also publicized new correctional ideas in his *American Journal of Education*, further attesting the close ties between educational and correctional reform movements in the nineteenth century. Barnard was an insightful commentator on learning environments in general; see *School Architecture* (New York: A. S. Barnes and Co., 1848).

26. Significantly, it was at this time that the phrase "reform school"

generally began to replace "house of refuge" in the correctional workers' lexicon. This change in language, one may hypothesize, gave symbolic verification to the emergence of a new group of penal reformers who, together with their peers in Europe, insisted they were the first to conceive of juvenile corrections in truly educational rather than punitive terms.

27. See Peirce, *Half-Century with Juvenile Delinquents*, especially pp. 162–63, 247, 256, and 268–69. I shall have more to say about the accuracy or inaccuracy of American perceptions in the epilogue.

28. I take the phrase "anti-institutional institution" from John Thomas's pioneering article, "Romantic Reform in America, 1815–1865," *American Quarterly* 17 (Winter 1965): 656–82. Jack Holl has made effective use of Thomas's concept in *Juvenile Reform in the Progressive Era* (Ithaca: Cornell University Press, 1971), although I believe the family reform school actually squares better with Thomas's meaning than the George Junior Republics.

29. A German enthusiast, Gustav Werner, was quoted by the commissioners of the Ohio Reform School as saying: "Only where persons are actuated by a proper feeling of love can children be made partakers of love, and this love may even excel a parent's love, in the formation of human character, if its wisdom be combined with holiness." Quoted in Mennel, *Thorns and Thistles*, p. 54. The increasing significance attributed to parental love in Victorian family relations will be discussed later in this chapter.

30. See Greta Fein and K. Alison Clarke-Stewart, *Day Care in Context* (New York: John Wiley and Sons, 1973); Charles Shireman, "How Can the Correctional School Correct?," *Crime and Delinquency* 6 (July 1960): 267–74; and George Gardner, "The Institution as Therapist," *The Child* 16 (January 1952): 70–72.

31. Mid-century fascination with relationships between environment and pedagogy of course went beyond the juvenile reformatory. In addition to the well-known utopian experiments of the period, the era saw the rise of urban parks, model tenements, suburban cottages, and new schoolroom designs, all of which, in different ways, attempted to neutralize pressures on the psyche fostered by the rapid growth of cities. See Albert Fein, *Frederic Law Olmstead and the American Environmental Tradition* (New York: George Braziller, 1972); Roy Lubove, *The Progressives and the Slums* (Pittsburgh: University of Pittsburgh Press, 1963); Mary Ryan, "American Society and the Cult of Domesticity, 1830–1860" (Ph.D. dissertation, University of California at Santa Barbara, 1971), pp. 226–32; Jean McClintock and Robert McClintock, *Henry Barnard's School Architecture* (New York: Teachers College Press, 1970); and, more generally, Morton White and Lucretia White, *The Intellectual versus the City* (Cambridge: Harvard University Press, 1962).

32. Probably the best review is K. Alison Clarke-Stewart, *Child Care in the Family*. Forthcoming.

33. My interpretation adheres in essentials to John Wirkkala, "Ju-

venile Delinquency and Reform in Nineteenth-Century Massachusetts: The Formative Era in State Care, 1846–1876" (Ph.D. dissertation, Clark University, 1973). I have also benefited from discussions with Barbara Brenzel, who is completing a study of the Lancaster School for Girls.

34. Writers on the correctional scene in Massachusetts often refer to this facility as "the first public training school for boys in the United States ...," Lloyd Ohlin, Robert Coates, and Alden Miller, "Radical Correctional Reform: A Case Study of the Massachusetts Youth Correctional System," *Harvard Educational Review* 44 (February 1974): 75. This is plainly wrong; cities had long funded houses of refuge in part or whole. Massachusetts created the first *state*-sponsored reformatory.

35. Quoted in Hawes, *Children in Urban Society*, p. 83.

36. The Rauhe Haus had been in operation since 1833. Hawes probably exaggerates in claiming that "By the early 1840s the Rauhe Haus had gained an international reputation as one of the most successful reformatories for juvenile delinquents in the world." The institution's reputation seems truly to have blossomed in the 1850s. See ibid., p. 79.

37. Lyman also wanted to set a maximum age entrance requirement of fourteen, which the legislature changed to sixteen. See ibid., pp. 82–83.

38. Secretary of the Board of State Charities, *First Annual Report* (Boston: State Printers, 1865), p. 171 (hereafter cited as Secretary, *First AR*).

39. See Samuel Howe, *A Letter to J. H. Wilkins, H. B. Rogers, and F. B. Fay, Commissioners of Massachusetts for the State Reform School for Girls* (Boston: Ticknor and Fields, 1854).

40. Quoted in Secretary, *First AR*, p. 203.

41. Trustees, *First AR*, p. 6.

42. By the time of the second convention in 1859, the Ohio State Reform School, the first family reform school for boys, was also in operation and widely heralded for its first two years' performance.

43. Additional detail on the various individuals involved and on the politics of correctional innovation in Massachusetts is contained in Wirkkala, "Juvenile Delinquency and Reform," passim.

44. Secretary, *First AR*, p. 179.

45. On the development of these supervisory agencies, see Mennel, *Thorns and Thistles*, pp. 65–70.

46. Secretary, *First AR*, p. 168.

47. Ibid., p. 180.

48. Ibid. See also the fascinating reminiscence by Joseph Allen, *Westboro' State Reform School Reminiscences* (Boston: Lockwood, Brooks and Co., 1877).

49. See Hawes, *Children in Urban Society*, chapter 6; Mennel, *Thorns and Thistles*, pp. 35–40, 46–48; and Rothman, *Discovery of the Asylum*, pp. 258–60.

50. This strain of thinking was much influenced by the widely

circulated report of New York's chief of police, George Matsell, in 1849; see Mennel, *Thorns and Thistles*, p. 32, and Hawes, *Children in Urban Society*, pp. 91–92. Attempts to "professionalize" the police accelerated greatly in this period; see Roger Lane, *Policing the City* (Cambridge: Harvard University Press, 1967), and James Richardson, *The New York Police* (New York: Oxford University Press, 1970).

51. See Miriam Langsam, *Children West* (Madison: State Historical Society of Wisconsin, 1964), and R. Richard Wohl, "The 'Country Boy' Myth and its Place in American Urban Culture: The Nineteenth-Century Contribution," *Perspectives in American History* 3 (1969): 77–158 for enlightening discussions of the intellectual context.

52. As observed earlier, the impact of new correctional ideas at mid-century cannot be fully understood without more extensive research on the particular social and political contexts in which those ideas took hold. Granted this, however, I still think it valid and important to examine the theory of anti-institutionalism on its own merits: first, because I believe ideas are independent moving forces in the lives of people, not simply reflex actions of underlying social processes or personal crises; second, because there is much evidence to indicate that the ideas were widely debated (if less frequently implemented) at the time. Even Rothman, *Discovery of the Asylum*, p. 259, who argues that Brace won few converts and was of little long-range influence, grants that his "position was by no means idiosyncratic" and that "something of a school formed about him." And Wohl, "The 'Country Boy' Myth," p. 108, suggests that imitation of Brace's ideas may have been more widespread than it is customary to think. In short, notwithstanding a paucity of relevant empirical research, there is good reason to examine the ideas as such, and to argue—with caution to be sure—about their probable place in the mid-century correctional dialogue. My position on the role of ideas in history is succinctly summarized by Peter Berger and Thomas Luckmann, *The Social Construction of Reality* (Garden City, N.Y.: Anchor Books, 1967), p. 128.

53. Charles Brace, *Short Sermons to Newsboys* (New York: Charles Scribner, 1866), p. 5.

54. Charles Brace, *Home Life in Germany* (New York: Charles Scribner, 1853), p. 29.

55. Ibid., pp. iv, 60.

56. Charles Brace, *The Best Method of Disposing of Our Pauper and Vagrant Children* (New York: Wynkoop, Hallenbeck and Thomas, 1859), p. 5.

57. Charles Brace, *The Norse-Folk* (New York: Charles Scribner, 1857), p. 311.

58. Though sympathetic to children, Brace's position on the poor adult was not very different from that of other charity spokespersons, including that of his local "rival," Robert Hartley. This becomes especially clear in his most famous book, *The Dangerous Classes of New York and Twenty Years' Work among Them* (New York: Wynkoop and Hallenbeck, 1872).

59. Brace, *Best Method*, pp. 10–11.

60. Charles Brace, *Address to the Theological Students of Harvard University* (Cambridge: n.p., 1881), p. 4.

61. Brace, *Best Method*, p. 4.

62. As I shall argue in chapter four regarding probation, the economic savings of noninstitutional programs have long been recognized. The argument was part of Brace's larger contention that institutional care was inadequate to the needs of an expanding, industrializing metropolis. Yet, interestingly, the legislature in New York did not endorse Brace's plan, thereby attesting its willingness to support institutional care at great cost. It would be fascinating to know whether the Tweed Ring was involved in correctional administration in New York and, if so, whether they actively opposed Brace's ideas in order to protect jobs for friends in the institutions.

63. Langsam, *Children West*, chapters 3, 4, and 5. Through 1890 the Children's Aid Society placed-out between two and three thousand children per year. That the children were not legally adopted facilitated parental cooperation—both the parents who gave up their children and those who received them—and also enhanced the leverage of the society to force receiving families to provide adequate care (at least in theory).

64. Wohl, "The 'Country Boy' Myth," pp. 107–21.

65. New York Children's Aid Society, *Fourth Annual Report* (New York: John P. Prall, 1857), p. 8.

66. On Howe, see Harold Schwartz, *Samuel Gridley Howe* (Cambridge: Harvard University Press, 1956), and Franklin Sanborn, *Dr. S. G. Howe, the Philanthropist* (New York: Funk and Wagnalls, 1891). Howe's work in public school reform and mental hospitals, of course, reveals that he was no dogmatic opponent of all philanthropic institutions. And Howe did serve for a while on the supervisory board of the original Boston House of Reformation. See Stanley Schultz, *The Culture Factory* (New York: Oxford University Press, 1973), and Gerald Grob, *The State and the Mentally Ill* (Chapel Hill: University of North Carolina Press, 1966).

67. Laura Richards, ed., *Letters and Journals of Samuel Gridley Howe*, 2 vols. (Boston: D. Estes and Co., 1909), 2: 512.

68. Massachusetts Board of State Charities, *Second Annual Report* (Boston: State Printers, 1866), p. xli (hereafter cited as Board, *Second AR*.

69. See Daniel Moynihan, *Maximum Feasible Misunderstanding* (New York: Free Press, 1969).

70. Much of the same impetus underlies recent efforts to bring volunteers into the correctional process, especially in juvenile courts. See, for example, Joe Morris, *First Offender* (New York: Funk and Wagnalls, 1970). The tie-in with more established "preventive" programs like Big Brothers and Big Sisters, and the recreational offerings of YMCAs, is even clearer.

71. Board, *Second AR*, p. xl.

72. Ibid., p. lxiii.

73. Ibid., pp. lxiii–lxiv.
74. Ibid., p. lxxv.
75. Ibid., p. lxxi.
76. Richards, *Letters and Journals of Samuel Gridley Howe*, p. 513.
77. Board, *Second AR*, p. lxxviii.
78. Ibid., p. lxxi.
79. Ibid., p. xlvi.
80. Ibid., pp. xlvi–xlvii.
81. Hawes, *Children in Urban Society*, p. 111. See my critique of the Hawes volume in "Traditionalism and Revisionism in Juvenile Correctional History," *Reviews in American History* 2 (March 1974): 59–65.
82. Thus I regard it as somewhat misleading to claim that growing endorsement of the family idea represented adoption of "the least original idea of the Brace program." Rothman, *Discovery of the Asylum*, pp. 259–60. The family reform school was not identified at all with Brace and, as Rothman himself argues, Brace's position was that "the prison atmosphere of the reformatories ... was a predictable phenomenon.... endemic to a system of institutionalization."
83. See Anthony Platt, *The Child Savers* (Chicago: University of Chicago Press, 1969), pp. 55–66, although Platt distorts the origins and meaning of the family reform school by seeing it, on the one hand, as a handmaiden of the Deweyan progressive education movement, and on the other, as integral to the adult reformatory movement of the late nineteenth century.
84. Books which have been helpful in my thinking on this subject include Richard Cloward and Lloyd Ohlin, *Delinquency and Opportunity* (New York: Free Press, 1960); Moynihan, *Maximum Feasible Misunderstanding;* Arthur Fink, *Causes of Crime* (Philadelphia: University of Pennsylvania Press, 1938); David Matza, "Subterranean Traditions of Youth," *Annals of the American Academy of Political and Social Science* 338 (November 1961): 102–18; Robert Merton, "The Social-Cultural Environment and Anomie," in Helen Witmer and Ruth Kotinsky, eds., *New Perspectives for Research on Juvenile Delinquency* (Washington: U.S. Department of Health, Education, and Welfare, 1956), pp. 24–32; and Leon Radzinowicz, *Ideology and Crime* (New York: Columbia University Press, 1966).
85. See John Davies, *Phrenology* (New Haven: Yale University Press, 1955). Mennel, *Thorns and Thistles*, pp. 78–79, deals briefly with the impact of phrenology, but does not satisfactorily pinpoint the nature of that influence.
86. See Timothy Smith, *Revivalism and Social Reform* (New York: Abingdon Press, 1957), and Carroll Rosenberg, *Religion and the Rise of the American City* (Ithaca: Cornell University Press, 1971).
87. See Anne Kuhn, *The Mother's Role in Childhood Education* (New Haven: Yale University Press, 1947); Ryan, "American Society and the Cult of Domesticity"; Bernard Wishy, *The Child and the Republic* (Philadelphia: University of Pennsylvania Press, 1968); E. Douglas Branch, *The Sentimental Years* (New York: D. Appleton-

Century Co., 1934); William Taylor, *Cavalier and Yankee* (New York: George Braziller, 1961); and Fred Pattee, *The Feminine Fifties* (New York: D. Appleton-Century Co., 1940).

88. Cf. Charles Strickland, "A Transcendentalist Father: The Child-Rearing Practices of Bronson Alcott," *Perspectives in American History* 3 (1969): 5–76.

89. To clinch this point it would be necessary to investigate the family lives of charity and correctional spokespersons. It would be interesting to know, for example, how representative was the experience of Illinois penal reformer Frederick Wines, whose inability to communicate with his own son, Arthur, was painfully evident in the years before Arthur's suicide. See Frederick Wines Papers, Illinois State Historical Society, Springfield, Illinois.

90. Two of the most troubling problems with recent writings on intrafamily relations in the nineteenth century are that we do not know how widely the newer techniques of affectional discipline were practiced, or, more basically, what segment of the population theoretically approved the new approaches. The same problems hold for analysis of affectional discipline in family reform schools. I do not claim to know precisely what portion of correctional administrators or lay reformers genuinely believed in affectional rehabilitative techniques, whether in the family or the reform school. My more modest goals here are, first, simply to point up a coincidence in the prescriptive literature on both institutions, and second, to show that juvenile corrections formed an integral part—wholly neglected by historians—of Victorian cultural aspirations. For a somewhat similar approach to the prescriptive pedagogical literature of the Victorian period, see Michael Katz, *The Irony of Early School Reform* (Cambridge: Harvard University Press, 1968), part 2.

91. Ryan, "American Society and the Cult of Domesticity," effectively ties the dissemination of new child-rearing ideas to technological advances in the publishing industry.

92. See Barbara Cross, *Horace Bushnell* (Chicago: University of Chicago Press, 1958), and Peter Slater, "Views of Children and Child Rearing during the Early National Period" (Ph.D. dissertation, University of California at Berkeley, 1971).

93. See Kuhn, *Mother's Role*, chapter 4.

94. See Robert Lynn and Elliot Wright, *The Big Little School* (New York: Harper and Row, 1970), chapters 1 and 2, and Edwin Rice, *The Sunday School Movement, 1780–1917, and the American Sunday School Union, 1817–1917* (Philadelphia: American Sunday School Union, 1917), for analyses of the transformation of Sunday schools from lower-class to middle-class institutions.

95. See Branch, *Sentimental Years*, pp. 292–95, and Kuhn, *Mother's Role*, chapter 4.

96. See Branch, *Sentimental Years*, pp. 295–314.

97. Ibid., pp. 278–86, and Davies, *Phrenology*.

98. See Kuhn, *Mother's Role*, pp. 109–19, 53–54.

99. Quoted in Ryan, "American Society and the Cult of Domesticity," p. 91.

100. Quoted in ibid.

101. Quoted in ibid., p. 92.

102. See Kuhn, *Mother's Role*, chapter 7.

103. Quoted in Ryan, "American Society and the Cult of Domesticity," p. 104.

104. Quoted in ibid.

105. Quoted in Kuhn, *Mother's Role*, p. 153.

106. See Ryan, "American Society and the Cult of Domesticity," pp. 217–19.

107. Quoted in ibid., p. 231.

108. See Katz, *Irony of Early School Reform*, part 2.

109. The single best book on the period in general remains Walter Houghton, *The Victorian Frame of Mind, 1830–1870* (New Haven: Yale University Press, 1957).

110. On Bushnell, see Cross, *Horace Bushnell*; on Downing, see Ryan, "American Society and the Cult of Domesticity," pp. 228–32; on Sigourney, see Gordon Haight, *Mrs. Sigourney, the Sweet Singer of Hartford* (New Haven: Yale University Press, 1930); on Beecher, see Kathryn Sklar, *Catharine Beecher* (New Haven: Yale University Press, 1973); and on Peabody, see Ruth Baylor, *Elizabeth Palmer Peabody* (Philadelphia: University of Pennsylvania Press, 1965).

Chapter 4

1. For representative views, see Margaret Rosenheim, ed., *Justice for the Child* (New York: Macmillan Co., 1962), passim; The President's Commission on Law Enforcement and Administration of Justice, *Juvenile Delinquency and Youth Crime* (Washington: U.S. Government Printing Office, 1967); Charles Chute, "The Juvenile Court in Retrospect," *Federal Probation* 13 (September 1949): 3–8; Herbert Lou, *Juvenile Courts in the United States* (Chapel Hill: University of North Carolina Press, 1927); and Ellen Ryerson, "Between Justice and Compassion: The Rise and Fall of the Juvenile Court" (Ph.D. dissertation, Yale University, 1970).

2. Anthony Platt, *The Child Savers* (Chicago: University of Chicago Press, 1969).

3. Contrast Platt's view with Sanford Fox, "Juvenile Justice Reform: An Historical Perspective," *Stanford Law Review* 22 (June 1970): 1187–1239, and Eric Fishman, "The Juvenile Court Movement, 1899–1921" (M.A. thesis, Columbia University, 1972).

4. The best work on Lindsey, in my estimation, is Peter Slater, "Judge Benjamin Barr Lindsey and the Denver Juvenile Court during the Progressive Era" (M.A. thesis, Brown University, 1965). Also useful are Charles Larsen, *The Good Fight* (Chicago: Quadrangle Books, 1972), Frances Huber, "The Progressive Career of Ben B. Lindsey, 1900–1920"

(Ph.D. dissertation, University of Michigan, 1963), and Stephanie Wallach, "Ben B. Lindsey and the Juvenile Court" (B.A. thesis, Barnard College, 1972).

5. Lindsey's literary output was enormous. For references, consult the bibliography.

6. Other leading advocates of the court kept their reservations about Lindsey to themselves. See Robert Mennel, *Thorns and Thistles* (Hanover, N.H.: University Press of New England, 1973), pp. 138–39.

7. One judge and reformer who attempted to imitate Lindsey in these several regards earned first praise and then scorn; see Steven Schlossman and Ronald Cohen, "The Music Man in Gary: Willis Brown and Child Saving in the Progressive Era," *Societas*, in press.

8. See especially Lawrence Cremin, *The Transformation of the School* (New York: Alfred A. Knopf, 1961), and Allen Davis, *American Heroine* (New York: Oxford University Press, 1973).

9. The differences are obvious in John Dewey, *Democracy and Education* (New York: Macmillan Co., 1916), and Jane Addams, *Twenty Years at Hull House* (New York: Macmillan Co., 1910), somewhat less obvious in John Dewey, *The School and Society* (Chicago: University of Chicago Press, 1899), and Jane Addams, *The Spirit of Youth and the City Streets* (New York: Macmillan Co., 1909).

10. This aspect of Dewey and Addams is strongly emphasized in the relevant essays in Clarence Karier et al., *Roots of Crisis* (Chicago: Rand McNally, 1973), and *History of Education Quarterly* vol. 15 (Spring 1975), and vol. 14 (Spring 1974). Davis, *American Heroine*, contends that the quest for acceptance and popularity was the leading motif in Addams's life although much of his own evidence tends to contradict his argument.

11. Admittedly, these are highly subjective judgments reached only after extensive reading. What the authors strikingly shared was an ability to reshape basic ideas to suit the demands of different audiences without sacrificing their essence. Dewey did this primarily by addressing current public issues and showing how his broader philosophy related to them; Addams by empathetic identification with those she proposed to assist; and Lindsey by the classic American technique of combining didactic sentimentalism with humor.

12. The societal framework for my interpretation draws upon diverse recent works, notably Robert Wiebe, *The Search for Order* (New York: Hill and Wang, 1967); Samuel Hays, *The Response to Industrialism* (Chicago: University of Chicago Press, 1957); Samuel Haber, *Efficiency and Uplift* (Chicago: University of Chicago Press, 1964); David Tyack, *The One Best System* (Cambridge: Harvard University Press, 1974); Raymond Callahan, *Education and the Cult of Efficiency* (Chicago: University of Chicago Press, 1962); Marvin Lazerson, *Origins of the Urban School* (Cambridge: Harvard University Press, 1971); Walter Drost, *David Snedden* (Madison: University of Wisconsin Press, 1967); John Higham, *Strangers in the Land* (New York: Atheneum, 1966); Michael Katz, *Class, Bureaucracy, and Schools* (New York: Praeger

Publishers, 1971); Robert Bremner, *From the Depths* (New York: New York University Press, 1956); Arthur Mann, *Yankee Reformers in the Urban Age* (Cambridge: Harvard University Press, 1954); Joel Spring, *Education and the Rise of the Corporate State* (Boston: Beacon Press, 1972); and Richard Hofstadter, *The Age of Reform* (New York: Alfred A. Knopf, 1955).

13. See Lazerson, *Origins of the Urban School;* Jeremy Felt, *Hostages of Fortune* (Syracuse: Syracuse University Press, 1965); Tyack, *One Best System;* and Sol Cohen, *Progressives and Urban School Reform* (New York: Bureau of Publications, Teachers College, 1964).

14. Two books from the Progressive period approximating this interpretation are Thomas Eliot, *The Juvenile Court and the Community* (New York: Macmillan Co., 1914), and Sophonisba Breckinridge and Edith Abbott, *The Delinquent Child and the Home* (New York: Russell Sage, 1912).

15. See especially, for modern perspectives, Jonathan Kozol, *Death at an Early Age* (Boston: Houghton Mifflin, 1967); Edgar Friedenberg, *The Disposal of Liberty and Other Industrial Wastes* (New York: Doubleday and Co., 1975); Peter Schrag and Diane Divoky, *The Myth of the Hyperactive Child and Other Means of Child Control* (New York: Pantheon Books, 1975); Charles Silberman, *Crisis in the Classroom* (New York: Random House, 1970); and Clarence Karier, *Shaping the American Educational State* (New York: Free Press, 1975).

16. For modern perspectives, see Lois Forer, *"No One Will Lissen"* (New York: Grossett and Dunlap, 1970), Lisa Richette, *The Throwaway Children* (New York: Dell Publishing Co., 1969), and Patrick Murphy, *Our Kindly Parent . . . The State* (New York: Viking Press, 1974).

17. Contrary to a common misconception, Ben Lindsey was not content to build the future of Denver's juvenile court on one charismatic personality; he consistently encouraged the expansion of probation services. See Mennel, *Thorns and Thistles*, p. 139.

18. Ibid., chapter 5; Fishman, "Juvenile Court Movement, 1899–1921," pp. 33–41, 55–74; James Collins, "The Juvenile Court Movement in Indiana," *Indiana Magazine of History* 28 (March 1932): 1–8; and George Curtis, "The Juvenile Court Movement in Virginia" (Ph.D. dissertation, University of Virginia, 1973),

19. On this matter historians are pretty much at the mercy of court sponsors, who emphasized the rigidity of traditional dispositional options to enhance the appeal of flexibility and discretion in the juvenile court. Fox, "Juvenile Justice Reform," p. 1212, senses that reformers exaggerated the degree of prior legal formality in children's cases, but the evidence at present is too skimpy to be sure. The same holds true for the rather ingenious argument of J. Lawrence Schultz, "The Cycle of Juvenile Court History," *Crime and Delinquency* 19 (October 1973): 457–76, that the juvenile court actually formalized the judicial response to juvenile crime. The subject requires extensive research in nineteenth-century court records and newspapers. The most trustworthy empirical

evidence, though far from conclusive, is in Platt, *Child Savers*, pp. 183–202.

20. The latter disposition, as noted in chapter two, was a recurrent one throughout the nineteenth century. Thus, it is difficult to assess its significance in accounting for correctional innovations at any particular time.

21. What follows is my synthesis of sundry primary sources; for specific references, consult the bibliography.

22. The attempt to locate the sources of crime within individual offenders has often been explained as a product of the "positivist" influence in late nineteenth-century sociology and criminology. See, for example, David Matza, *Delinquency and Drift* (New York: John Wiley and Sons, 1964), chapter 1; Platt, *Child Savers*, chapter 1; and Elliot Currie, "Managing the Minds of Men: The Reformatory Movement, 1865–1920" (Ph.D. dissertation, University of California at Berkeley, 1973). This interpretation, in my judgment, overstates the impact of formal criminological theory on early twentieth-century social reform movements and understates continuities in explanations for juvenile crime over the course of the nineteenth century (I shall elaborate this point later in the chapter). It also diverts attention from the moralistic, exhortatory quality of correctional theory during most of the Progressive era.

23. The role of detention in modern juvenile justice and in the early juvenile court movement has received little scholarly attention, even though, as I shall demonstrate in chapter eight, it was central to correctional practice. On modern uses see Ronald Goldfarb, *Jails, the Ultimate Ghetto* (Garden City, N.Y.: Anchor Books, 1975), and Margaret Rosenheim, "Detention Facilities and Temporary Shelters," in Donnell Pappenfort, Dee Kilpatrick, and Robert Roberts, eds., *Child Caring* (Chicago: Aldine Publishing Co., 1973), pp. 253–99.

24. That is, each of these aims was explicit in the promotional literature, although the punitive features were downplayed. Thus, one cannot argue that the later uses of detention were "unintended" or "latent." Rather, they were part and parcel of the early movement.

25. It remains unclear to me whether these statutes were intended primarily to hold parents criminally liable or to facilitate prosecution of other "contributors" to delinquency, such as saloon keepers, pimps, etc.

26. This is my surmise from the primary sources; I have no specific piece of empirical data to substantiate it.

27. Although this issue gave rise to more litigation than any other. See, for example, Mill v. Brown, 88 Pacific Reporter (Utah), 609 (1907), and Robison v. Wayne Circuit Judges, 151 Michigan 315 (1908).

28. See Mennel, *Thorns and Thistles*, pp. 149–50.

29. Though probation existed in various forms before the twentieth century, only Massachusetts had truly integrated it into its correctional system, and even there, its administration and ostensible purposes were altered after the advent of the juvenile court. A sophisticated study of

probation, as ideology and institution, is badly needed before we can realistically assess the impact of the juvenile court. A useful though outdated and uncritical overview is Nicholas Timasheff, *One Hundred Years of Probation, 1841–1941* (New York: Fordham University Press, 1941).

30. Thus I disagree rather sharply with Platt, *Child Savers*, p. 135, who argues that "the child savers . . . recommended increased imprisonment as a means of removing delinquents from corrupting influences." My assumption here is that Platt is referring to long-term institutionalization in reformatories. The statistical evidence he offers to support his contention, pp. 140–41, in no way does so because he does not compare the situation before and after the establishment of the juvenile court.

31. Thus Progressive juvenile reformers were far more enthusiastic than Brace and Howe about the rehabilitative potential of family reform schools; see ibid., pp. 55–66.

32. I am referring here only to long-term institutionalization. Short-term detention was quite another matter.

33. Charles Heusiler, "Probation Work in Children's Courts," *Charities* 11 (7 November 1903): 400.

34. Harvey Hurd, "Juvenile Court Law," *Charities* 13 (7 January 1905): 328.

35. Heusiler, "Probation Work," p. 400.

36. Frederic Almy, "Juvenile Courts in Buffalo," *Annals of the American Academy of Political and Social Science* 20 (July 1902): 283–84.

37. Heusiler, "Probation Work," p. 400.

38. Thus the significance of both change and continuity in the ideals of Victorian and Progressive juvenile justice. The juvenile court provided new means, suggested a new locale, and expanded the clientele for the application of affectional discipline. Perhaps the best overall statement of juvenile court ideology is in Hannah Schoff, *The Wayward Child* (Indianapolis: Bobbs-Merrill Co., 1915).

39. Interestingly, I have never confronted this argument in the historical literature on the juvenile court, even among revisionists who attack the benevolent intent of the Progressive reformers.

40. Almy, "Juvenile Courts in Buffalo," p. 281.

41. Heusiler, "Probation Work," p. 401.

42. See Carl Kaestle, ed., *Joseph Lancaster and the Monitorial School Movement* (New York: Teachers College Press, 1973).

43. Much the same contention might be made for the growing appeal of foster care during this period; see Homer Folks, *The Care of Destitute, Neglected, and Delinquent Children* (New York: Macmillan Co., 1902).

44. See Lou, *Juvenile Courts in the U.S.*, pp. 14–18. The extent to which various types of judges began informally to hear children's cases separately probably goes far beyond available information.

45. The reformers did, though, eventually carry the segregation principle one step further, insisting upon separation of neglected and delin-

quent youth during court hearings. See Bernard Flexner, "The Juvenile Court as a Social Institution," *Survey* 23 (5 February 1910): 608.

46. See Timasheff, *One Hundred Years of Probation*, and Charles Chute and Marjorie Bell, *Crime, Courts, and Probation* (New York: Macmillan Co., 1956), chapter 4.

47. This type of explanation, expressed with varying degrees of subtlety, appears in the previously cited works of Pickett, Mennel, Hawes, and Rothman.

48. See Mennel, *Thorns and Thistles*, chapter 4.

49. On Folks see Walter Trattner, *Homer Folks* (New York: Columbia University Press, 1968).

50. Homer Folks, "The Care of Delinquent Children," National Conference of Charities and Correction, *Proceedings* (Boston: George H. Ellis, 1891), pp. 137–39.

51. Another representative spokesman in this vein was Hastings Hart. See *Preventive Treatment of Neglected Children* (New York: Russell Sage, 1910).

52. L. D. Drake, "Do Reform Schools Reform?," National Conference of Charities and Correction, *Proceedings* (Boston: George H. Ellis, 1897), pp. 126–27.

53. In pointing to a growing pessimism regarding the ability of reformatories to rehabilitate, I do not want to suggest that widespread faith in them is essential to their political viability. Corrections forms part of a larger network of law enforcement, administrative, and political agencies which often, at least for short periods, function independently of popular and legislative opinion. See Sheldon Messinger, "Strategies of Control" (Ph.D. dissertation, University of California at Berkeley, 1969).

54. Remarkably, this subject has never been treated in all its variety. Two useful works of broad scope are Walter Trattner, *Crusade for the Children* (Chicago: Quadrangle Books, 1970), and Nancy Weiss, "Save the Children: A History of the Children's Bureau, 1903 to 1918" (Ph.D. dissertation, University of California at Los Angeles, 1974).

55. Although I have several disagreements with Platt, *Child Savers*, on the intellectual underpinnings of the juvenile court movement, his is the only book which treats the court mainly as a cultural product.

56. See especially Cremin, *Transformation of the School*, Dorothy Ross, *G. Stanley Hall* (Chicago: University of Chicago Press, 1972), and Bremner, *From the Depths*.

57. See Bernard Wishy, *The Child and the Republic* (Philadelphia: University of Pennsylvania Press, 1968), part 2.

58. Ibid., p. 115.

59. See Michael Katz, *The Irony of Early School Reform* (Cambridge: Harvard University Press, 1968), part 2.

60. See Ross, *G. Stanley Hall*, and Steven Schlossman, "G. Stanley Hall and the Boys' Club: Conservative Applications of Recapitulation Theory," *Journal of the History of the Behavioral Sciences* 9 (April 1973): 140–47.

61. See William Forbush, *The Boy Problem* (Boston: Pilgrim Press, 1902).

62. Charles Bernheimer and Jacob Cohen, *Boys' Clubs* (New York: Baker and Taylor Co., 1914), pp. 19–20.

63. See especially *The Spirit of Youth and the City Streets*.

64. The early twentieth century, though, also saw the maturing of a new strain of hereditarian thinking on delinquency causation; see Currie, "Managing the Minds of Men," pp. 258–59, and Peter Tyor, "Segregation or Surgery: The Mentally Retarded in America, 1850–1920" (Ph.D. dissertation, Northwestern University, 1972). Consider Platt, *Child Savers*, p. 43 on this subject: "The preoccupation with the 'natural' criminal was replaced by a concern for the 'nurtured' criminal.... Except for a brief period in the 1930s, the idea that criminals are born rather than made disappeared from correctional polemics." I consider this misleading in at least two significant ways. First, it belies continuities in the environmentalist explanation of juvenile crime from the early nineteenth to the early twentieth centuries. And second, as Currie and Tyor show, the role of biological ideas in delinquency causation theory was actually more important after, not before, the so-called Age of Social Darwinism gave way to the Progressive era. Still, when all is said and done on this subject, it remains clear that the principal explanation for juvenile crime in the Progressive era, just as in the Jacksonian, was environmental—a bad home and community make a bad boy.

65. The best work still remains Bremner, *From the Depths*.

66. See Roy Lubove, *The Professional Altruist* (Cambridge: Harvard University Press, 1965), Nathan Huggins, *Protestants against Poverty* (Westport, Conn.: Greenwood Publishing Corp., 1971), and Kenneth Kusmer, "The Function of Organized Charity in the Progressive Era: Chicago as a Case Study," *Journal of American History* 60 (December 1973): 657–78.

67. On Hunter, see Peter d'A Jones, Introduction in Robert Hunter, *Poverty* (New York: Harper and Row, 1965); on Wald, see Robert Duffus, *Lillian Wald* (New York: Macmillan Co., 1939).

68. See Currie, "Managing the Minds of Men"; Tyor, "Segregation or Surgery"; Rudolph Vecoli, "Sterilization: A Progressive Measure?," *Wisconsin Magazine of History* 43 (Spring 1960): 190–202; and Donald Pickens, *Eugenics and the Progressive Era* (Nashville: Vanderbilt University Press, 1968).

69. This is conjecture only, although bits and pieces of evidence in the previously cited works of Currie, Tyor, Vecoli, and Pickens are suggestive. For many who found sterilization morally offensive, a massive institution building program probably was the preferred response to "congenital" delinquency.

70. Neither Bremner, *From the Depths*, nor anyone else examines this point. The key issue for social policy may not have centered on individualistic versus environmentalistic explanations of poverty—that old standard in social welfare history—but rather on changing perceptions

of the *penetrability* of urban immigrant subcultures. I have examined the antebellum position in "The 'Culture of Poverty' in Ante-Bellum Social Thought," *Science and Society* 38 (Summer 1974): 150–66.

71. See the previously cited works of Currie, Tyor, Vecoli, and Pickens.

72. See Bremner, *From the Depths*, and Lubove, *Professional Altruist*, chapter 1.

73. Almy, "Juvenile Courts in Buffalo," p. 283.

74. There were obvious continuities here with the "friendly visiting" campaign of the late nineteenth century and, indeed, with the work of Robert Hartley's Association for Improving the Condition of the Poor in the antebellum period. But, in my judgment, it was only in the Progressive era that the emphasis shifted away from a punitive regard for "efficiency" in alms distribution toward a more therapeutic interest in reeducating the adult poor. See Huggins, *Protestants against Poverty*; Kusmer, "Function of Organized Charity"; Lubove, *Professional Altruist*; and Carroll Rosenberg, *Religion and the Rise of the American City* (Ithaca: Cornell University Press, 1971), chapter 9.

75. This was most obvious in the case of Ben Lindsey, who was heavily influenced by the Gospel preacher Lyman Abbott. In fact, to understand what Lindsey meant in saying that "love" should be the foundation stone of future criminal law, one must read Abbott's *Christianity and Social Problems* (Boston: Houghton, Mifflin and Co., 1896). On the importance of the Social Gospel to Progressive social reform, see Henry May, *Protestant Churches and Industrial America* (New York: Harper and Bros., 1949), Aaron Abell, *The Urban Impact on American Protestantism, 1865–1900* (Cambridge: Harvard University Press, 1943), and Robert Handy, *The Social Gospel in America, 1870–1920* (New York: Oxford University Press, 1966).

76. On the early aims of Sunday schools, see Carl Kaestle, *The Evolution of an Urban School System* (Cambridge: Harvard University Press, 1973), pp. 120–26.

77. Robert Wiebe, *Search for Order*, p. 169, has written: "If humanitarian progressivism had a central theme, it was the child. He united the campaigns for health, education, and a richer city environment, and he dominated much of the interest in labor legislation.... The most popular version of legal and penal reform also emphasized the needs of youth." True enough, but this ever-popular theme should not obscure the new focus on the family as an irreplaceable social unit, and on the child as intermediary between reformers and the adult immigrant poor.

78. In addition to numerous works by Dewey, see Edward Ross, *Social Control* (New York: Macmillan Co., 1901); Arthur Calhoun, *A Social History of the American Family*, 3 vols. (Cambridge: Arthur H. Clark Co., 1917–19); Elsie Parsons, *The Family* (New York: G. P. Putnam's Sons, 1912); and Willystine Goodsell, *A History of the Family as a Social and Educational Institution* (New York: Macmillan Co., 1915).

79. On Lee, see Lawrence Finfer, "Leisure as Social Work in the

Urban Community: The Progressive Recreation Movement, 1890–1920" (Ph.D. dissertation, Michigan State University, 1974).

80. Joseph Lee, "The Integrity of the Family as a Vital Issue," *Survey* 23 (4 December 1909): 305–13.

81. Ibid., p. 313.

82. Ibid., pp. 305–6.

83. Given Lee's concern for the preservation of the family, it was surprising that in his role as leader of nationwide recreational reform he did not emphasize planned play activities within families. The motto that families which play together, stay together apparently emerged later, becoming part of the "togetherness" theme in post–World War II family relations. See Peter Filene, *Him/Her/Self* (New York: Harcourt Brace Jovanovich, 1975), chapter 6, and Joel Spring, "Mass Culture and School Sports," *History of Education Quarterly* 14 (Winter 1974): 483–500.

84. David Kennedy, *Birth Control in America* (New Haven: Yale University Press, 1970), p. 40.

85. The most articulate opposition came from a group warranting systematic study, the National Divorce Reform League, which changed its name and broadened the range of its concerns in 1897, becoming the National League for the Protection of the Family.

86. Kennedy, *Birth Control*, p. 49, and William O'Neill, *Divorce in the Progressive Era* (New Haven: Yale University Press, 1967).

87. An innovative work discussing the issue in this context is Elaine May, "The Pursuit of Domestic Perfection: Marriage and Divorce in Los Angeles, 1890–1920" (Ph.D. dissertation, University of California at Los Angeles, 1975).

88. This was evident in the proceedings of diverse charity organizations throughout the country, for instance, the Wisconsin Conference of Charities and Correction, where rising divorce rates became a catch-all explanation for a wide range of social ills. The National League for the Protection of the Family also used divorce as a take-off point for examining related social problems.

89. See Kusmer, "Function of Organized Charity."

90. Mark Leff, "Consensus for Reform: The Mothers'-Pension Campaign in the Progressive Era," *Social Service Review* 47 (September 1973): 398.

91. Ibid.

92. The social philosophy underlying the pension campaign was succinctly stated at the famous White House Conference of 1909, quoted in ibid., p. 400: "Home life is the highest and finest product of civilization. It is the great molding force of mind and of character. Children should not be deprived of it except for urgent and compelling reasons. Children of parents worthy of character, suffering from temporary misfortune and children of reasonably efficient and deserving mothers who are without the support of the normal breadwinner, should, as a rule, be kept with their parents, such aid being given as may be necessary to maintain suitable homes for the rearing of the children.... Except in

unusual circumstances, the home should not be broken up for reasons of poverty, but only for considerations of inefficiency and immorality."

93. See David Rothman, *The Discovery of the Asylum* (Boston: Little, Brown and Co., 1971), chapter 9.

94. Quoted in Margaret Steinfels, *Who's Minding the Children?* (New York: Simon and Schuster, 1973), p. 51.

95. Ibid., pp. 50–52.

96. The reality behind the popular perception is examined in Jom Kingsdale, "The 'Poor Man's Club': Social Functions of the Urban Working Class Saloon," *American Quarterly* 25 (October 1973): 269–90.

97. Much work remains to be done on this neglected social movement. For basic information see Emma Weigley, "It Might Have Been Euthenics: The Lake Placid Conference and the Home Economics Movement," *American Quarterly* 26 (March 1974): 79–96. For the economic and technological context, see Heidi Hartmann, "Capitalism and Women's Work in the Home, 1900–1930" (Ph.D. dissertation, Yale University, 1974).

98. See Caroline Hunt, *The Life of Ellen H. Richards* (Boston: Whitcomb and Barrows, 1912).

99. Ellen Richards, *Euthenics, the Science of Controllable Environment* (Boston: Whitcomb and Barrows, 1910), p. 56.

100. An excellent ideological analysis is Barbara Ehrenreich and Deidre English, "The Manufacture of Housework," *Socialist Revolution* 5 (October–December 1975): 5–40. See also Weiss, "Save the Children," pp. 224–25. The fascinating *Journal of Home Economics* provided a professional outlet for the new, aggressively feminine discipline of domestic science.

101. For brief mentions, see William O'Neill, *The Woman Movement* (Chicago: Quadrangle Books, 1969), pp. 48–49, and Robert Riegel, *American Women* (Rutherford, N.J.: Fairleigh Dickinson University Press, 1970), p. 293.

102. See Steven Schlossman, "Before Home Start: Notes toward a History of Parent Education in America, 1897–1929," *The Harvard Educational Review* 46 (August 1976): 436–67.

103. Mrs. Theodore Birney, "Address of Welcome," The National Congress of Mothers, *The Work and Words of the National Congress of Mothers* (New York: D. Appleton and Co., 1897), pp. 7–8.

104. Mrs. Mary Dickinson, "Response to Address of Welcome," ibid., p. 18. This viewpoint actually came to prevail among the third, if not the second, generation of college women, according to William Chafe, *The American Woman* (New York: Oxford University Press, 1972), pp. 103–7.

105. Mrs. A. Jennesse Miller, "Mother's Relation to the Sound Physical Development of Her Child," The National Congress of Mothers, *Work and Words*, pp. 120, 118.

106. Miss Frances Newton, "The Mother's Greatest Needs," ibid., p. 153.

107. Mrs. Lucy Bainbridge, "Mothers of the Submerged World—Day Nurseries," ibid., p. 49.

108. Ibid.

109. Ibid., p. 50.

110. Ibid., p. 51.

111. The same faith, though expressed on a considerably more sophisticated level, underlay the theory and practice of the Children's Bureau, according to Weiss, "Save the Children."

Introduction to Part 2

1. Of the many books on these diverse subjects, three have influenced me most: Gerald Grob, *The State and the Mentally Ill* (Chapel Hill: University of North Carolina Press, 1966), Michael Katz, *The Irony of Early School Reform* (Cambridge: Harvard University Press, 1968), and Laurence Veysey, *The Emergence of the American University* (Chicago: University of Chicago Press, 1965).

2. The Chicago court was the object of several dissertations in the 1920s and 1930s at the University of Chicago, most completed under the direction of Ernest Burgess. These provide a wealth of untapped data.

3. Grob, *State and Mentally Ill*, has attempted to demonstrate cycles of achievement and failure in therapeutic policy at mental hospitals. Without evaluating the persuasiveness of his argument, it can simply be noted that there are better scientific grounds for viewing various types of mental aberration as "illness" than there are for viewing juvenile delinquency as pathology—Thomas Szasz notwithstanding.

4. See, generally, Edwin Schur, *Radical Non-Intervention* (Englewood Cliffs, N.J.: Prentice-Hall, 1973), and Paul Lerman, *Community Treatment and Social Control* (Chicago: University of Chicago Press, 1975).

5. The data on reformatories are unquestionably superior in New York and Massachusetts; on juvenile courts, they are superior in New York and Illinois.

6. Oftentimes one hears today that questions about implementation and financial resources divert attention from larger questions about correctional concept and theory. Christopher Lasch, for example, argues against the danger of being co-opted by administrators of institutions who plead they could "get the job done" if better financed and appreciated. See *The World of Nations* (New York: Random House, 1973), chapter 1. While Lasch has a point, I see no reason to view the issues as mutually exclusive—except, that is, for purposes of empirical analysis, for they are not equally demonstrable.

Chapter 5

1. My understanding of Wisconsin corrections today derives from several discussions between 1970 and 1975 with administrators in the

Division of Corrections, State Department of Public Welfare, Madison; with various personnel at the state's two main reform schools for boys; with personnel at Milwaukee's reform school for girls, home for dependent children, and juvenile court; from various published documents of the Division of Corrections, for example, *Corrections in the Wisconsin Tradition* (Madison: State Department of Public Welfare, 1965); from diverse unpublished master's theses at the School of Social Work, University of Wisconsin, Madison; and from newspaper files on recent institutional developments in the archives of the Kettle Moraine School for Boys and the Waukesha Public Library. I have also benefited from informal discussions with citizens of Waukesha about corrections in general and the role of the reformatory in their community.

2. One of the more intriguing aspects of my visit to Kettle Moraine in 1970 was the amount of disagreement among different segments of the staff on labor as a therapeutic agent. Many staff members, notably those who had worked in the old institution at Waukesha (and were protected in their jobs by civil service) felt that inmates were dangerously idle. There were too few work opportunities and insufficient monies to fund other innovative and, presumably, therapeutic programs. The reformatory, they believed, smacked too much of a boarding school. "All the punks do," one employee remarked, "is shoot baskets [in the modern gym] and shoot pool."

3. Actually, there was much in common between the goals of Victorian correctional reformers and those of "milieu therapy" advocates in the 1960s, whose ideas underlay initial programs at Kettle Moraine. For an analysis of the difficulties of applying "milieu therapy," see Howard Polsky, *Cottage Six* (New York: Russell Sage, 1962).

4. Several personnel did express concern, however, about the institution's location. Around 75 percent of the inmates were black, the bulk from Milwaukee, and the institution was too far away for many of their families to visit. Even if one owns a car, the institution is none too easy to locate and also, as several inmates found out, none too easy to escape from, despite relatively lax internal surveillance. The incongruity of an institution housing mainly urban blacks in an all-white rural community did not escape local townsfolk.

5. On the pervasiveness of these concerns in early midwestern cities, see Richard Wade, *The Urban Frontier* (Cambridge: Harvard University Press, 1959). On the "crisis mentality" in antebellum eastern cities, see Stanley Schultz, *The Culture Factory* (New York: Oxford University Press, 1973) and David Rothman, *The Discovery of the Asylum* (Boston: Little, Brown and Co., 1971).

6. Bayrd Still, *Milwaukee* (Madison: State Historical Society of Wisconsin, 1948), p. 112. I have relied heavily on this book for understanding the social and political scene in nineteenth- and early twentieth-century Milwaukee, although I have supplemented it with selective reading of Republican and Democratic English-language newspapers.

7. Still, *Milwaukee*, pp. 81–85, 111–32, 216–21.

8. At least I have failed to locate such speeches or extensive news-

paper references, relying mainly on the index to the *Milwaukee Sentinel* (nineteenth century only), located in the local history room of the Milwaukee Public Library.

9. Thus, the danger of taking as typical the pattern of institution-founding in New York, Boston, or Philadelphia.

10. See *Milwaukee Sentinel*, 28 February 1861.

11. Ibid., 13 December 1861.

12. Ibid., 28 February 1861.

13. See *Private and Local Laws of Wisconsin*, 1857, chapter 318, and 1859, chapter 192. Unfortunately it has proven impossible to trace the role of jails in juvenile justice for most of the nineteenth century, other than to acknowledge that many, perhaps the great majority of youth arrested for crime, vagrancy, incorrigibility, etc. spent time in jail in lieu of, or preliminary to, sentences in the reformatory. As we shall see, the "jail problem" was also a major issue in the juvenile court movement nearly a half-century later.

14. Wisconsin legislative journals and the scattered references to legislative happenings in Madison newspapers were of little use in determining political alignments on reformatory affairs.

15. I have culled information on the commissioners from the index to the *Milwaukee Sentinel*, to which I refer the reader for specific dates.

16. To assess Bacon's wealth, I have used manuscript census data.

17. On Waupun, see Miriam Langsam, "The Nineteenth-Century Wisconsin Criminal: Ideologies and Institutions" (Ph.D. dissertation, University of Wisconsin, 1967).

18. My information on the political history of Waukesha derives from reading the *Waukesha Democrat*, 1858–60, and the *Waukesha Freeman*, 1859–60.

19. See *Waukesha Democrat*, 5 October 1858.

20. Interestingly, the Wisconsin delegation was not even included on the official roster of states in attendance. One is left to wonder how many other states sent representatives whose presence went unrecorded.

21. *Waukesha Republican*, as quoted in the *Milwaukee Sentinel*, 17 September 1857.

22. *Waukesha Democrat*, January to June, 1858.

23. Ibid., June to July, 1858.

24. Ibid., June, 1858 to June, 1859.

25. Ibid., 5 October 1858.

26. *Waukesha Freeman*, 7 June 1859.

27. Ibid., 7 February 1860.

28. To be sure, the commissioners were chagrined. Even though their ideas were ignored, they protested the tendency to refer to the facility as a "house of refuge" rather than a "reform school," a difference in language whose symbolic significance has previously been noted. While many newspapers referred to the institution in 1860 and after as a "house of refuge," the legislature, responding to a direct request from the commissioners, had changed its name officially to "State Reform

School" in 1859.

29. See, for example, *Waukesha Freeman,* 8 May 1860.

30. Ever since the Jacksonian period, a relatively long stay—two years at least—had been considered necessary to effect a total change in character. Cogswell's emphasis on the need for lengthy commitments was not indicative of a major shift in the ideology of treatment in this period. Rather, it was probably an indirect response to legislators who, for reasons that remain unclear, did not endorse indeterminate sentencing in the original law. Cogswell was reacting to an anomaly, not invoking a new idea.

31. Managers of the State Reform School, *First Annual Report* (Madison: State Printer, 1860), p. 36 (all reformatory reports issued by the managers hereafter cited as Managers, *First AR, Second AR, Third AR,* etc., with specific date of issue).

32. Corruption in state benevolent institutions was actually quite common in Wisconsin, or so the newspapers of the early 1860s suggested in their sensationalistic reports on the state mental hospital at Delavan.

33. The creation of separate cells rather than dormitories was probably the sharpest rebuff to the commissioners who sponsored a family reform school.

34. Managers, *First AR,* 1860, p. 21.

35. Ibid., p. 7.

36. Commissioners Appointed to Locate and Erect a State Reform School for Juvenile Delinquents, *Fourth Annual Report* (Madison: State Printer, 1860), p. 1.

37. I have culled information on the managers from the index to the *Milwaukee Sentinel,* to which I refer the reader for specific dates.

38. On Elmore see "Reminiscences of Andrew E. Elmore," Wisconsin State Historical Society, *Proceedings* (Madison: State Historical Society of Wisconsin, 1910), pp. 190–204, and Frank Bruno, *Trends in Social Work, 1874–1946* (New York: Columbia University Press, 1948), pp. 16–17.

39. See Jonathan Messerli, *Horace Mann* (New York: Alfred A. Knopf, 1973).

40. *Milwaukee Sentinel,* 14 June 1860. In 1851 Barrett settled in Wautema, Wisconsin, where he represented that section of the state in a newly formed county government. After moving to Milwaukee he began his own medical and surgical practice, devoting spare time to assembling a sophisticated nature collection and to church activities. Rufus King frequently publicized Barrett's diverse activities in his newspaper, and the two were obviously good friends. Unfortunately, I have been unable to trace where Barrett was born, reared, and educated.

41. Managers, *First AR,* 1860, pp. 14, 20, 21. He was much less confident about girls, however—if no longer virgins, they were as good as dead.

42. See ibid., p. 36 and passim.

43. See Carl Kaestle, *The Evolution of an Urban School System*

(Cambridge: Harvard University Press, 1973), p. 10.

44. Managers, *First AR*, 1860, p. 25.

45. It is unclear whether Barrett maintained a specific denominational tie; at times he seemed like a Congregationalist, at other times not.

46. Managers, *Third AR*, 1862, p. 1206.

47. Managers, *First AR*, 1860, p. 21, and Managers, *Fourth AR*, 1863, p. 408.

48. All calculations derive from raw data in the yearly reports.

49. Managers, *Second AR*, 1861, pp. 2, 8.

50. Managers, *First AR*, 1860, p. 21. This law was especially important to Barrett because the first inmates, committed for short periods, suffered "relapses" and thereby jeopardized the institution's public image at just the time he was straining to build public support. See Managers, *Third AR*, 1862, p. 1206. Data on offenses committed by inmates are contained in appendix one, table 1.

51. Barrett and the managers had tried unsuccessfully to convince legislators to draw reformatory appropriations from the state's common school fund in order to emphasize the institution's educational objectives. Barrett also encouraged Waukesha public school students to visit the reformatory and commingle with inmates.

52. Managers, *First AR*, 1860, p. 33.

53. Managers, *Third AR*, 1862, p. 1206.

54. Managers, *First AR*, 1860, pp. 27, 32.

55. *Waukesha Democrat*, 14 August, 18 September, 5 February 1861; *Milwaukee Sentinel*, 7 April 1861.

56. *Waukesha Democrat*, 14 April 1863.

57. "Four of the inmates of the State Reform School made their escape, and of course, as usual, made tracks for Milwaukee. Yesterday afternoon Policeman McCarthy caught one of the boys, and while taking him to the Police Station, observed another." *Milwaukee Sentinel*, 2 September 1861.

58. Ibid.

59. Ibid., 14 December 1861.

60. Ibid., 18 December 1861.

61. Managers, *Fourth AR*, 1863, p. 422.

62. Ibid., p. 423.

63. *Milwaukee Sentinel*, 16 January 1864.

64. Managers, *Sixth AR*, 1865, p. 377.

65. Ibid., pp. 381–82.

Chapter 6

1. *Waukesha Plaindealer*, 16 January 1866; *Milwaukee Sentinel*, 27 April 1866.

2. *Milwaukee Sentinel*, 17 April 1866.

3. Managers of the State Reform School, *Seventh Annual Report*

(Madison: State Printer, 1866), pp. 228–29 (all reformatory reports issued by the managers hereafter cited as Managers, *First AR, Second AR, Third AR,* etc., with specific date of issue).

4. Ibid., p. 229.

5. On the Chicago superintendent, see Wiley Sanders, ed., *Juvenile Offenders for a Thousand Years* (Chapel Hill: University of North Carolina Press, 1970), pp. 392–97.

6. I have been unable to find out more about this convention, either who attended or what the range of subjects was.

7. Managers, *Seventh AR,* 1866, pp. 229–30.

8. I do not in the least mean to suggest that if Hendrickson were actually the man some thought him to be, the family reform school would have achieved its goals. That is entirely a different matter. However, given the paucity of evidence, it could be argued that as early as 1866 the differences between Hendrickson and Barrett were clear, that the choice of Hendrickson for superintendent represented a conscious change in correctional policy. Since neither the managers nor anyone else gave any indication that this was the case, I have not argued it, but the possibility remains.

9. Wines's magnum opus was *The State of Prisons and of Child-Saving Institutions in the Civilized World* (Cambridge, Mass.: J. Wilson and Son, 1880). Wines, like Hendrickson, was something of a transitional figure in corrections; his ideas pointed in the direction of a "science" of criminology, yet were clearly imbued with the moral fervor typical of antebellum reformers.

10. Born in upstate New York in 1817, Hendrickson had attended Rensselaer Academy for four years before teaching public school. He came to Wisconsin in 1855, assuming the principalship of a Whitewater school before becoming county superintendent of schools in Waukesha in 1861. An active churchman, he became a deacon of the Methodist Episcopal Church. Hendrickson was Wisconsin's delegate to the Prison and Reform Congress in Cincinnati in 1870 and to the International Penitentiary Congress in London in 1872. See *The History of Waukesha County, Wisconsin* (Chicago: Western Historical Company, 1880), pp. 815–16.

11. Managers, *Sixteenth AR,* 1875, p. 37.

12. On the subject generally see Robert Mennel, *Thorns and Thistles* (Hanover, N.H.: University Press of New England, 1973), chapter 3; Joseph Hawes, *Children in Urban Society* (New York: Oxford University Press, 1971), chapter 11; and Anthony Platt, *The Child Savers* (Chicago: University of Chicago Press, 1969), chapter 2.

13. Managers, *Twelfth AR,* 1871, p. 22.

14. For a somewhat similar argument regarding developments in the Massachusetts State Reform School, see Michael Katz, *The Irony of Early School Reform* (Cambridge: Harvard University Press, 1968), pp. 181–82, 207–8. The impact of hereditarian thinking on mental hospitals was also clear; see Gerald Grob, *The State and the Mentally Ill* (Chapel Hill: University of North Carolina Press, 1966), chapters 6 and 7.

15. Managers, *Fifteenth AR*, 1874, p. 35.

16. Ibid., p. 37. This proposal gained Hendrickson a certain degree of nationwide notoriety, as witnessed by the report in U.S. Bureau of Education, *Circulars of Information, Number 6*, quoted in Robert Bremner et al., eds., *Children and Youth in America*, 3 vols. (Cambridge: Harvard University Press, 1970–74), 2 (1971): 466.

17. Managers, *Seventeenth AR*, 1876, p. 33. For a similar argument about the intentions of Jacksonian reformers, see David Rothman, *The Discovery of the Asylum* (Boston: Little, Brown and Co., 1971), passim.

18. Managers, *Seventeenth AR*, 1876, p. 33.

19. It should be pointed out here that, as during Barrett's tenure, Hendrickson's wife served as matron and his two daughters as teachers. With the family design intact, however, it was necessary to hire many more overseers to act as surrogate parents. In practice it proved difficult to attract mature couples, if only because they were required to live full-time in the institution. Most cottages (it seems from the scanty evidence) were supervised by single men, some even by unmarried men and women (to the superintendent's obvious chagrin). It would be fascinating to know what admixture of humanitarian aspirations, personal frustrations, and authoritarian drives led mature men and women to spend twenty-four hours per day, at nominal salaries, as voluntary inmates of correctional institutions. It needs also to be pointed out that neither the Rauhe Haus nor the Colonie Agricole relied mainly on women to administer affectional discipline. It may be that the desire to have mature couples in male reformatories was unique to America.

20. Managers, *Thirteenth AR*, 1872, p. 20.

21. Managers, *Seventeenth AR*, 1876, p. 14.

22. Managers, *Eleventh AR*, 1870, p. 20.

23. "We must work the inmate to reform and educate him, but not expressly to bring in a revenue to the institution." Managers, *Twelfth AR*, 1871, p. 15.

24. In developing the following interpretation, I have relied more on my own observations of reform schools in New York, Pennsylvania, and Wisconsin than on a particular theoretical schema. For imaginative discussion of how managerial and rehabilitative considerations are intertwined in correctional institutions, see Erving Goffman, *Asylums* (Garden City, N.Y.: Doubleday and Co., 1961); Gresham Sykes, *The Society of Captives* (Princeton: Princeton University Press, 1958); Elliot Studt, Sheldon Messinger, and Thomas Wilson, *C-Unit* (New York: Russell Sage, 1968); and Sheldon Messinger, "Strategies of Control" (Ph.D. dissertation, University of California at Berkeley, 1969).

25. This is not to say that the use of classification systems for managerial purposes was "caused" by the new climate of opinion, only that the latter made the former more obvious and provided a nonmanagerial rationale.

26. Managers, *Fifteenth AR*, 1874, p. 33.

27. Again, this argument draws on my own perception of how classi-

fication systems serve to enhance managerial prerogatives and facilitate new strategies of internal control.

28. See U.S. Bureau of Education, *Circulars of Information, Number 6*, quoted in Bremner et al., *Children and Youth*, p. 466.

29. This, again, appears to have been the effect of Hendrickson's innovations. Given the scant evidence, one dare not pronounce too authoritatively on his motives.

30. See Messinger, "Strategies of Control."

31. Implicit in this analysis, of course, is a series of assumptions about the legislature which my empirical data support only in part. I know much less than I would like to about what individual politicians and parties thought of juvenile corrections. Still, the evidence does suggest that legislators, while not indifferent to "progressive" correctional ideas, were equally concerned about (1) running the facility as cheaply as possible, which often meant forcing inmates to produce marketable goods or at least defray internal operating expenses, and (2) never appearing to "coddle" offenders against the law. Only rarely in the history of the reform school did legislators fully support correctional ideas which did not promise some economic payoff in return. This was true not only in the institution's early history but also in the early twentieth century (which lies beyond the present study), when the attempt to incorporate a full-scale vocational training program failed due to lack of financing.

32. See *Milwaukee Sentinel*, 25 April 1877; 1 March 1880.

33. Managers, *Eighth AR*, 1867, p. 378.

34. *Milwaukee Sentinel*, 21 November 1881. The procedure seems to have been used most often by stepfathers to get rid of their wives' children by previous marriages.

35. A check of the occupations of the managers over several decades suggests that, as at the beginning, most continued to be businessmen within easy traveling distance of the institution. Religious rivalries (to be discussed shortly) also suggested that most were Protestant.

36. Managers, *Seventeenth AR*, 1876, pp. 9–10.

37. I shall discuss changes in statewide supervision of Wisconsin benevolent institutions in greater detail in the following chapter. The best source on this subject is Donald Berthrong, "Social Legislation in Wisconsin, 1836–1900" (Ph.D. dissertation, University of Wisconsin, 1951).

38. See especially Ray Billington, *The Protestant Crusade, 1800–1860* (New York: Macmillan Co., 1938).

39. *Milwaukee Sentinel*, 22 July 1872. Data on ethnic backgrounds of inmates provides the only gauge for determining religious affiliations. See appendix one, table 2.

40. Ibid., 11 June 1875.

41. The whole subject of Catholic education was an especially lively one in the 1870s and 1880s. See Neil McCluskey, ed., *Catholic Education in America* (New York: Teachers College Press, 1964), pp. 127–74.

42. See *Milwaukee Sentinel*, 22 July 1875; 4 January 1881.

43. Thus the danger of jumping to conclusions about how a person is likely to behave on the basis of mere occupation or status identifications.

44. See *Milwaukee Sentinel*, 7 December 1881.

45. Ibid., 11 March 1880; 7 December 1881.

46. Ibid., 3 October 1879.

47. Ibid.

48. Ibid., 30 September, 12 December 1879.

49. Elmore's "professional" opinion of Sleep, I suspect, was mixed with elements of guilt and nostalgia. As president of the Wisconsin State Board of Charities and Reform and a founder of the recently established National Conference of Charities and Correction, he no longer had time to watch over the institution that had sparked his interest in charitable affairs. But he recognized in Sleep the antithesis of his old friend Moses Barrett and thought that Rockwood (who soon became co-editor of the state teacher association's *Journal of Education*) might be able to revitalize earlier correctional ideals. On Elmore's developing views, see Andrew Elmore, "Report of the Committee on Reformatories and Houses of Refuge," National Conference of Charities and Correction, *Proceedings* (Boston: George H. Ellis, 1885), pp. 84–86.

50. Born in England in 1848, Sleep had come to America in 1857. He became a reformatory employee at age twenty-one. See *The History of Waukesha County, Wisconsin*, p. 828, and *Wisconsin Necrology* (a series of newspaper obituaries in the Wisconsin State Historical Society).

51. *Milwaukee Sentinel*, 25 November, 29 November 1881.

52. Ibid., 25 November 1881.

53. This fascinating, if somewhat commonsensical idea raises a host of interesting questions about how institutions maintain equilibrium. Sykes's discussion of the subject in *Society of Captives*, is excellent but really does not address issues that are bound to be different in juvenile institutions.

54. *Milwaukee Sentinel*, 19 July 1881.

55. Ibid., 21 November 1881.

56. Ibid.

57. Ibid.

58. Ibid.

59. Ibid., 22 November 1881. Whether the profit-sharing arrangement was begun by Sleep, or whether it developed along with large-scale manufacturing at the institution under Hendrickson, is unclear.

60. Ibid., 21 November 1881.

61. Ibid., 23 November 1881.

62. Ibid., 25 November 1881. "The defense reminded us of the mother's apology for her daughter's accident out of marriage. The good lady said: it was a small baby." *Waukesha Democrat*, 3 December 1881.

63. *Milwaukee Sentinel*, 19 December 1881.

64. Ibid., 8 December, 17 December 1881.

65. Ibid., 13 December 1881.

66. Unfortunately, I have been unable to learn much about actual uses of parole revocation by administrators of the reform school. The few manuscript records available suggest that the threat of parole revocation could not have been very great, if only because the institution had difficulty keeping track of ex-inmates' whereabouts.

67. *Milwaukee Sentinel*, 26 November, 3 December, 10 December, 20 December 1881.

68. Ibid., 1 December, 8 December, 10 December 1881; 3 January 1882. The "high walls" were not really as high as implied, nor was the institution physically barricaded from the rest of the community. Indeed several trains passed the reformatory every day on a track that ran right through its grounds. Moreover, the community had begun to develop around the institution. That the reformatory seemed like a fortress suggested more about people's attitudes than anything else.

69. Ibid., 15 April 1883.

Chapter 7

1. The situation is different today, although much work remains to be done. I have found the following books most helpful: Alfred Kahn, *A Court for Children* (New York: Columbia University Press, 1953); Robert Emerson, *Judging Delinquents* (Chicago: Aldine Publishing Co., 1969); Lisa Richette, *The Throwaway Children* (New York: Dell Publishing Co., 1969); Lois Forer, *"No One Will Lissen"* (New York: Grosset and Dunlap, 1970); William Stapleton and Lee Teitelbaum, *In Defense of Youth* (New York: Russell Sage, 1972); and Patrick Murphy, *Our Kindly Parent . . . The State* (New York: Viking Press, 1974).

2. It remains for historians to find out, however, just how many courts did keep reasonably complete records, both statistical and stenographic. I was pleasantly surprised by the quality of stenographic records in Milwaukee. If Milwaukee is typical in this regard, there is a wealth of unexplored documentary material in cities throughout the country awaiting historical analysis.

3. The legal guidelines for gaining entrance to court records vary and are imprecise. It is unclear to me whether records are better or worse guarded today than they were in the early twentieth century. Although it is not easy for historians to gain access to the records, social workers, educationists, military, and business personnel often gain entry informally through personal contacts with court staff.

4. A recent book and one typical of several written in this vein is Murray Levine and Adeline Levine, *A Social History of Helping Services* (New York: Appleton-Century-Crofts, 1970). The ideology of the social work profession needs analysis of the same kind Lawrence Cremin gave to education in *The Wonderful World of Ellwood Patterson Cubberley* (New York: Teachers College Press, 1965), although Roy Lubove, *The Professional Altruist* (Cambridge: Harvard University Press, 1965) is an excellent start.

5. This criticism includes Anthony Platt's revisionist book, *The Child Savers* (Chicago: University of Chicago Press, 1969), a provocative interpretation of the court based mainly on the reexamination of traditional documentary sources.

6. Of the numerous books and articles which fit into this interpretive pattern, see especially Julian Mack, "The Juvenile Court," *Harvard Law Review* 23 (December 1909): 104–22, and Bernard Flexner and Roger Baldwin, *Juvenile Courts and Probation* (New York: Century, 1912).

7. See Orman Ketcham, "The Unfulfilled Promise of the American Juvenile Court," in Margaret Rosenheim, ed., *Justice for the Child* (New York: Macmillan Co., 1962), pp. 22–43.

8. See Platt, *Child Savers*.

9. As shown in chapter four, the economic savings of noninstitutional treatment were quite *explicitly* advanced in the Progressive era.

10. See Rudolph Vecoli, "Sterilization: A Progressive Measure?," *Wisconsin Magazine of History* 43 (Spring 1960): 190–202, and Peter Tyor, "Segregation or Surgery: The Mentally Retarded in America, 1850–1920" (Ph.D. dissertation, Northwestern University, 1972).

11. In providing this overview, I have relied, as earlier, on local newspapers as well as official institutional reports. The newspapers were notable during the decade after 1882 for the lack of attention given reformatory affairs, as contrasted with earlier and later periods.

12. See Donald Berthrong, "Social Legislation in Wisconsin, 1836–1900" (Ph.D. dissertation, University of Wisconsin, 1951), pp. 207–9.

13. *Waukesha Democrat*, 11 July 1891.

14. Ibid.

15. Ibid., 18 July 1891.

16. Ibid., 24 October 1891. Carney was of course wrong, thereby attesting the low profile Sleep managed to maintain during most of his administration.

17. Ibid., 21 November, 24 November 1891; 27 February 1892.

18. Ibid., 12 March 1892.

19. Ibid., 13 February, 20 February 1892.

20. Ibid., 2 July 1892.

21. Ibid., 20 February, 16 July 1892.

22. The view certainly was one component in the growth of the George Junior Republics, although it needs to be noted that these catered to a slightly older clientele than generally appeared in juvenile court. See Jack Holl, *Juvenile Reform in the Progressive Era* (Ithaca: Cornell University Press, 1971).

23. An insightful overview of social thought and Progressive politics in Wisconsin is David Thelen, *The New Citizenship* (Columbia, Mo.: University of Missouri Press, 1972). Still, there is no substitute for primary sources. The quickest avenue into reformist thinking in Wisconsin is through the writings of the state's leading sociologist, child psychologist, and penologist—Edward Ross, Michael O'Shea, and John Gillin, respectively. All three wrote extensively for popular as well as professional audiences, and all lectured frequently before local civic

groups. Only Ross has received sufficient attention. See Julius Wein-berg, *Edward Alsworth Ross and the Sociology of Progressivism* (Madison: State Historical Society of Wisconsin, 1972), and Chris-topher Lasch, *The New Radicalism in America, 1889–1963* (New York: Alfred A. Knopf, 1965), chapter 5. The bibliography lists a variety of less familiar primary sources for understanding the social and intel-lectual backdrop of correctional innovations in Wisconsin.

24. Though not earlier, as Sallee McNamara argues in "The Record Re-Examined: The Stalwarts, the Progressives, Education, and Public Welfare in Wisconsin" (M.A. thesis, University of Wisconsin, 1965), chapter 3.

25. Wisconsin State Conference of Charities and Correction, *Pro-ceedings* (Madison: State Printer, 1897), p. 66.

26. Ibid., pp. 66–67.

27. Ibid.

28. Ibid.

29. See especially Nathan Huggins, *Protestants against Poverty* (Westport, Conn.: Greenwood Publishing Corp., 1971), and Lubove, *Professional Altruist*, chapter 1.

30. Thelen, *New Citizenship*, pp. 114–15.

31. These changes can be traced in the annual reports from 1894 to 1919, the major changes occurring from 1899 to 1905.

32. See Lubove, *Professional Altruist*, chapters 1 and 2. Historians have generally not made fine enough distinctions among the diverse charity spokespersons in the late nineteenth and early twentieth-cen-turies. For instance, to lump Mary Richmond—even the early Mary Richmond—with most other writers is to miss the artistry she consid-ered essential to turn human interactions into levers of social and moral uplift.

33. See Keith Melder, "Ladies Bountiful: Organized Women's Benev-olence in Early Nineteenth-Century America," *New York History* 68 (July 1967): 231–54.

34. See pp. 75–78.

35. The boys' club is a neglected social institution of the Progressive period, though one of the most popular throughout the country. I have briefly investigated its theoretical underpinnings in "G. Stanley Hall and the Boys' Club: Conservative Applications of Recapitulation Theory," *Journal of the History of the Behavioral Sciences* 9 (April 1973): 140–47. It would be interesting to know in how many other cities the boys' club provided the key focal point for female reform efforts, as contrasted, for instance, with social settlements, which often receive a disproportionate share of attention.

36. See pp. 67–68.

37. See Kathryn Sklar, *Catharine Beecher* (New Haven: Yale Univer-sity Press, 1973), chapter 15.

38. The annual reports sometimes included information on how dif-ferent staff members, especially the paid superintendent, spent their time.

39. See Hugh Knapp, "The Social Gospel in Wisconsin, 1890–1912" (M.A. thesis, University of Wisconsin, 1968).

40. The other was led by Reverend Herbert Jacobs, also a Congregationalist, who participated in municipal politics while running the city's best known Protestant settlement house. See Ruth Harman and Charlotte Lekachman, "The 'Jacobs' House," *Wisconsin Magazine of History* 16 (March 1933): 252–84. The other religiously inspired settlement in Milwaukee was run by the Federated Jewish Charities and led by Lizzie Kander, author of the *Settlement Cookbook*. See Ann Waligorski, "Social Action and Women: The Experience of Lizzie Black Kander" (M.A. thesis, University of Wisconsin, 1969).

41. On Titsworth, see Knapp, "Social Gospel in Wisconsin," passim; Thelen, *New Citizenship*, pp. 99–110; and Titsworth's *The Moral Evolution* (Milwaukee: Press of Swain and Tate Co., 1899), especially pp. 62–71, 100–113.

42. With the cooperation of Reverend William Edge, I was able to use church membership lists from 1898 to 1904 contained in the basement of Plymouth Church.

43. Scattered information suggests that as early as the 1870s, well-to-do, religiously motivated women in Milwaukee were visiting children in jails. It is unclear whether this persisted without break through the 1890s.

44. I have traced developing interest in the Chicago Juvenile Court in the pages of the *Milwaukee Sentinel* from 1900 to 1901.

45. See Platt, *Child Savers*, chapter 4, on the role of women in Chicago. I shall have more to say about the sponsorship of the court in chapter eight.

46. Marion Ogden, now in her late nineties, confirmed this interpretation for me in a letter dated May 13, 1974: "We based our law definitely on the Chicago law. I worked on that myself."

47. Miss Ogden's letter, quoted above, continued: "There was practically no opposition in Madison. That was because the bill demanded almost no expenditure by the County Board. It was also due to the fact that Mrs. Van Wyck, secretary of the Boys' Club, had seen that the bill was acceptable before it was introduced."

48. In the early stages of the juvenile court movement, most reformers genuinely believed it was preferable to have voluntary probation officers rather than salaried ones. Voluntary officers, the argument went, would not be subject to political intimidation and would be motivated solely by their concern for children. One of the reasons paid probation officers came to be preferred throughout the country within less than a decade was that volunteers found the job more demanding, in time and energy, than they had anticipated. It also may be that other reform activities drew them away. In any case, though standards varied before the founding of the National Probation Association in 1907, fifty to sixty children were generally considered the absolute limit for effective treatment.

49. Whether a lack of financing of probation indicated that a signifi-

cant gap existed between reformers and the citizenry on the virtues of noninstitutional treatment is, obviously, an important issue but one which I have been unable to determine by reading newspapers and legislative journals. For intriguing modern-day perspectives on popular attitudes toward children which speak indirectly to this issue, see Justine Polier, "The Myth that our Society is Child-Centered," *New York Times*, 25 January 1972, and Joyce Maynard, "The Monster Children," *Newsweek*, 26 July 1976.

50. State v. Scholl, 167 Milwaukee 504 (1918). See also Milwaukee Industrial School v. The Supervisors of Milwaukee County, 40 Wisconsin 328 (1876), and Wisconsin Industrial School for Girls v. Clark County, 103 Wisconsin 651 (1899).

51. Laws of Wisconsin, 1901, Chapter 90.

52. As the decision in State v. Scholl indicated, the legislature later withdrew this right after court decisions in other states affirmed the constitutionality of juvenile courts with or without provision for juries.

53. See Boys' Busy Life Club, *Annual Report* (Milwaukee: n.p., 1904), pp. 28–29.

54. For an excellent description and diagram of the layout, see Bernard Flexner, "The Juvenile Court as a Social Institution," *Survey* 23 (5 February 1910): 622–23.

55. See *Milwaukee Sentinel*, 3 February 1905; *Milwaukee Journal*, 22 May 1905, both references part of the Juvenile Court File located in the Legislative Reference Bureau, State Capitol Building, Madison.

56. See note 49, and *Milwaukee Sentinel*, 3 February, 29 May 1905.

57. These are my calculations based on the unpublished Annual Reports of the Chief Probation Officer, located in the archives of the Milwaukee Juvenile Court and beginning in 1905.

58. The role of religious rivalries in Chicago juvenile justice is ably discussed in Sanford Fox, "Juvenile Justice Reform: An Historical Perspective," *Stanford Law Review* 22 (June 1970): 1187–1239, although one need not accept Fox's exclusion of other equally important issues in accounting for the rise of the court. See also Robert Mennel, *Thorns and Thistles* (Hanover, N.H.: University Press of New England, 1973), pp. 140–42.

59. As noted in chapter six, religious controversies probably also subsided because the school lost its evangelical tone in the latter part of the century. By the early twentieth century it had switched allegiances to the "religion" of vocational education, a subject needing more study, since it formed a little-known part of the larger vocational education movement.

60. I judge this to be the custom, although my conclusion rests on the somewhat risky attempt to evaluate religious and ethnic affiliations on the basis of clients' last names.

61. I will examine the backgrounds of probation officers in chapter eight.

62. My ideas on this subject have been influenced by an insightful article on Progressive political innovations. See Samuel Hays, "The

Politics of Reform in Municipal Government in the Progressive Era,"
Pacific Northwest Quarterly 55 (October 1964): 157–69.

63. See the incredible series of articles on the Chicago Juvenile Court
in the *Real Estate News* for 1917–18, contained in the Juvenile Court File
of the Legislative Reference Bureau. On Denver, see Francis Huber,
"The Progressive Career of Ben B. Lindsey, 1900–1920" (Ph.D. dissertation, University of Michigan, 1963), and Ben Lindsey and Harvey
O'Higgins, *The Beast* (New York: Doubleday, Page, 1910).

64. See, for example, *Milwaukee Journal*, 18 November 1908.

65. This controversy continued from 1908 well into the 1940s. See
Milwaukee Journal, 6 January, 30 January 1909; *Milwaukee Free Press*,
2 February, 11 February, 24 February, 2 March 1909; *Milwaukee Daily
News*, 10 February, 20 February, 6 March 1909.

66. A letter of Chief Probation Officer Zuerner to a Madison col-
league in 1919 is most revealing: "We have the best Juvenile Court law
in the United States, and the only point that I can see is that we have not
enough officers to do justice to the work." Collected in the unpublished
Annual Report of 1920.

67. For the court's favorable public image and rare statements of
purpose and method, see *Milwaukee Free Press*, 20 August 1905; 12
March 1906; 27 March, 11 August, 10 December 1907; *Milwaukee
Sentinel*, 16 November 1905; 22 December 1907; *Evening Wisconsin*, 5
February 1909.

Chapter 8

1. My own assessment was confirmed in a survey conducted by the
National Probation Association under the direction of Francis Hiller,
Probation in Wisconsin (New York: National Probation Association,
1926), pp. 54–99. Although the report praised Milwaukee relative to
other jurisdictions in the state, it left little doubt that record-keeping
procedures everywhere, especially before 1920, were extraordinarily
sloppy. It may not have been coincidental that Zuerner retired shortly
after publication of the report.

2. Even today we know next to nothing about this phase of the
probation officer's work. Attention continues to focus on hearings in
court, not on the role of probation officers, truant officers, guidance
counselors, and law enforcement agents who try to resolve potentially
justiciable cases out of court. Scholarly neglect of the probation officer
today is understandable in light of his somewhat passive role in processing cases for court appearance. But in the Progressive era, as we shall
see, the probation officer was anything but passive; he did not simply
administer cases brought to his attention by others, but sought out
potentially justiciable cases on his own.

3. Let me make it clear that in this chapter as in the next, I am using
the twelve hundred case sample mainly for the trial transcripts contained therein, not as a data base for most of the statistical analysis. The

case sample raised a host of issues requiring extensive investigation, for example, the court's role in administering mothers' pensions and the relation of mothers' pensions to the city's and state's other welfare apparatus. These are important subjects, to be sure, and should be integral to future research on the social history of the juvenile court. But I have decided not to discuss them at present.

4. In chapters five and six, I paid little systematic attention to this subject because even less information was available.

5. In addition to Milwaukee city directories, I have used the following: the *Wisconsin Necrology*, located in the State Historical Society at Madison; William Bruce, *History of Milwaukee, City and County* (Chicago: S. J. Clarke Publishing Co., 1922); John Gregory, ed., *History of Milwaukee, Wisconsin* (Chicago: S. J. Clarke Publishing Co., 1931); Jerome Watrous, ed., *Memoirs of Milwaukee County* (Madison: Western Historical Association, 1909); Andrew Aikens and Lewis Proctor, *Men of Progress* (Milwaukee: Evening Wisconsin Co., 1897); and John Berryman, *History of the Bench and Bar of Wisconsin*, 2 vols. (Chicago: H. C. Hooper, Jr., and Co., 1898).

6. Of the many, many books and articles dealing with this subject directly and indirectly, I have found the following most useful: Richard Hofstadter, *The Age of Reform* (New York: Alfred A. Knopf, 1955); Michael Katz, *Class, Bureaucracy, and Schools* (New York: Praeger Publishers, 1971); Christopher Lasch, *The New Radicalism in America, 1889–1963* (New York: Alfred A. Knopf, 1965); Marvin Lazerson, *Origins of the Urban School* (Cambridge: Harvard University Press, 1971); Anthony Platt, *The Child Savers* (Chicago: University of Chicago Press, 1969); Nathan Glazer and Daniel Moynihan, *Beyond the Melting Pot* (Cambridge: M.I.T. Press, 1963); Colin Greer, *The Great School Legend* (New York: Basic Books, 1972); Robert Wiebe, *The Search for Order* (New York: Hill and Wang, 1967); David Hammack, "The Centralization of New York City's Public School System, 1896: A Social Analysis of a Decision" (M.A. thesis, Columbia University, 1969); Diane Ravitch, *The Great School Wars* (New York: Basic Books, 1974); David Tyack, *The One Best System* (Cambridge: Harvard University Press, 1974); and Robert Buroker, "From Voluntary Association to Welfare State: Social Welfare Reform in Illinois, 1890–1920" (Ph.D. dissertation, University of Chicago, 1973).

7. However extensive the above literature may appear at first glance, there has been remarkably little effort to distinguish between those who sponsored and those who ran new institutions. The importance of this distinction is clearly revealed in Lee Rainwater, "The Revolt of the Dirty-Workers," *Trans-action* 5 (November 1967): 2, 64.

8. That is, of course, when they worked at all. In numerous cases it was obvious that for many males work was seasonal. Many others seemed to drift from one job to another for short periods. Family income was often boosted, though, by rent from boarders, by income from wives' performing domestic labor in middle-class homes, and by salaries from children. I attempted to deal with occupational and finan-

cial information more systematically, but gave up the project once it became clear how scattered the data were and how sloppily they had been collected.

9. The frequently radical shifting of street locations in Milwaukee in the intervening years makes it essential to rely on maps from the time period, which are available in the city directories. I have also used maps in the local history room of the Milwaukee Public Library.

10. This represented nearly three-quarters of the individuals I originally set out to trace, leaving a sizable portion unaccounted for. Numerous historians have noted that many poor people were never listed in city directories because of their transiency. One can hypothesize that those who could be located were more stable in their employment and family situations than those not listed, and hence, that there is probably considerable upward distortion in the occupational distribution I discovered. My impression is that the "average" parent in court was somewhat poorer and more occupationally undifferentiated than the directory listings suggest. On use of directories, see Stephan Thernstrom, *The Other Bostonians* (Cambridge: Harvard University Press, 1973).

11. Here I am drawing from my sample of twelve hundred cases. Because of the way I took the sample, taking at least fifty cases from every year and at different times of the year, it is likely that I included the great majority of volunteer probation officers.

12. This is a critical linkage which I have been unable to explore in the depth it deserves. As will become clear in chapter nine, the ties between the court and public school officials were especially close, largely due to the efforts of Hasso Pestalozzi, a descendant of Johann Pestalozzi, who served as the city's head truant officer as well as a volunteer probation officer.

13. Thus I do not want to deny the continued linkage between the court and the city's elite, only to show that whatever ties existed were indirect and that there was a wider range of individuals involved than might at first be suspected. Moreover, as will shortly become evident, the significance of volunteers to the court's daily work diminished rapidly after 1905.

14. Oral communication to the author. Miss Ogden attended in 1894–95 and then returned to Milwaukee due to illness.

15. Here I am drawing from my sample of twelve hundred cases. I know for certain that other judges heard juvenile cases during this period, but these four definitely heard most of them.

16. Of course, one could take the approach that *because* most judges and clientele had similar ethnic and religious backgrounds, their behavior conformed to certain patterns. It seems to me, however, that other variations in the judges' backgrounds make it wise simply to abandon the effort to portray them as a "type" and to accept the complexity of the situation without seeking an explanatory shortcut.

17. Thus, my interpretation of judges and probation officers forms a variation on a theme advanced by David Thelen to explain the charac-

ter of reform efforts in Progressive Wisconsin. Thelen's emphasis, like mine, is on a common orientation toward social change and social amelioration among the middle-class in Wisconsin. See David Thelen, *The New Citizenship* (Columbia, Mo.: University of Missouri Press, 1972).

18. In several years the number of out-of-court settlements was almost as high as the number of new delinquency cases. In most years the ratio varied between 1:2 and 2:3. For example, in 1908 there were 380 out-of-court settlements and 704 new delinquency cases; in 1918 there were 990 out-of-court settlements and 1,054 new delinquency cases. Except for one year (1911) there appears to have been a rise in the total number of out-of-court settlements each year (although a lack of data between 1912 and 1916 makes it impossible to be sure). Whether the probation staff actually succeeded in settling cases out of court that might previously have been justiciable is, however, another matter and one which, as the evidence will suggest shortly, is doubtful.

19. This proportion would increase to approximately one out of four if I were to include several cases in which probation officers, based on their intimate knowledge of local communities, initiated proceedings on their own. I would like to thank Sheldon Messinger for pointing out to me how radically different referral patterns are today, with the great majority of referrals coming from police. Unfortunately, it is difficult to trace the sources of referral in cases that actually came to court.

20. My evidence tends to conform to the hypothesis advanced by J. Lawrence Schultz that "immigrants, racial minorities and poor parents may have welcomed an expansion of state police power as a means of controlling ungovernable children, relieving the burdens of under-financed child-rearing and restoring order to turbulent neighborhoods. In fact, parents often availed themselves of the courts' broad jurisdiction to discipline or rid themselves of their own children." J. Lawrence Schultz, review of *The Child Savers*, by Anthony Platt, in *Yale Law Journal* 82 (January 1973): 633. It should be pointed out, however, that this practice was not unique to the Progressive era, although the juvenile court facilitated the procedure. Poor parents had long been sending their children to reformatories on the charge of "incorrigibility."

21. In this and the following chapter, I have changed the names of all parents, children, neighbors, etc., although I have attempted to retain their particular ethnic content. Thus a Mr. Simon might become a Mr. Epstein but not a Mr. Rodriguez.

22. It remains unclear to me whether this use of detention and probation was recorded on official records. If not, the statistical data on both could be seriously misleading.

23. This assumes, of course, that a random distribution of cases was recorded in the particular log book which has survived. I believe, though, that this was so, and that probation officers were more concerned about the harmful effects of court appearances on girls than on boys.

24. The treatment of girls by probation officers was perplexing indeed. Before discovering the log book, I had only the information in trial transcripts to go on, and based on that information I had concluded that probation officers generally responded hysterically to the sexual experiences of young girls. These same officers, however, seemed to behave differently in cases not brought to court, even when the ostensible offenses were identical. The officers' subjective evaluation of the girls' "character," personal appearance, mannerisms, etc., much influenced the decision on whether to bring them to court (even more so than was the case with boys). Also, of course, the different responses in and out of court may reflect nothing more than the different types of documentary evidence available.

25. I shall have more to say about the juvenile court as an agent of surveillance and control in the epilogue.

26. Certainly there was nothing in the newspapers in the years 1905–7 to indicate a great increase, in absolute terms, of want or crime. Whether a notable demographic shift occurred is difficult to determine from federal census data. But it is clear that, despite continuing immigration to the city, the growth of the age-specific population was not as great as the growth of new intake. Given the extraordinarily vague definitions of delinquency that prevailed and the many different agencies through which children could come to the court's attention, mere statistical correlations between intake and age-specific population would contribute little to understanding the centrality of discretion in the court's operations.

27. This was the chief probation officer's own explanation for the court's increasing intake in the years after 1905. For example, in the unpublished Annual Report of 1917 he affirmed: "The increased number of cases in Juvenile Court does not argue that juvenile delinquency has increased, but on the contrary, that the activities of the different agencies for the correction of delinquents has increased, notably the Police Department, Detective Bureau, Sheriff's Office and the Probation Department." Whenever he requested new probation officers, it was not to cope with apparent recent increases in crime but to give officers more opportunities to "prevent" crime through early intervention.

28. So Judge Neelen, quoted in the unpublished Annual Report of 1911, reported: "The Probation Officers in making their visits and attending to their routine duties are always on the alert to any unusual complaints, statements, or occurrences. They feel it necessary to take note of everything, no matter how apparently trivial or unimportant it may be, as sometimes the slightest hint leads to developments of great importance. In this way they have, during the past three months, discovered and brought before the Juvenile Court a great number of children charged with immorality, as well as many cases of negligence and dependency where minor children are involved." And in the Annual Report of 1917 Zuerner commended his officers for a recent crackdown "in bringing to justice any adult persons who in any shape,

manner or form contribute to the delinquency of minors. The arrest and prosecution of such persons has, to a certain extent, lessened the opportunities for vice and curtailed the number of complaints from all over the County. This part of the work takes the officers, both men and women, into all kinds of disreputable resorts, saloons, dance halls, pool-rooms, bowling alleys, etc., both during the day and night." Clearly, then, the probation officers did not wait to have cases brought to their attention by established law enforcement agencies.

29. Thus Zuerner would consistently aver that sixty probationers were the maximum for effective treatment, and at the same time call for greater vigilance by probation officers to "delinquency-producing" conditions in previously unsupervised parts of the community. Plainly he wanted it both ways, whether he could have it or not.

30. Although it is clear that certain officers tended to receive special types of cases, this alone will not account for the wide disparities in individual caseloads among the paid staff.

31. There were, however, numerous instances of probationary periods as short as one month and as long as six years. In many instances it simply was impossible to determine, either from the yearly statistical data or the individual case reports, how long the probationary periods lasted.

32. A dearth of nineteenth-century data makes it impossible to say, however, whether this was a smaller percentage of committals per total youth prosecuted than was true before the court.

33. On this issue today, see Paul Lerman, *Community Treatment and Social Control* (Chicago: University of Chicago Press, 1975).

Chapter 9

1. Because the majority of transcripts dealt with cases in which children were removed from their homes, either temporarily or permanently, there remains some doubt as to the typicality of the cases. Did the court and clientele behave in different ways in the great majority of cases where probation was the main remedy? I have tried to minimize the possibility of distortion by including testimony from seven cases which did *not* result in long-term removal of a child from his home. In my estimation, these cases did not reveal a qualitative difference in courtroom interactions or intake procedures. As we shall see, just because a child was sent to an institution did not mean that the circumstances of the case were so extreme as to invalidate the evidence for purposes of generalization. Finally, it is impossible to say why transcripts were included in some cases not leading to removal of a child and why they were not included in others. It is also unclear why some cases leading to committal did not include transcripts.

2. As in chapter eight, I have changed or not specified the names of all participants in court. I have also not given the exact number of each case, although I have included the approximate date. These were pre-

conditions for my using the court records.

3. I do not know the frequency of fines. But the presence of fines in Milwaukee never evoked constitutional challenge as it did in Michigan. See Robison v. Wayne Circuit Judges, 151 Michigan 315 (1908).

4. See Sanford Fox, "Juvenile Justice Reform: An Historical Perspective," *Stanford Law Review* 22 (June 1970): 1187–1239.

5. Since my sample included several dozen mothers' pension cases, in which attorneys were not allowed, the percentage of delinquency or neglect cases in which attorneys appeared was a little higher.

6. For obvious reasons it is difficult to write about this phenomenon dispassionately. My own point of view is well-expressed in William Ryan, *Blaming the Victim* (New York: Random House, 1972). Barbara Brenzel highlights the central role of parents in the committal process in the nineteenth century in "Lancaster Industrial School For Girls: A Social Portrait of a Nineteenth-Century Reform School for Girls," *Feminist Studies*, forthcoming.

7. Unfortunately, I cannot be more precise about the exact proportion because the records often fail to specify how a child was initially brought into court, e.g., a parent could swear out a complaint of "incorrigibility" after his child had already been arrested for an actual crime or a probation officer rather than a parent could charge a child with "incorrigibility."

8. On girls in court, see the brief commentary in appendix two, table 3. I am engaged on further research on this subject.

9. Boarders appear most often to have been relatives.

10. This is my reading of the law and likely legal strategies. In practice the issue arose very infrequently.

11. To say this is not to imply that the juvenile court movement would have succeeded in its rehabilitative goals with more or better staff members. It is simply to highlight what the evidence most clearly demonstrates. That I have serious reservations about the juvenile court movement and "progressive" correctional ideas in general will be obvious in the epilogue. For a modern perspective which most closely approximates my analysis of the past, see Robert Emerson, *Judging Delinquents* (Chicago: Aldine Publishing Co., 1969).

Epilogue

1. Bradford Peirce, *A Half-Century with Juvenile Delinquents* (New York: D. Appleton and Co., 1869), passim.

2. See especially Anthony Platt, *The Child Savers* (Chicago: University of Chicago Press, 1969), passim.

3. An excellent example is Edwin Schur, *Radical Non-Intervention* (Englewood Cliffs, N.J.: Prentice-Hall, 1973).

4. Justine Polier, "The Myth That Our Society is Child-Centered," *New York Times*, 25 January 1972.

5. A useful recent collection of contemporary opinion is Margaret

Rosenheim, ed., *Pursuing Justice for the Child* (Chicago: University of Chicago Press, 1976). See especially the penetrating discussion by Paul Nejelski, "Diversion: Unleashing the Hound of Heaven?" Pp. 94–118.

6. Paul Lerman, *Community Treatment and Social Control* (Chicago: University of Chicago Press, 1975), passim.

Bibliography

Books

Abbott, Lyman. *Christianity and Social Problems*. Boston: Houghton, Mifflin and Co., 1896.

Abell, Aaron. *The Urban Impact on American Protestantism, 1865–1900*. Cambridge: Harvard University Press, 1943.

Addams, Jane. *The Spirit of Youth and the City Streets*. New York: Macmillan Co., 1909.

———. *Twenty Years at Hull House*. New York: Macmillan Co., 1910.

Aikens, Andrew, and Proctor, Lewis. *Men of Progress*. Milwaukee: Evening Wisconsin Co., 1897.

Albion, Robert. *The Rise of New York Port*. New York: Charles Scribner's Sons, 1939.

Allen, Francis. *The Borderland of Criminal Justice*. Chicago: University of Chicago Press, 1964.

Allen, Joseph. *Westboro' State Reform School Reminiscences*. Boston: Lockwood, Brooks and Co., 1877.

Barnard, Henry. *Reformatory Education*. Hartford: F. C. Brownell, 1857.

———. *School Architecture*. New York: A. S. Barnes and Co., 1848.

Barnes, Harry. *The Evolution of Penology in Pennsylvania*. Indianapolis: Bobbs-Merrill Co., 1927.

Barrows, Samuel. *Children's Courts in the United States.* Washington: U.S. Government Printing Office, 1904.

Baylor, Ruth. *Elizabeth Palmer Peabody.* Philadelphia: University of Pennsylvania Press, 1965.

Bender, Thomas. *Toward an Urban Vision.* Lexington, Ky.: University Press of Kentucky, 1975.

Berger, Peter, and Luckmann, Thomas. *The Social Construction of Reality.* Garden City, N.Y.: Anchor Books, 1967.

Bernheimer, Charles, and Cohen, Jacob. *Boys' Clubs.* New York: Baker and Taylor Co., 1914.

Berryman, John. *History of the Bench and Bar of Wisconsin.* 2 vols. Chicago: H. C. Hooper, Jr., and Co., 1898.

Billington, Ray. *The Protestant Crusade, 1800–1860.* New York: Macmillan Co., 1938.

Blassingame, John. *The Slave Community.* New York: Oxford University Press, 1972.

Brace, Charles. *Address to the Theological Students of Harvard University.* Cambridge: n.p., 1881.

———. *The Best Method of Disposing of our Pauper and Vagrant Children.* New York: Wynkoop, Hallenbeck and Thomas, 1859.

———. *The Dangerous Classes of New York and Twenty Years' Work among Them.* New York: Wynkoop and Hallenbeck, 1872.

———. *Home Life in Germany.* New York: Charles Scribner, 1853.

———. *The Norse-Folk.* New York: Charles Scribner, 1857.

———. *Short Sermons to Newsboys.* New York: Charles Scribner, 1866.

Branch, E. Douglas. *The Sentimental Years.* New York: D. Appleton-Century Co., 1934.

Breckinridge, Sophonisba, and Abbott, Edith. *The Delinquent Child and the Home.* New York: Russell Sage, 1912.

Bremner, Robert. *From the Depths.* New York: New York University Press, 1956.

——— et al., eds. *Children and Youth in America.* 3 vols. Cambridge: Harvard University Press, 1970–74.

Bruce, William. *History of Milwaukee, City and County.* Chicago: S. J. Clarke Publishing Co., 1922.

Bruno, Frank. *Trends in Social Work, 1874–1946.* New York: Columbia University Press, 1948.

Calhoun, Arthur. *A Social History of the American Family.*

3 vols. Cleveland: Arthur H. Clark Co., 1917–19.

Callahan, Raymond. *Education and the Cult of Efficiency.* Chicago: University of Chicago Press, 1962.

Carpenter, Joseph. *Life and Work of Mary Carpenter.* London: Macmillan and Co., 1879.

Carpenter, Mary. *Juvenile Delinquents, Their Condition and Treatment.* London: W. F. G. Cash, 1853.

———. *Reformatory Schools for the Children of the Perishing and Dangerous Classes, and for Juvenile Offenders.* London: C. Gilpin, 1851.

Chafe, William. *The American Woman.* New York: Oxford University Press, 1972.

Chevalier, Louis. *Laboring Classes and Dangerous Classes in Paris During the First Half of the Nineteenth Century.* New York: H. Fertig, 1973.

Chute, Charles, and Bell, Marjorie. *Crime, Courts, and Probation.* New York: Macmillan Co., 1956.

Clarke-Stewart, K. Alison. *Child Care in the Family.* Forthcoming.

Cloward, Richard, and Ohlin, Lloyd. *Delinquency and Opportunity.* New York: Free Press, 1960.

Coffey, W. A. *Inside Out, or An Interior View of the Newgate State Prison.* New York: Printed by the author, 1823.

Cohen, Sol. *Progressives and Urban School Reform.* New York: Bureau of Publications, Teachers College, 1964.

Cole, Larry. *Our Children's Keepers.* Greenwich: Fawcett Publications, 1974.

Collins, P. A. W. *Dickens and Crime.* New York: St. Martin's Press, 1962.

Corrections in the Wisconsin Tradition. Madison: State Department of Public Welfare, 1965.

Corwin, Edward. *The "Higher Law" Background of American Constitutional Law.* New York: Great Seal Books, 1955.

Cremin, Lawrence. *The Transformation of the School.* New York: Alfred A. Knopf, 1961.

———. *The Wonderful World of Ellwood Patterson Cubberley.* New York: Teachers College Press, 1965.

Cross, Barbara. *Horace Bushnell.* Chicago: University of Chicago Press, 1958.

Davies, John. *Phrenology.* New Haven: Yale University Press, 1955.

Davis, Allen. *American Heroine.* New York: Oxford University

Press, 1973.

Demos, John. *A Little Commonwealth.* New York: Oxford University Press, 1970.

DeVoe, Elijah. *The Refuge System; or, Prison Discipline Applied to Juvenile Delinquents.* New York: J. R. M'Gown, 1848.

Dewey, John. *Democracy and Education.* New York: Macmillan Co., 1916.

———. *The School and Society.* Chicago: University of Chicago Press, 1899.

Dreeben, Robert. *On What is Learned in School.* Reading, Mass.: Addison-Wesley Publishing Co., 1968.

Drost, Walter. *David Snedden.* Madison: University of Wisconsin Press, 1967.

Duffus, Robert. *Lillian Wald.* New York: Macmillan Co., 1939.

Eliot, Thomas. *The Juvenile Court and the Community.* New York: Macmillan Co., 1914.

Emerson, Robert. *Judging Delinquents.* Chicago: Aldine Publishing Co., 1969.

Ensign, Forest. *Compulsory School Attendance and Child Labor.* Iowa City: Athens Press, 1921.

Erikson, Kai. *Wayward Puritans.* New York: John Wiley and Sons, 1966.

Fein, Albert. *Frederic Law Olmstead and the American Environmental Tradition.* New York: George Braziller, 1972.

Fein, Greta, and Clarke-Stewart, K. Alison. *Day Care in Context.* New York: John Wiley and Sons, 1973.

Felt, Jeremy. *Hostages of Fortune.* Syracuse: Syracuse University Press, 1965.

Filene, Peter. *Him/Her/Self.* New York: Harcourt Brace Jovanovich, 1975.

Fink, Arthur. *Causes of Crime.* Philadelphia: University of Pennsylvania Press, 1938.

Flaherty, David. *Privacy in Colonial New England.* Charlottesville: University Press of Virginia, 1972.

Flexner, Bernard, and Baldwin, Roger. *Juvenile Courts and Probation.* New York: Century, 1912.

Folks, Homer. *The Care of Destitute, Neglected, and Delinquent Children.* New York: Macmillan Co., 1902.

Forbush, William. *The Boy Problem.* Boston: Pilgrim Press, 1902.

Forer, Lois. *"No One Will Lissen".* New York: Grosset and Dunlap, 1970.

Friedenberg, Edgar. *The Disposal of Liberty and Other Industrial Wastes.* New York: Doubleday and Co., 1975.

Friedman, Lawrence. *A History of American Law.* New York: Simon and Schuster, 1973.

Gay, Peter. *The Enlightenment.* 2 vols. New York: Alfred A. Knopf, 1966–69.

George, B. James. *Gault and the Juvenile Court Revolution.* Ann Arbor: Institute of Continuing Legal Education, 1968.

Glazer, Nathan, and Moynihan, Daniel. *Beyond the Melting Pot.* Cambridge: M.I.T. Press, 1963.

Goffman, Erving. *Asylums.* Garden City, N.Y.: Doubleday and Co., 1961.

Goldfarb, Ronald. *Jails, the Ultimate Ghetto.* Garden City, N.Y.: Anchor Press, 1975.

Goldmark, Pauline, ed. *West Side Studies.* New York: Survey Associates, 1914.

Goodsell, Willystine. *A History of the Family as a Social and Educational Institution.* New York: Macmillan Co., 1915.

Gottleib, David, ed. *Children's Liberation.* Englewood Cliffs, N.J.: Prentice-Hall, 1973.

Greer, Colin. *The Great School Legend.* New York: Basic Books, 1972.

Gregory, John, ed. *History of Milwaukee, Wisconsin.* Chicago: S. J. Clarke Publishing Co., 1931.

Griscom, John. *A Year in Europe.* 2 vols. New York: Collins and Jannay, 1824.

Griscom, John H. *Memoir of John Griscom.* New York: R. Carter Brothers, 1859.

Grob, Gerald. *The State and the Mentally Ill.* Chapel Hill: University of North Carolina Press, 1966.

Gumbert, Edgar, and Spring, Joel. *The Superschool and the Superstate.* New York: John Wiley and Sons, 1974.

Haber, Samuel. *Efficiency and Uplift.* Chicago: University of Chicago Press, 1964.

Haight, Gordon. *Mrs. Sigourney, the Sweet Singer of Hartford.* New Haven: Yale University Press, 1930.

Handlin, Oscar, and Handlin, Mary. *Commonwealth; A Study of the Role of Government in the American Economy.* New York: New York University Press, 1947.

Handy, Robert. *The Social Gospel in America, 1870–1920.* New York: Oxford University Press, 1966.

Hart, Hastings. *Preventive Treatment of Neglected Children.* New York: Russell Sage, 1910.

Hart, Nathaniel, comp. *Documents Relative to the House of Refuge.* New York: Mahlon Day, 1832.

Hartz, Louis. *Economic Policy and Democratic Thought.* Cambridge: Harvard University Press, 1948.

Haskins, George. *Law and Authority in Early Massachusetts.* New York: Macmillan Co., 1960.

Hawes, Joseph. *Children in Urban Society.* New York: Oxford University Press, 1971.

Hays, Samuel. *The Response to Industrialism.* Chicago: University of Chicago Press, 1957.

Higham, John. *Strangers in the Land.* New York: Atheneum, 1966.

Hiller, Francis. *Probation in Wisconsin.* New York: National Probation Association, 1926.

History of Education Quarterly. Vols. 14 (Spring 1974) and 15 (Spring 1975).

The History of Waukesha County, Wisconsin. Chicago: Western Historical Co., 1880.

Hofstadter, Richard. *The Age of Reform.* New York: Alfred A. Knopf, 1955.

———. *Anti-Intellectualism in American Life.* New York: Alfred A. Knopf, 1963.

Holl, Jack. *Juvenile Reform in the Progressive Era.* Ithaca: Cornell University Press, 1971.

Houghton, Walter. *The Victorian Frame of Mind, 1830–1870.* New Haven: Yale University Press, 1957.

Howard, Derek. *John Howard.* London: Christopher Johnson, 1958.

Howe, Samuel. *A Letter to J. H. Wilkins, H. B. Rogers, and F. B. Fay, Commissioners of Massachusetts for the State Reform School for Girls.* Boston: Ticknor and Fields, 1854.

Huggins, Nathan. *Protestants against Poverty.* Westport, Conn.: Greenwood Publishing Corp., 1971.

Hunt, Caroline. *The Life of Ellen H. Richards.* Boston: Whitcomb and Barrows, 1912.

Hunter, Robert. *Poverty.* New York: Harper and Row, 1965.

Hurst, J. Willard. *The Growth of American Law.* Boston: Little, Brown and Co., 1950.

———. *Law and the Conditions of Freedom in the Nineteenth-Century United States.* Madison: University of Wisconsin Press, 1956.

James, Howard. *Children in Trouble.* New York: Pocket Books, 1971.

James, Sydney. *A People among Peoples.* Cambridge: Harvard University Press, 1963.

Jones, Peter d'A. Introduction to *Poverty*, by Robert Hunter. New York: Harper and Row, 1965.

Kaestle, Carl. *The Evolution of an Urban School System.* Cambridge: Harvard University Press, 1973.

———, ed. *Joseph Lancaster and the Monitorial School Movement.* New York: Teachers College Press, 1973.

Kahn, Alfred. *A Court for Children.* New York: Columbia University Press, 1953.

Kanter, Rosabeth. *Commitment and Community.* Cambridge: Harvard University Press, 1972.

Karier, Clarence. *Shaping the American Educational State.* New York: Free Press, 1975.

——— et al. *Roots of Crisis.* Chicago: Rand McNally, 1973.

Katz, Michael. *Class, Bureaucracy, and Schools.* New York: Praeger Publishers, 1971.

———. *The Irony of Early School Reform.* Cambridge: Harvard University Press, 1968.

———. *School Reform: Past and Present.* Boston: Little, Brown and Co., 1971.

Kennedy, David. *Birth Control in America.* New Haven: Yale University Press, 1970.

Kiefer, Monica. *American Children through Their Books.* Philadelphia: University of Pennsylvania Press, 1948.

Kittrie, Nicholas. *The Right to be Different.* Baltimore: Johns Hopkins Press, 1971.

Knapp, Samuel, ed. *The Life of Thomas Eddy.* New York: Conner and Cooke, 1834.

Kozol, Jonathan. *Death at an Early Age.* Boston: Houghton Mifflin, 1967.

Kuhn, Anne. *The Mother's Role in Childhood Education.* New Haven: Yale University Press, 1947.

Kutler, Stanley. *Privilege and Creative Destruction.* Little, Brown and Co., 1971.

Lane, Roger. *Policing the City.* Cambridge: Harvard University Press, 1967.

Langsam, Miriam. *Children West.* Madison: State Historical Society of Wisconsin, 1964.

Larsen, Charles. *The Good Fight.* Chicago: Quadrangle Books, 1972.

Lasch, Christopher. *The New Radicalism in America, 1889–1963.* New York: Alfred A. Knopf, 1965.

———. *The World of Nations.* New York: Random House, 1973.

Lazerson, Marvin. *Origins of the Urban School.* Cambridge: Harvard University Press, 1971.

Lerman, Paul. *Community Treatment and Social Control.* Chicago: University of Chicago Press, 1975.

Levine, Murray, and Levine, Adeline. *A Social History of Helping Services*. New York: Appleton-Century-Crofts, 1970.

Lewis, W. David. *From Newgate to Dannemora*. Ithaca: Cornell University Press, 1965.

Lindsey, Ben, and O'Higgins, Harvey. *The Beast*. New York: Doubleday, Page, 1910.

Lockridge, Kenneth. *A New England Town*. New York: W. W. Norton & Co., 1970.

Lou, Herbert. *Juvenile Courts in the United States*. Chapel Hill: University of North Carolina Press, 1927.

Lubove, Roy. *The Professional Altruist*. Cambridge: Harvard University Press, 1965.

———. *The Progressives and the Slums*. Pittsburgh: University of Pittsburgh Press, 1963.

Lynn, Robert, and Wright, Elliot. *The Big Little School*. New York: Harper and Row, 1970.

Maestro, Marcello. *Cesare Beccaria and the Origins of Penal Reform*. Philadelphia: Temple University Press, 1973.

———. *Voltaire and Beccaria as Reformers of Criminal Law*. New York: Columbia University Press, 1942.

Mann, Arthur. *Yankee Reformers in the Urban Age*. Cambridge: Harvard University Press, 1954.

Mann, Horace. *Account of the Hamburgh Redemption Institute*. N.p.: 1843.

Mannheim, Hermann, ed. *Pioneers of Criminology*. Chicago: Quadrangle Books, 1960.

Marx, Leo. *The Machine in the Garden*. New York: Oxford University Press, 1964.

Matza, David. *Delinquency and Drift*. New York: John Wiley and Sons, 1964.

May, Henry. *Protestant Churches and Industrial America*. New York: Harper and Brothers, 1949.

McCadden, Joseph. *Education in Pennsylvania, 1801–1835*. Philadelphia: University of Pennsylvania Press, 1937.

McClintock, Jean, and McClintock, Robert. *Henry Barnard's School Architecture*. New York: Teachers College Press, 1970.

McCluskey, Neil, ed. *Catholic Education in America*. New York: Teachers College Press, 1964.

McKelvey, Blake. *American Prisons*. Chicago: University of Chicago Press, 1936.

Mennel, Robert. *Thorns and Thistles*. Hanover, N.H.: University Press of New England, 1973.

Merton, Robert. "The Social-Cultural Environment and Anomie." In *New Perspectives for Research on Juvenile Delinquency*, pp. 24–32. Edited by Helen Witmer and Ruth Kotinsky. Washington: U.S. Department of Health, Education, and Welfare, 1956.

Messerli, Jonathan. *Horace Mann*. New York: Alfred A. Knopf, 1973.

Meyers, Marvin. *The Jacksonian Persuasion*. Stanford: Stanford University Press, 1957.

Miller, Kenneth. *Immigrant Life in New York City*. New York: Macmillan Co., 1949.

Mohl, Raymond. *Poverty in New York, 1783–1825*. New York: Oxford University Press, 1971.

Morgan, Edmund. *The Puritan Family*. Rev. ed. New York: Harper and Row, 1966.

Morris, Joe. *First Offender*. New York: Funk and Wagnalls, 1970.

Moynihan, Daniel. *Maximum Feasible Misunderstanding*. New York: Free Press, 1969.

Murphy, Patrick. *Our Kindly Parent . . . The State*. New York: Viking Press, 1974.

O'Neill, William. *Divorce in the Progressive Era*. New Haven: Yale University Press, 1967.

———. *The Woman Movement*. Chicago: Quadrangle Books, 1969.

Owen, David. *English Philanthropy, 1660–1960*. Cambridge: Harvard University Press, 1964.

Parsons, Elsie. *The Family*. New York: G. P. Putnam's Sons, 1912.

Pattee, Fred. *The Feminine Fifties*. New York: D. Appleton-Century Co., 1940.

Peirce, Bradford. *A Half-Century with Juvenile Delinquents*. New York: D. Appleton and Co., 1869.

Perkinson, Henry. *The Imperfect Panacea*. New York: Random House, 1968.

Phillipson, Coleman. *Three Criminal Law Reformers: Beccaria, Bentham, Romilly*. London: J. M. Dent and Sons, Ltd., 1923.

Pickens, Donald. *Eugenics and the Progressive Era*. Nashville: Vanderbilt University Press, 1968.

Pickett, Robert. *House of Refuge*. Syracuse: Syracuse University Press, 1969.

Piven, Frances, and Cloward, Richard. *Regulating the Poor*. New York: Random House, 1971.

Platt, Anthony. *The Child Savers*. Chicago: University of Chicago Press, 1969.

———. "The Triumph of Benevolence: The Origins of the Juvenile Justice System in America." In *Criminal Justice in America*, pp. 356–89. Edited by Richard Quinney. Boston: Little, Brown and Co., 1974.

Polsky, Howard. *Cottage Six.* New York: Russell Sage, 1962.

Pomerantz, Sidney. *New York, an American City, 1783–1803.* New York: Columbia University Press, 1938.

The President's Commission on Law Enforcement and Administration of Justice. *Juvenile Delinquency and Youth Crime.* Washington: U.S. Government Printing Office, 1967.

Prize Essays on Juvenile Delinquency. Philadelphia: Edward C. and John Biddle, 1855.

Radzinowicz, Leon. *A History of English Criminal Law and its Administration from 1750.* 4 vols. London: Stevens and Sons, Ltd., 1948–68.

———. *Ideology and Crime.* New York: Columbia University Press, 1966.

Ravitch, Diane. *The Great School Wars.* New York: Basic Books, 1974.

Rice, Edwin. *The Sunday School Movement, 1780–1917, and the American Sunday School Union, 1817–1917.* Philadelphia: American Sunday School Union, 1917.

Richards, Ellen. *Euthenics, the Science of Controllable Environment.* Boston: Whitcomb and Barrows, 1912.

Richards, Laura, ed. *Letters and Journals of Samuel Gridley Howe.* 2 vols. Boston: D. Estes and Co., 1909.

Richardson, James. *The New York Police.* New York: Oxford University Press, 1970.

Richette, Lisa. *The Throwaway Children.* New York: Dell Publishing Co., 1969.

Riegel, Robert. *American Women.* Rutherford, N.J.: Fairleigh Dickinson University Press, 1970.

Rosenberg, Carroll. *Religion and the Rise of the American City.* Ithaca: Cornell University Press, 1971.

Rosenheim, Margaret. "Detention Facilities and Temporary Shelters." In *Child Caring*, pp. 253–99. Edited by Donnell Pappenfort, Dee Kilpatrick, and Robert Roberts. Chicago: Aldine Publishing Co., 1973.

———, ed. *Justice for the Child.* New York: Macmillan Co., 1962.

———, ed. *Pursuing Justice for the Child.* Chicago: University of Chicago Press, 1976.

Ross, Dorothy. *G. Stanley Hall.* Chicago: University of Chicago

Press, 1972.

Ross, Edward. *Social Control.* New York: Macmillan Co., 1901.

Rothman, David. *The Discovery of the Asylum.* Boston: Little, Brown and Co., 1971.

Ryan, William. *Blaming the Victim.* New York: Random House, 1972.

Sanborn, Franklin. *Dr. S. G. Howe, the Philanthropist.* New York: Funk and Wagnalls, 1891.

Sanders, Wiley, ed. *Juvenile Offenders for a Thousand Years.* Chapel Hill: University of North Carolina Press, 1970.

Schoff, Hannah. *The Wayward Child.* Indianapolis: Bobbs-Merrill Co., 1915.

Schrag, Peter, and Divoky, Diane. *The Myth of the Hyperactive Child and Other Means of Child Control.* New York: Pantheon Books, 1975.

Schultz, Stanley. *The Culture Factory.* New York: Oxford University Press, 1973.

Schur, Edwin. *Radical Non-Intervention.* Englewood Cliffs, N.J.: Prentice-Hall, 1973.

Schwartz, Harold. *Samuel Gridley Howe.* Cambridge: Harvard University Press, 1956.

Sedgwick, Catherine. *Memoir of Joseph Curtis, A Model Man.* New York: Harper and Brothers, 1858.

Silberman, Charles. *Crisis in the Classroom.* New York: Random House, 1970.

Sklar, Kathryn. *Catharine Beecher.* New Haven: Yale University Press, 1973.

Smith, Timothy. *Revivalism and Social Reform.* New York: Abingdon Press, 1957.

Sommers, Charles. *Memoir of the Rev. John Stanford, D.D.* New York: Swords, Stanford and Co., 1835.

Spargo, John. *The Bitter Cry of the Children.* New York: Macmillan, 1906.

Spring, Joel. *Education and the Rise of the Corporate State.* Boston: Beacon Press, 1972.

Stapleton, William, and Teitelbaum, Lee. *In Defense of Youth.* New York: Russell Sage, 1972.

State Board of Control of Wisconsin. *Aid to Dependent Children in Wisconsin, 1913–33.* Madison: n.p., 1934.

Steinfels, Margaret. *Who's Minding the Children?* New York: Simon and Schuster, 1973.

Still, Bayrd. *Milwaukee.* Madison: State Historical Society of Wisconsin, 1948.

Studt, Elliot; Messinger, Sheldon; and Wilson, Thomas. *C-Unit.*

New York: Russell Sage, 1968.

Sykes, Gresham. *The Society of Captives*. Princeton: Princeton University Press, 1958.

Taylor, William. *Cavalier and Yankee*. New York: George Braziller, 1961.

Teeters, Negley. *The Cradle of the Penitentiary*. Philadelphia: Pennsylvania Prison Society, 1955.

Thelen, David. *The New Citizenship*. Columbia, Mo.: University of Missouri Press, 1972.

Thernstrom, Stephan. *The Other Bostonians*. Cambridge: Harvard University Press, 1973.

Thistlethwaite, Frank. *America and the Atlantic Community*. New York: Harper and Row, 1963.

Timasheff, Nicholas. *One Hundred Years of Probation, 1841–1941*. New York: Fordham University Press, 1941.

Titsworth, Judson. *The Moral Evolution*. Milwaukee: Press of Swain and Tate Co., 1899.

Tobias, J. J. *Urban Crime in Victorian England*. New York: Schocken Books, 1972.

Trattner, Walter. *Crusade for the Children*. Chicago: Quadrangle Books, 1970.

———. *Homer Folks*. New York: Columbia University Press, 1968.

Travis, Thomas. *The Young Malefactor*. New York: Thomas Y. Crowell, 1908.

Tyack, David. *The One Best System*. Cambridge: Harvard University Press, 1974.

Tyler, Alice. *Freedom's Ferment*. Minneapolis: University of Minnesota Press, 1944.

Vanderbilt, John, Jr. *An Address Delivered in the New York Free School ... on the Introduction of Fifty Orphan and Helpless Children, Belonging to the Masonic Fraternity*. New York: Southwick and Pelsue, 1810.

Veysey, Laurence. *The Emergence of the American University*. Chicago: University of Chicago Press, 1965.

Wade, Richard. *The Urban Frontier*. Cambridge: Harvard University Press, 1959.

Warner, Sam. *The Private City*. Philadelphia: University of Pennsylvania Press, 1968.

Watrous, Jerome, ed. *Memoirs of Milwaukee County*. Madison: Western Historical Association, 1909.

Weinberg, Julius. *Edward Alsworth Ross and the Sociology of Progressivism*. Madison: State Historical Society of Wisconsin.

White, Morton, and White, Lucretia. *The Intellectual Versus the City*. Cambridge: Harvard University Press, 1962.

Wiebe, Robert. *The Search for Order*. New York: Hill and Wang, 1967.

Wines, Frederick. *The State of Prisons and of Child-Saving Institutions in the Civilized World*. Cambridge, Mass.: J. Wilson and Son, 1880.

Wisconsin Women's Suffrage Association. *Wisconsin Legislators and the Home*. Madison: n.p., 1914.

Wishy, Bernard. *The Child and the Republic*. Philadelphia: University of Pennsylvania Press, 1968.

Wood, Stephen. *Constitutional Politics in the Progressive Era*. Chicago: University of Chicago Press, 1971.

Zuckerman, Michael. *Peaceable Kingdoms*. New York: Alfred A. Knopf, 1970.

Articles

"A New Piece of Social Machinery." *Charities* 13 (7 January 1905): 323–24.

Almy, Frederic. "Juvenile Courts in Buffalo." *Annals of the American Academy of Political and Social Science* 20 (July 1902): 283–84.

Baker, Herbert. "The Court and the Delinquent Child." *American Journal of Sociology* 26 (September 1920): 176–86.

Banner, Lois. "Religious Benevolence as Social Control: A Critique of an Interpretation." *Journal of American History* 60 (June 1973): 23–41.

Barrows, Samuel. "The Delinquent." *Charities and the Commons* 21 (16 January 1909): 690–91.

Beitler, Judge Abraham. "The Juvenile Court in Philadelphia." *Annals of the American Academy of Political and Social Science* 20 (July 1902): 271–76.

Belden, Evelina. "The Boys' Court of Chicago: A Record of Six Months' Work." *American Journal of Sociology* 20 (May 1915): 731–44.

Björkman, Frances. "The Children's Court in American City Life." *Review of Reviews* 33 (March 1906): 305–11.

Brenzel, Barbara. "Lancaster Industrial School for Girls: A Social Portrait of a Nineteenth-Century Reform School for Girls." *Feminist Studies*, in press.

Chute, Charles. "The Juvenile Court in Retrospect." *Federal Probation* 13 (September 1949): 3–8.

———. "Juvenile Probation." *Annals of the American Academy*

of Political and Social Science 105 (January 1923): 223–28.

Cogan, Neil. "Juvenile Law, Before and After the Entrance of 'Parens Patriae.'" *South Carolina Law Review* 22 (Spring 1970): 147–81.

Collins, James. "The Juvenile Court Movement in Indiana." *Indiana Magazine of History* 28 (March 1932): 1–8.

Ehrenreich, Barbara, and English, Deidre. "The Manufacture of Housework." *Socialist Revolution* 5 (October–December 1975): 5–40.

Eliot, Charlotte. "Before and After in St. Louis." *Charities* 11 (7 November 1903): 430–32.

Flexner, Bernard. "The Juvenile Court as a Social Institution." *Survey* 23 (5 February 1910): 607–38.

———. "The Juvenile Court—Its Legal Aspects." *Annals of the American Academy of Political and Social Science* 36 (July 1910): 49–56.

Flexner, Bernard, and Oppenheimer, Reuben. "The Legal Aspect of the Juvenile Court." *American Law Review* 57 (January 1923): 65–96.

Foster, Charles. "The Urban Missionary Movement, 1814–1837." *Pennsylvania Magazine of History and Biography* 75 (January 1951): 47–65.

Fox, Sanford. "Juvenile Justice Reform: An Historical Perspective." *Stanford Law Review* 22 (June 1970): 1187–1239.

Franklin, Sara. "A Workshop of a Probation Officer." *Charities* 11 (7 November 1903): 414–16.

Friday, Lucy. "The Work of the Probation Officer among Children." *Charities* 13 (7 January 1905): 357–59.

Furfey, Paul. "The Juvenile Court Movement." *Thought* 6 (September 1931): 207–27.

Gardner, George. "The Institution as Therapist." *The Child* 16 (January 1952): 70–72.

Haniphy, Joseph. "Juvenile Courts." *Educational Review* 49 (May 1915): 489–502.

Harman, Ruth, and Lekachman, Charlotte. "The 'Jacobs' House." *Wisconsin Magazine of History* 16 (March 1933): 252–84.

Hays, Samuel. "The Politics of Reform in Municipal Government in the Progressive Era." *Pacific Northwest Quarterly* 55 (October 1964): 157–69.

Henderson, Charles. "Juvenile Courts." *Charities* 13 (7 January 1905): 340–43.

Heusiler, Charles. "Probation Work in Children's Courts." *Charities* 11 (7 November 1903): 399–401.

Horwitz, Morton. "The Emergence of an Instrumental Conception of American Law, 1780–1820." *Perspectives in American History* 5 (1971): 287–328.

Hurd, Harvey. "Juvenile Court Law." *Charities* 13 (7 January 1905): 327–28.

Hurley, T. D. "Development of the Juvenile Court Idea." *Charities* 11 (7 November 1903): 423–25.

Jeffrey, Kirk. "The Family as Utopian Retreat from the City." *Soundings* 55 (Spring 1972): 21–41.

Kelsey, C. "The Juvenile Court of Chicago and its Work." *Annals of the American Academy of Political and Social Science* 17 (March 1901): 298–304.

Kingsdale, Jom. "The 'Poor Man's Club': Social Functions of the Urban Working Class Saloon." *American Quarterly* 25 (October 1973): 269–90.

Kusmer, Kenneth. "The Function of Organized Charity in the Progressive Era: Chicago as a Case Study." *Journal of American History* 60 (December 1973): 657–78.

Lathrop, Julia. "The Development of the Probation System in a Large City." *Charities* 13 (7 January 1905): 344–49.

Lee, Joseph. "The Integrity of the Family as a Vital Issue." *Survey* 23 (4 December 1909): 305–13.

Leff, Mark. "Consensus for Reform: The Mothers'-Pension Campaign in the Progressive Era." *Social Service Review* 47 (September 1973): 397–417.

Lenroot, Katharine. "The Evolution of the Juvenile Court." *Annals of the American Academy of Political and Social Science* 105 (January 1923): 223–28.

Liazos, Alexander. "Class Oppression: The Functions of Juvenile Justice." *The Insurgent Sociologist* 1 (Fall 1974): 2–24.

Lindsey, Ben. "The Boy and the Court." *Charities* 13 (7 January 1905): 350–57.

———. "My Lesson From the Juvenile Court." *Survey* 23 (February 1910): 652–56.

———. "Love and the Criminal Law." *Journal of Education* 70 (2 and 16 September, 2 October 1909): 203–4, 258–59, 344, respectively.

———. "The New Juvenile Court of Denver." *Charities and the Commons* 18 (3 August 1907): 469–70.

———. "Present Outlook for Juvenile Court and Probation." *Child-Welfare Magazine* 4 (December 1909): 101–4.

———. "The Public School and Morality." *Journal of Education* 70 (August 1909): 150–51.

———. "Saving the Citizenship of Tomorrow." *Charities and the Commons* 15 (March 1906): 757–58.

———. "Some Experiences in the Juvenile Court of Denver."

Charities 11 (7 November 1903): 403–13.

Lindsey, Edward. "The Juvenile Court from the Lawyer's Stand-point." *Annals of the American Academy of Political and Social Science* 52 (March 1914): 140–48.

Mack, Julian. "The Juvenile Court." *Harvard Law Review* 23 (December 1909): 104–22.

Matza, David. "Subterranean Traditions of Youth." *Annals of the American Academy of Political and Social Science* 338 (1961): 102–18.

May, Margaret. "Innocence and Experience: The Evolution of the Concept of Juvenile Delinquency in the Mid-Nineteenth Century." *Victorian Studies* 17 (September 1973): 7–29.

Mayer, Julius. "The Child of the Large City." *Charities* 11 (7 November 1903): 417–23.

Maynard, Joyce. "The Monster Children." *Newsweek*, 26 July 1976.

Melder, Keith. "Ladies Bountiful: Organized Women's Benevolence in Early Nineteenth-Century America." *New York History* 68 (July 1967): 231–54.

Ohlin, Lloyd, Coates, Robert, and Miller, Alden. "Radical Correctional Reform: A Case Study of the Massachusetts Youth Correctional System." *Harvard Educational Review* 44 (February 1974): 74–111.

Polier, Justine. "The Myth That Our Society is Child-Centered." *New York Times*, 25 January 1972.

Rainwater, Lee. "The Revolt of the Dirty-Workers." *Trans-action* 5 (November 1967): 2, 64.

Reeder, R. R. "To Country and Cottage." *Charities* 13 (7 January 1905): 364–67.

Rendleman, Douglas. "Parens Patriae: From Chancery to the Juvenile Court." *South Carolina Law Review* 23 (Spring 1971): 205–59.

Renn, Donna. "The Right to Treatment and the Juvenile." *Crime and Delinquency* 19 (October 1973): 477–84.

Schlossman, Steven. "Before Home Start: Notes toward a History of Parent Education in America, 1879–1929." *The Harvard Educational Review* 46 (August 1976): 436–37.

———. "The 'Culture of Poverty' in Ante-Bellum Social Thought." *Science and Society* 38 (Summer 1974): 150–66.

———. "G. Stanley Hall and the Boys' Club: Conservative Applications of Recapitulation Theory." *Journal of the History of the Behavioral Sciences* 9 (April 1973): 140–47.

———. "Traditionalism and Revisionism in Juvenile Correctional History." *Reviews in American History* 2 (March 1974): 59–65.

Schlossman, Steven, and Cohen, Ronald. "The Music Man in Gary: Willis Brown and Child Saving in the Progressive Era." *Societas,* in press.

Schoff, Hannah. "Pennsylvania's Unfortunate Children." *Charities* 11 (7 November 1903): 425–28.

Schultz, J. Lawrence. "The Cycle of Juvenile Court History." *Crime and Delinquency* 19 (October 1973): 451–76.

———. Review of *The Child Savers,* by Anthony Platt. *Yale Law Journal* 82 (January 1973): 629–38.

Shireman, Charles. "How Can the Correctional School Correct?" *Crime and Delinquency* 6 (July 1960): 267–74.

Spring, Joel. "Mass Culture and School Sports." *History of Education Quarterly* 14 (Winter 1974): 483–500.

Strickland, Charles. "A Transcendentalist Father: The Child-Rearing Practices of Bronson Alcott." *Perspectives in American History* 3 (1969): 5–76.

Teeters, Negley. "The Early Days of the Philadelphia House of Refuge." *Pennsylvania History* 27 (April 1960): 165–87.

Thomas, John. "Romantic Reform in America, 1815–1865." *American Quarterly* 17 (Winter 1965): 656–82.

Vecoli, Rudolph. "Sterilization: A Progressive Measure?" *Wisconsin Magazine of History* 48 (Spring 1960): 190–203.

Waite, Edward. "The Outlook for the Juvenile Court." *Annals of the American Academy of Political and Social Science* 105 (January 1923): 229–42.

Weigley, Emma. "It Might Have Been Euthenics: The Lake Placid Conference and the Home Economics Movement." *American Quarterly* 26 (March 1974): 79–96.

Williamson, Emily. "Probation and Juvenile Courts." *Annals of the American Academy of Political and Social Science* 20 (July 1902): 259–67.

Wohl, R. Richard. "The 'Country Boy' Myth and its Place in American Urban Culture: The Nineteenth-Century Contribution." *Perspectives in American History* 3 (1969): 77–158.

Wolkin, Robert. "The Economic Side of Parental Responsibility." *Charities* 13 (7 January 1905): 324–25.

Proceedings and Reports

Bainbridge, Mrs. Lucy. "Mothers of the Submerged World—Day Nurseries." The National Congress of Mothers. *The Work and Words of the National Congress of Mothers.* New York: D. Appleton and Co., 1897, pp. 47–54.

Birney, Mrs. Theodore. "Address of Welcome." The National Congress of Mothers. *The Work and Words of the National Congress of Mothers*. New York: D. Appleton and Co., 1897, pp. 6–10.

Boston Common Council. *Report of a Committee Appointed to Investigate Alleged Abuses at the House of Reformation and House of Correction*. Boston: City Printer, 1864.

Charles, H. W. "The Problem of the Reform School." *Proceedings of the Child Conference for Research and Welfare*. New York: G. E. Stechert and Co., 1910, pp. 84–93.

Commissioners Appointed to Locate and Erect a State Reform School for Juvenile Delinquents [name varies]. *Annual Reports*, 1857 through 1860. Madison: State Printer.

Commissioners for Locating and Building House of Reformation for Juvenile and Female Offenders against the Laws." *First Annual Report*. Manchester, N.H.: State Printer, 1856.

Dickinson, Mrs. Mary. "Response to Address of Welcome." The National Congress of Mothers. *The Work and Words of the National Congress of Mothers*. New York: D. Appleton and Co., 1897, pp. 11–20.

Drake, L. D. "Do Reform Schools Reform?" National Conference of Charities and Correction. *Proceedings*. Boston: George H. Ellis, 1897, pp. 125–27.

Elmore, Andrew. "Report of the Committee on Reformatories and Houses of Refuge." National Conference of Charities and Correction. *Proceedings*. Boston: George H. Ellis, 1885, pp. 84–86.

Federated Jewish Charities of Milwaukee. *Annual Reports*, 1905, 1907. Milwaukee: n.p.

Flexner, Bernard. "A Decade of the Juvenile Court." National Conference of Charities and Correction. *Proceedings*. Fort Wayne, Ind.: The Archer Printing Co., 1910, pp. 105–16.

Folks, Homer. "The Care of Delinquent Children." National Conference of Charities and Correction. *Proceedings*. Boston: George H. Ellis, 1891, pp. 136–44.

———. "The Probation System; Its Value and Limitations." *Proceedings of the Child Conference for Research and Welfare*. New York: G. E. Stechert and Co., 1910, pp. 224–32.

Hart, Hastings. "Advantages and Disadvantages of the Placing-Out System." National Congress of Mothers. *Report*. National Congress of Mothers, 1905, pp. 256–63.

Henderson, Charles. "Theory and Practice of the Juvenile Court." National Conference of Charities and Correction. *Proceedings*. Fred J. Heer, 1904, pp. 358–69.

Hurley, Timothy. "Juvenile Probation." National Conference of

Charities and Correction. *Proceedings.* Indianapolis: William B. Burford, 1907, pp. 225–32.

Lindsey, Ben. "The Child and the Community." National Education Association. *Addresses and Proceedings.* Winona, Minn.: National Education Association, 1909, pp. 737–43.

———. "Childhood and Morality." National Education Association. *Addresses and Proceedings.* Winona, Minn.: National Education Association, 1909, pp. 146–57.

———. "The Nation's Boy Problem." National Congress of Mothers. *Report.* National Congress of Mothers, 1904, pp. 21–26.

———. "The Reformation of Juvenile Delinquents through the Juvenile Court." National Conference of Charities and Correction. *Proceedings.* Fred J. Heer, 1903, pp. 206–29.

Mack, Julian. "Juvenile Courts as Part of the School System of the Country." National Conference of Charities and Correction. *Proceedings.* Fort Wayne, Ind.: Fort Wayne Printing Co., 1908, pp. 369–83.

———. "The Juvenile Court; The Judge and the Probation Officer." National Conference of Charities and Correction. *Proceedings.* Fred J. Heer, 1906, pp. 123–31.

Managers and Superintendents of Houses of Refuge and Schools of Reform in the United States. *Proceedings of the First Convention.* New York: Wynkoop, Hallenbeck and Thomas, 1857.

Managers of the State Reform School [name varies]. *Annual Reports,* 1860 through 1920. Madison: State Printer.

Massachusetts Board of State Charities. *Annual Reports,* 1865, 1866. Boston: State Printer.

Miller, Mrs. A. Jennesse. "Mother's Relation to the Sound Physical Development of Her Child." The National Congress of Mothers. *The Work and Words of the National Congress of Mothers.* New York: D. Appleton and Co., 1897, pp. 117–22.

Milwaukee Associated Charities. *Annual Reports,* 1894 through 1919. Milwaukee: n.p.

Milwaukee Boys' Busy Life Club. *Annual Reports,* 1899 through 1910. Milwaukee: n.p.

Milwaukee-Downer College. *Catalogues,* 1890 through 1910. Milwaukee: n.p.

Milwaukee Mission Kindergarten Association. *Annual Reports,* 1892, 1907. Milwaukee: n.p.

Milwaukee Social Economics Club. *Minutes,* 1893 through 1910. Milwaukee: n.p.

Newton, Miss Frances. "The Mother's Greatest Needs." The National Congress of Mothers. *The Work and Words of the National Congress of Mothers.* New York: D. Appleton and Co., 1897, pp. 148–54.

New York Children's Aid Society. *Fourth Annual Report.* New York: John P. Prall, 1857.

New York Public School Society. *An Address of the Trustees of the Public School Society . . . Respecting the Extension of their Public Schools.* New York: J. Seymour, 1828.

New York Society for the Prevention of Pauperism. *Report on the Penitentiary System.* New York: Mahlon Day, 1822.

New York Sunday School Union. *First Annual Report.* New York: Printed by the Union, 1817.

Ramsey, Mrs. Anna. "Juvenile Court and Probation Work." National Congress of Mothers. *Report.* n.p.: National Congress of Mothers, 1905, pp. 28–38.

"Reminiscences of Andrew E. Elmore." Wisconsin State Historical Society. *Proceedings.* Madison: State Historical Society of Wisconsin, 1910, pp. 190–204.

Report of the Commissioners on the State Reform School to His Excellency the Governor of the State of New Hampshire. Manchester: State Printer, 1852.

Rogers, Mrs. Helen. "The Probation System of the Juvenile Court of Indianapolis." National Conference of Charities and Correction. *Proceedings.* Fred J. Heer, 1904, pp. 369–79.

Stubbs, Judge George. "The Mission of the Juvenile Court." National Conference of Charities and Correction. *Proceedings.* Fred J. Heer, 1904, pp. 350–57.

Thurston, Henry. "Some Phases of the Probation Work of the Juvenile Court." National Conference of Charities and Correction. *Proceedings.* Fred J. Heer, 1905, pp. 177–85.

Trustees of the State Industrial School for Girls at Lancaster. *First Annual Report.* Boston: State Printers, 1857.

Wisconsin Branch, American Institute of Criminal Law and Criminology. *Proceedings of the Conference on Criminal Law and Criminology.* Madison: State Printer, 1909.

Wisconsin State Conference of Charities and Correction. *Annual Proceedings,* 1888, 1893, 1894, 1897, 1911–20. Madison: State Printer.

Woman's Christian Friendly Society. *Annual Reports,* 1890, 1893. Milwaukee: n.p.

Woman's Club of Wisconsin. *Annual Reports,* 1884, 1887, 1903. Milwaukee: n.p.

Young Women's Christian Association. *Annual Reports,* 1888, 1895. Milwaukee, n.p.

Dissertations and Theses

Baghdadi, Mania. "Protestants, Poverty and Urban Growth: A Study of the Organization of Charity in Boston and New York, 1820–1865." Ph.D. dissertation, Brown University, 1975.

Berthrong, Donald. "Social Legislation in Wisconsin, 1836–1900." Ph.D. dissertation, University of Wisconsin, 1951.

Brownsword, Alan. "Educational Ideas in Early Wisconsin, 1849–1870." M.A. thesis, University of Wisconsin, 1958.

Buroker, Robert. "From Voluntary Association to Welfare State: Social Welfare Reform in Illinois, 1890–1920." Ph.D. dissertation, University of Chicago, 1973.

Currie, Elliot. "Managing the Minds of Men: The Reformatory Movement, 1865–1920." Ph.D. dissertation, University of California at Berkeley, 1973.

Curtis, George. "The Juvenile Court Movement in Virginia." Ph.D. dissertation, University of Virginia, 1973.

Cutler, William. "Philosophy, Philanthropy, and Public Education: A Social History of the New York Public School Society, 1805–1853." Ph.D. dissertation, Cornell University, 1960.

Duffy, Julia. "The Proper Objects of a Gratuitous Education." Ph.D. dissertation, Teachers College, Columbia University, 1968.

Ekirch, Arthur, Jr. "Thomas Eddy: His Ideas and Interests." M.A. thesis, Columbia University, 1938.

Finfer, Lawrence. "Leisure as Social Work in the Urban Community: The Progressive Recreation Movement, 1890–1920." Ph.D. dissertation, Michigan State University, 1974.

Finkelstein, Barbara. "Governing the Young: Teacher Behavior in American Primary Schools, 1820–1880; A Documentary History." Ed.D. dissertation, Teachers College, Columbia University, 1970.

Fishman, Eric. "The Juvenile Court Movement, 1899–1921." M.A. thesis, Columbia University, 1972.

Font, John. "Protestant Christian Socialism in Germany, 1848–1896; Wichern, Stoeker, Naumann: The Search for a New Social Ethic." Ph.D. dissertation, University of Minnesota, 1969.

Hammack, David. "The Centralization of New York City's Public School System, 1896: A Social Analysis of a Decision." M.A. thesis, Columbia University, 1969.

Hartmann, Heidi. "Capitalism and Women's Work in the Home, 1900–1930." Ph.D. dissertation, Yale University, 1974.

Houston, Susan. "The Impetus to Reform: Urban Crime,

Poverty and Ignorance in Ontario, 1850–1875." Ph.D. dissertation, University of Toronto, 1974.

Huber, Frances. "The Progressive Career of Ben B. Lindsey, 1900–1920." Ph.D. dissertation, University of Michigan, 1963.

Knapp, Hugh. "The Social Gospel in Wisconsin, 1890–1912." M.A. thesis, University of Wisconsin, 1968.

Langsam, Miriam. "The Nineteenth Century Wisconsin Criminal: Ideologies and Institutions." Ph.D. dissertation, University of Wisconsin, 1967.

May, Elaine. "The Pursuit of Domestic Perfection: Marriage and Divorce in Los Angeles, 1890–1920." Ph.D. dissertation, University of California at Los Angeles, 1975.

McNamara, Salle. "The Record Re-Examined: The Stalwarts, the Progressives, Education, and Public Welfare in Wisconsin." M.A. thesis, University of Wisconsin, 1965.

Messinger, Sheldon. "Strategies of Control." Ph.D. dissertation, University of California at Berkeley, 1969.

Remick, Cecile. "The House of Refuge of Philadelphia." Ed.D. dissertation, University of Pennsylvania, 1975.

Resch, John. "Anglo-American Efforts in Penal Reform, 1850–1900: The Work of Thomas Barwicke Lloyd Baker." Ph.D. dissertation, Ohio State University, 1969.

Ryan, Mary. "American Society and the Cult of Domesticity, 1830–1860." Ph.D. dissertation, University of California at Santa Barbara, 1971.

Ryerson, Ellen. "Between Justice and Compassion: The Rise and Fall of the Juvenile Court." Ph.D. dissertation, Yale University, 1970.

Salsgiver, Richard. "Child Reform in Pittsburgh, 1890–1915: The Development of the Juvenile Court and the Allegheny County Industrial and Training School for Boys." Ph.D. dissertation, Carnegie Mellon University, 1975.

Schupf, Harriet. "The Perishing and Dangerous Classes: Efforts to Deal with the Neglected, Vagrant and Delinquent Juvenile in England, 1840–1875." Ph.D. dissertation, Columbia University, 1971.

Slater, Peter. "Judge Benjamin Barr Lindsey and the Denver Juvenile Court during the Progressive Era." M.A. thesis, Brown University, 1965.

———. "Views of Children and Child Rearing during the Early National Period." Ph.D. dissertation, University of California at Berkeley, 1971.

Stack, John. "Social Policy and Juvenile Delinquency in England

and Wales, 1815–1875." Ph.D. dissertation, University of Iowa, 1974.

Tyor, Peter. "Segregation or Surgery: The Mentally Retarded in America, 1850–1920." Ph.D. dissertation, Northwestern University, 1972.

Waligorski, Ann. "Social Action and Women: The Experience of Lizzie Black Kander." M.A. thesis, University of Wisconsin, 1969.

Wallach, Stephanie. "Ben B. Lindsey and the Juvenile Court." B.A. thesis, Barnard College, 1972.

Weiss, Nancy. "Save the Children: A History of the Children's Bureau, 1903 to 1918." Ph.D. dissertation, University of California at Los Angeles, 1974.

Wirkkala, John. "Juvenile Delinquency and Reform in Nineteenth-Century Massachusetts: The Formative Era in State Care, 1846–1876." Ph.D. dissertation, Clark University, 1973.

Legal Cases

Commonwealth v. Fisher. 213 Pennsylvania 48 (1905).
Ex parte Becknell. 51 Pacific Reporter (Ca.) 692 (1897).
Ex parte Crouse. 4 Wharton (Pa.) 9 (1838).
In re Sharp. 15 Idaho 120 (1908), 96 Pac. 563.
Mill v. Brown. 88 Pacific Reporter (Utah) 609 (1907).
Milwaukee Industrial School v. The Supervisors of Milwaukee County. 40 Wisconsin 328 (1876).
Petition of Alexander Ferrier. 103 Illinois 367 (1882).
The People v. Turner. 55 Illinois 280 (1870).
Robison v. Wayne Circuit Judges. 151 Michigan 315 (1908).
State v. Ray. 63 New Hampshire 405 (1886).
State v. Scholl. 167 Milwaukee 504 (1918).
Wisconsin Industrial School v. Clark County. 103 Wisconsin 651 (1899).

Newspapers

Milwaukee Sentinel.
Waukesha Democrat.
Waukesha Freeman.
Waukesha Plaindealer.

Archival Materials

Archives of the Milwaukee Juvenile Court, 1901–20. Unpub-

lished. Located at the Milwaukee Children's Court, Milwaukee. (Use restricted, and by permission only.)

Case Book, 1914–1916. Unpublished. Located at the Milwaukee Children's Court, Milwaukee. (Use restricted, and by
permission only.)

Chief Probation Officer of the Milwaukee Juvenile Court.
Annual Reports, 1905 through 1929. Unpublished. Located at
the Milwaukee Children's Court, Milwaukee. (Use restricted,
and by permission only.)

Miscellaneous

Miss Marion Ogden to Author, letter of May 13, 1974.

"This Child is Rated X." Film shown on NBC in spring of
1971.

Stanford, John. Petition of January 21, 1812. Stanford Papers.
New York Historical Society.

Wisconsin Necrology. Unpublished. Located in State Historical
Society of Wisconsin, Madison.

Laws of Wisconsin, 1850 through 1920. Madison: State Printer.

Milwaukee Juvenile Court File. Located in the Legislative Reference Bureau, State Capitol Building, Madison.

Index

Abbott, Edith, 230 n. 14
Abbott, Lyman, 235 n. 75
Abell, Aaron, 235 n. 75
Ackerly, George, 52
Addams, Jane: and Ben Lindsey,
    56–57, 229 nn. 8, 9, 10, 11;
    and use of G. Stanley Hall's
    ideas, 68, 234 n. 63; and social
    reform, 68–69; and views of the
    poor, 70; and acquaintance with
    Milwaukee reformers, 137
Adolescence and delinquency,
    67–68, 168–69
Adult delinquency statutes: as
    integral to juvenile court move-
    ment, 60, 62; compared to
    nineteenth-century practices,
    60, 231 n. 26; goals of, 60, 231
    n. 25; and necessity for sep-
    arate legal proceedings, 60, 231
    n. 27; and family courts, 60; in
    Milwaukee Juvenile Court, 139,
    183, 201, 251 n. 55, 258 n. 10
Affectional discipline. *See* Affec-
    tional treatment
Affectional treatment: theory of,
    38–39, 40–41; and Victorian
    child-rearing methods, 49–53,
    66; theory versus practice of,
    50, 53, 227 n. 90; and proba-
    tion, 61–62; Homer Folks on,
    65; and Progressive child-
    rearing methods, 66–67, 235
    n. 75; and National Congress of
    Mothers, 77–78; discussed at
    opening ceremonies of Wis-

285